BORED
TO
DISTRACTION

SUNY series in Latin American
and Iberian Thought and Culture

Jorge J. E. Gracia and Rosemary Geisdorfer Feal, editors

BORED
TO
DISTRACTION

Cinema of Excess in End-of-the-Century
Mexico and Spain

Claudia Schaefer

STATE UNIVERSITY OF NEW YORK PRESS

Published by
State University of New York Press, Albany

For information, address State University of New York Press,
90 State Street, Suite 700, Albany, NY 12207

Production by Marilyn P. Semerad
Marketing by Michael Campochiaro

Library of Congress Cataloging-in-Publication Data

Schaefer, Claudia, 1949–
    Bored to distraction : cinema of excess in end-of-the-century Mexico
and Spain / Claudia Schaefer.
        p. cm — (SUNY series in Latin American and Iberian thought and culture)
    Includes bibliographical references and index.
        ISBN 0–7914–5887-3 (alk. paper) — ISBN 0–7914–5888–1 (pbk. : alk. paper)
    1. Motion pictures—Mexico—History.   2. Motion pictures—Spain—History.
I. Title.   II. Series

    PN1993.5.M4S32 2003
    791.43'0972—dc21
                                                                                2002045253

10 9 8 7 6 5 4 3 2 1

Contents

List of Illustrations   vii

Acknowledgments   ix

1   At the Millennium: Boredom Theory and
Middle-Class Desires   1

2   Jaime Humberto Hermosillo's *La tarea*:
Not Your Average Afterschool Special   27

3   How I Spent My Summer Vacation: *Danzón* and the
Myth of Getting Away from It All   55

4   *Amores perros*: Throwing Politics to the Dogs   83

5   Still Just a Dress Rehearsal?: From Archibaldo de la Cruz
to Penélope Cruz   109

6   The Demonic Side of Modernity: Waiting for Satan
at the Movies   135

7   A Few Last Words:
Waiting in the Anteroom of the Twenty-First Century   163

Notes   175

Works Cited   185

Index   195

Illustrations

Figure 1.1. The look of the new   13

Figure 1.2. The demise of the old   13

Figure 1.3. Recovering audiences   19

Figure 3.1. María Rojo (Julia, left) and Daniel Rergis
             (Carmelo, right)   61

Figure 3.2. Víctor Carpinteiro (Rubén, left) and
             María Rojo (Julia, right)   68

Figure 3.3. María Rojo (Julia)   69

Figure 3.4. Tito Vasconcelos (Susy)   71

Figure 4.1. Vanessa Bauche and Gael García Bernal   94

Figure 4.2. Gael García Bernal   95

Figure 4.3. Goya Toledo and Alvaro Guerrero   97

Figure 4.4. Emilio Echevarría   100

Figure 5.1. Víctor (Liberto Rabal) visits his mother's grave   121

Figure 5.2. Head shot of Elena (Francesca Neri)   124

Figure 5.3. Partners David (Javier Bardem) and Sancho
             (José Sancho)   126

Figure 6.1. Father Angel Berriartúa (Alex Angulo)   147

Figure 6.2. Classmates Angela (Ana Torrent) and Chema
             (Fele Martínez)   153

Figure 6.3. Director Bosco (Eduardo Noriega)   158

Figure 6.4. Angela (Ana Torrent)   160

Acknowledgments

Films are two-edged swords. How one develops a fascination with the movies is so very far removed from the more technical and rigorous process of criticism. As far as the mysteries of darkened theaters are concerned, I have to thank my grandmother Helen Evanchik for letting me perch on her arthritic knees to watch John Wayne fight the Battle of Pork Chop Hill in an almost-empty suburban movie theater, escaping boredom during a summer heat wave. This is the first film I can remember ever seeing. More taken by the Duke and his escapades than I was at age five or so, I found her enthusiasm over the sights and sounds of battle infinitely more interesting and puzzling than what was on screen. She could imagine a war she had missed experiencing in the flesh, because she had left Russia long before, perhaps only through Hollywood's version of the events, complete with an American victory. Hours after the matinee session was over she could recall the details of the soldiers and the dialogue they had spoken. I myself can relive the event of accompanying her to the theater much more than the plot of the film (although I guess I certainly know the story's outcome).

Later on, I found another spirit whose dreams were fostered in movie theaters. During the same decades, almost a continent away and in a culture far removed from suburban Long Island, Raúl Rodríguez-Hernández found stories portrayed on screen that transported him both back in time and all the way across the ocean to distant realms. Mexico's openness to European films and cultures brought Italy, Poland, the Soviet Union, Spain, and other countries right to his doorstep. As a teenage theater employee, making popcorn and sandwiches for the daily crowds, carrying heavy cases to the post office to be transported to the next small-town theater, and helping change the title letters on the marquee, he had the rare opportunity (outside characters in the novels of Manuel Puig or in *Cinema Paradiso*) to see more movies than anyone else I know. So taken was he by those images that, almost miraculously and often monstrously, he still retains plots and faces from the features that changed several times a week in those days. Obviously, an inquiry today about a film elicits more than a few perfunctory words and our conversations about the movies have been enlightening in so many senses. Raúl has been the bridge between watching and analyzing; without his input I would still be sitting in the dark.

Now for my debt to others who have contributed to my critical interest in films and to this project in particular. I am grateful to my University of Rochester film classes over the past several years for their sometimes vexing, but more frequently enticing, comments regarding the Mexican and Spanish directors and productions we have studied. I have learned from them that fresh eyes see such very different things in a film, things that are easily dismissed but which in more than one instance have led me to think again about what had appeared to be familiar images. I appreciate their difficulties with talking about movies and the efforts many of them have made to find the language to do so. Maybe what one of them has called making her think "in the fifth dimension" was the best way of describing this complex process.

Without the help of Kathleen Vernon I would probably still be looking for photos to illustrate this book, and without her technical suggestions and production information it would have taken me twice as long to get all the legalities taken care of. For this, and for her loyal support over quite a number of years, I thank her from the bottom of my heart. Aside from being a pioneer in Almodóvar studies, she is a true colleague.

I gratefully acknowledge the generous support of the Program for Cultural Cooperation Between Spain's Ministry of Culture and North American Universities for a grant to begin the research for this book. I also thank Dean Thomas LeBlanc of The College of Arts and Sciences for allowing me time off from teaching to pursue this and other projects, and for his understanding of the need to upgrade my computer every once in a while.

Thanks to Ron Mandelbaum (and researchers Buddy Weiss and Pierre Montiel) at Photofest who found me perfect photo illustrations for chapter 4. I am especially grateful to El Deseo, Altavista Films and Zeta Films, Lola Films, Cinematográfica Macondo, and Las Producciones del Escorpión for their kind permission to reprint film stills and for their incredibly rapid response to my requests.

Last but not least, I am forced to admit that the term "boredom" has been ringing in my ears since childhood, when my siblings and I were frequently accused of complaining that there was nothing to do after the school year ended. So in some subconscious way, I guess I have been brought full circle to a maternal admonition to find some way to fill those empty hours. Of course, the suggestion always was to read a book. From the depths of academia today I can only remark that you should be careful what you wish for. . . .

AT THE MILLENNIUM
Boredom Theory and Middle-Class Desires

Among the discourses on which twentieth-century, turn-of-the- millennium society is articulated are those of liberation (from the tyranny of
the state, from cultural and economic isolation, from nationalism and into
globalism), those of progress or advancement toward a common set of
goals, those of the entitlement of the private, individual subject to pursue a
dream or "get ahead," and those of the self-made entrepreneur whose
spirit and drive are combined with a boundless energy for work into an
equation for singular enrichment and success. Within what is by now the
cliché of a globalization of social factors and economic systems, the visible
images of such overarching ideologies are hard to miss in the media, and a
sense of natural privilege frequently ensues from an identification with the
processes of this global culture. Consumers are convinced that everyone
wants into the banquet of what Jameson refers to as "that 'inner' frontier"
("Class and Allegory" 288) of the market that has replaced the real geographic frontiers of the historical past. All seek their avowedly guaranteed
place at the table filled with inestimable quantities of goods and rewards.
The spaces left to explore and conquer—especially for the wages of investment capital but also for the ardent consumer—belong to a daily life
whose material expressions of social forces and interests surround us at
every turn. While we may feel suspended somewhere between our desires
and their fulfillment, entranced by the call of the sirens but not knowing

which way to look first, still other commodities are in production to keep us wanting even more.

Though we may propose to take possession of our world by buying it up in bits and pieces, or by freezing it in the frames of photographic stills or in digitized CD images, our investment in it merely effects an uneasy comfort with what remains beyond the scope of our consciousness. As Jameson reminds the citizen/consumer whose identity is no longer unlinked from the ability to acquire merchandise or services, "[c]ultural products are full of surprises" ("Class and Allegory" 289). Such commodities may not respond to its desires as the community imagines they will, and they indeed may even elicit feelings of uncanniness in the unwary consumer, reminding us of those unstated motivations or "forgotten" resources that have helped us acquire what the market has to offer or perhaps have influenced what is for sale from the outset. It might take lots of old-fashioned detective work to uncover the sources of wealth of today's world-class consumers, as well as the cultural forces which mold the products available to them (us).

As pedestrians make their way down the broad sidewalks of the Avenida Reforma in downtown Mexico City or stroll along the Gran Vía in Madrid, the half-smiling face of Bill Gates dances in the wind on the covers of international magazines displayed in kiosks. It reminds all passersby that they too can, in theory, make a quantity of money so vast that there won't even be anything left to buy unless new things come along in the meantime. In the public's enthralled gaze, wealth accumulates faster than its expenditure. Besides becoming exhausted by trying to find ways to invest it or to discover new items to purchase, one is frustrated by the fact that the possible objects of consumption do not keep pace with purchasing power. We must mark time in anticipation of the new, and the now is where (and when) that marching-in-place occurs. We have all heard about the beginning of Microsoft in someone's garage, or a start-up company taking its first steps into the market with a couple of hundred dollars invested by an uncle or a neighbor. The fantasies of wealth, endless consumption, and limitless leisure time are conjured up to fill our otherwise routine everyday lives with the tantalizing but vague images of something new and different somewhere down the road. Even making money is no longer sufficiently exciting but merely the tediously monotonous repetition of successful ventures in anticipation of more of the same; once the formula has been mastered it becomes a given in the course of everyday life and not a challenge.

At the end of the twentieth century and as we moved through the portal into the twenty-first, it is the trend toward privatization—of industry, of services, of education, of all thoughts and opinions previously shared in the agora of civic society—that most greatly inflects our perception of the tedium of daily life. If each and every one of us is told we have the chance to pursue our personal fantasies—which are driven, of course, by the economies of desire produced through and around us—we will be able to buy into both the dream and its concomitant unlimited leisure, beginning with early retirement and ending with luxury living in some comfortable clime where no one speaks of markets unless they have to do with some remote idea of the mythical sources of our comfort. Given the recent shift in the global workforce toward so-called voluntary overtime (we need just recall the year 2000 public transit workers' strike in Los Angeles in protest over the proposed cessation of such extra benefits for masses of bus drivers and rail conductors), the growing phenomenon of the workaholic, shorter lunch hours or the advent of the power lunch in which work takes precedence over food (or actually nourishes us more than traditional victuals), the abolition of the tradition of the siesta and the two-part workday, mandatory vacation time that accrues by year's end, and the virtual office which creates literally no division between the space of the home and the space of work (or for that matter between the hours of work and hours off the job), it goes without saying that there is a mythology about labor that intrudes on all aspects of modern life. A great part of that mythology is that if one does not toil, one would be hard-pressed to fill the empty space and endless hours in the days, weeks, months, and years of a lifetime. Idle hands are still considered in demonic terms, much as they were during Puritan times; as long as one fills the black hole of time with profitable activity, then any feelings of emptiness, nostalgia, or anxiety can be kept at bay. The terms of the equation are easily strung together: the opportunity for work, made easier and increasingly more lucrative by the technological advances of modernity, added to the accumulation of wealth, yields time off—both long-term and short-term. Then comes the time when we are left to decide what to do with the flip side of labor: leisure. We may turn to work to forget other aspects of our lives, but even leisure time is converted into a sort of work since we burn calories, strenuously exert ourselves to acquire flat abs, and create energy drinks that allow us to have more endurance so that we "produce" better workouts.

Both Patricia Meyer Spacks and Patrice Petro have recently explored the notion of boredom, the first from a historical perspective and the second with a focus on a specific period. Each addresses provocatively as well the cultural supposition that leisure (the time filled by boredom, one surmises) signals an absence of action, a void to be filled with something other than "work" or production. Such a hypothesis rests on the conviction that leisure could become a threat to the immediate psychological as well as economic health of the individual, or to his or her future status in society, since it indicates an inadequate amount of significant activity or, in the extreme, none at all. As a measure of the current state of social values, boredom or tedium or routine is meaningfully and intimately linked to societal conceptions of work as well as to certain cultural perceptions of time and history. The element of the boring intrudes when one can almost feel the laborious passage of time, when the real struggle is not to earn enough to survive (what we might call a basic sense of remunerated labor), but to find something to do with the surplus of everything, from finances to time. Work, then, no longer fulfills a function other than occupying the spaces made available by the incessant passage of time. Not so much the actual loss of the exceptional or the remarkable but a horror of its devaluation into the mundane often produces the grounds for tedium. This is sometimes accompanied by a feeling of anguish over such a loss, while other times not even that intrudes on the familiar feeling of inertia. The naturalizing of the images of both extreme poverty and inordinate wealth—especially by global media resources—leaves the spaces between them to be haunted by a sense of continuity of the same to which neither pole seemingly falls victim: the win-all or lose-all excesses lie elsewhere. The mythical middle-of-the-road security of the middle classes removes, in their own eyes, the obstacles of either resounding failure or overwhelming achievement. It celebrates acquired certainty (risks disappear or are deemed minimal) and expectations for more of the same; having escaped the depths, one longs for the economic peaks but marks time in between. Boredom may be the indicator of a frozen moment when, as a collectivity, we look backward, or it may imply a momentary paralysis as a community faces the future. The year 2000 proved to be such a juncture.

While Spacks traces the origins of the term "boredom" from the eighteenth century through the cultural changes wrought on its interpretation by nineteenth-century industrialization and modernization into the reign of the twentieth-century European subject, Petro centers her discussion on the writings of Georg Simmel and Walter Benjamin, who inhabit the spaces already affected by the arrival of modernity. In particular Petro examines the primacy of the visual media—film and photography—as they became the primary instruments for recording how innovative or extraordinary events and inventions were domesticated and naturalized into the mundane. We might think of the rise of modern photography and its oppositional stance to the painterly vision of the world as an indicator of this historical moment when society acquired a new window on the world through the lens of the camera. Or we might recall how British actor and director Charlie Chaplin parodied the boredom of the factory workplace in his early silent films set in modernizing and alienating cityscapes, making the little tramp both recognizable and filled with pathos for the viewer. It is the representation of this liminality at another historical juncture, the concurrence of both "before" and "after" in a post-twentieth-century expanse filled with singular expectation and terror, that interests me for trying to historically and aesthetically locate the genres and codes of contemporary Hispanic cinema. How boredom is put on display as a relic of daily life as one century closes and another looms large on the horizon, and how the audience might be seized by the moment, despite its own professed lethargy, and thrust into an energized and awakened consciousness, are two of the areas on which I would like to focus in contemporary Mexico and Spain. I recognize that some might find here a less-than-joyous celebration of popular culture as the liberator of us all, along the lines of what critic John Fiske has touted as the vehicle of expression for the subordinate masses in which pleasure and social resistance unite in jubilant subversion (54). Yet despite some fundamental differences between an absolute vision of present opportunity (Fiske) and a more limited one of future potentiality (Benjamin), Fiske and Benjamin coincide in discerning that the sites of popular culture—all of the aspects that constitute the life of the everyday—are filled with power. Benjamin never fails to envision boredom not as the source of a lamentation over closure but as fuel for possibility, a time from which to dig out. From its lethargic depths one might be roused to a clearer vision of society's contradictions. As Highmore asserts, "Benjamin doesn't remain within the melancholy realm often ascribed to him. His project is an attempt to redeem the everyday experience of modernity from silence" (65). I propose that through the end-of-the-century cinema of excess such silence is broken.

The time sensed as a filler between events is the vast, lumbering domain of social boredom. Qualified as a subjective experience of material reality, as Petro notes, the feeling of banality inhabits a "time without event, when nothing happens" (265). At least this is what the individual subject discerns: it is the experience of nonexperience, the realm of before-and-after described previously. When we sift back through the dusty documents of recorded history—to excavate things that did happen, one assumes, as opposed to limitless waiting and expectation for something, anything, to break the monotony extending across the daily horizon—we encounter only those distant, staccato echoes of beginnings and endings. What we hear in the endlessness of unmeasured flow is the sound of tedium; what we see is a fog of nonevents, a haze that leaves us bewildered as to their interconnectedness or even their association with some sense of historical "reality." Before and after those moments when we decide that we are witnessing history-in-the-making, we have time to spend, time to kill, time on our hands, spare time, free time, and time to pass, finding in routine both a strange yet simultaneously uncanny security of endless repetitions and a reminder of the inescapable drudgery of these undifferentiated moments. Seen as a pathology, one could find that boredom is a symptom of something gone awry in society; its physical manifestation "masks another condition" (Spacks x) which is generally then culturally encoded, normally within the realm of discontent, dullness, and disinterest. We do not desperately seek boredom, but it comes to us along with the territories of capital, wealth, and consumer desire. It is the ghost that haunts excess; it is the shadow cast by desire.

But even the production of desires can acquire a distinct sense of monotony, for we can predict, or have the feeling that we can, that many other desires will inevitably come along. That is the way of the market. What we want today is merely one step on the road of a greater critical mass. The accumulation of fantasies does not predicate their fulfillment as an end but rather their irremediable and inescapable challenge to us to engage with them. Like the hording of economic capital, accumulated desire(s) must be dealt with either through expenditure or sublimation, through excessive consumption or internalized longing. And it is in the interlude of solicited and then sublimated desire that we might come to frame our vision of boredom as a type of paralysis or "incapacity" (Spacks 165) to take action on either external or internal challenges. This leads Spacks to conclude that the psyche is wounded by such an impasse and she proposes that in literary texts "psychosis and boredom are tropes for one another" (165) as visible signs of the frustration of a desire once aroused and then repressed. This moment would then, in some general sense, belong to the stilled fraction of time perceived by Foucault when that inseparable conjunction of prohibition and resistance reaches some instant of stalemate. Things grind to a halt and we do not appear capable of moving on; time stands still as it were and appears to deny the existence of desire. Yet all the while the existence of a sense of impasse implies desire's role in the emotional blockage. In other words, there must be something to block in order for an impediment to exist. The forms of psychosis and the violence they do to the subject and to the nation are two of the aspects of the films I shall examine, from Almodóvar's recovery of Buñuel's vision of the bourgeoisie's repressions to González Iñárritu's transference of political violence to the bloodlines of the family.

In his incisive study of the everyday life and social vision of the Mexican middle classes, Gabriel Careaga concludes his discussion of similar aspects of society with a proposal for an aesthetics. In his view, middle-class woes exaggerate the sense of impediment or blockage into the spectacular theater of melodrama as a substitute for yet another absence: history. The desire for goods, coupled with a lack of historical vision (as to social origins or a pre-text for existence), projects one lack atop another. The result is a lament carried over the top as the only source of social presence for classes who feel left out of a greater national vision. Rather than seek a true prehistory of the present, however, which might lead to contested terrains of legitimacy, the middle classes wallow in excessive expenditure, as witnessed in the conventions of the genre of melodrama. To counteract absence, they exhibit overwhelming presence. Careaga sums up his argument in this manner:

> Son los hombres y las mujeres de la clase media que suben y bajan, luchando desesperadamente por tener mayor movilidad social, que aspiran a más cosas, que se irritan, que se enojan, dentro de una tradición melodramática porque cuando se carece de conciencia trágica, ha dicho alguna vez Carlos Fuentes, de razón histórica o de afirmación personal, el melodrama la suple, es un sustituto, una imitación, una ilusión de ser. Esta clase media vive la mayor parte del tiempo . . . [s]oñando en querer ser otra cosa, siempre envidiando al otro que no es como él . . . , siempre deseando y frustrándose. (It is the men and women of the middle classes that rise and fall, desperately fighting for greater social mobility, that aspire to more things, that get incensed, that become angry, [all] within a tradition of the melodramatic because when there is no conscience of tragedy, as Carlos Fuentes once said, melodrama steps in to take its place, it becomes a substitute, an imitation, the illusion of being. This middle class lives the majority of the time . . . dreaming about wanting to be something else . . . , always envious of those who are different, . . . always desiring and being frustrated; 61).

Dreams of riches, fame, and social recognition are blocked by the knowledge (even if repressed for the time being) of being caught in the middle, constantly disappointed and frustrated by lost opportunities and deferred gratification but ever impelled by social pressures to dream on. Want and lack go hand-in-hand; they play off one another on a daily basis much as desire and the law are codependent. The more one finds to desire, the more the lack is manifested and compensated for with excessive detail. If one is forced to wait for that elusive something down the road, then at least this can be done with the greatest sense of exaggeration one can muster. So the codes of melodrama step in to attempt to fill the void of both past (lack) and future (desire). It makes social classes between two extremes more visible.

Of course, routine may be envisioned as all the more overwhelming if represented in the hyper-mode of melodrama, which forces and twists it into condensed images of affect at every turn in order to invest each passing minute with visible signs of meaning. When we feel that there is no longer any sense to the passage of time we endure, no action worth the effort, then it must be imbued with not just signifiers, but accumulated signifiers whose meanings pile up like so much rubbish on a refuse heap. Contrary to Walter Benjamin's Angel of History "who would like to stand still" to take stock of such remains, the stasis of boredom seems to make one oblivious to the need for a "leap out of this movement [of evolutionary progress]" (Bolz and Van Reijen 42). Even as Benjamin retains his faith in a (divine) revelation amidst the debris, the steady if lethargic momentum of the banal folds back on the gaze of the onlooker and impedes either clarity of vision or messianic hope. But the mundane may also be all the more evocative of a latent panic—of which we may be only dully aware—if it is removed from our line of sight altogether but continues to stalk us from among the shadows. When routine is the anchor we search for in a sea of extraordinarily violent and traumatic images, it becomes all the more discernible for its absence. In a crisis, banality is reassurance. Tossed about on the sea of blood and mayhem, the spectator is cast adrift from any moorings of certainty about self or surroundings. The cinema of excess, therefore, gives us one extreme or the other, taking away the artificial reassurance of the middle ground: either boredom on screen is even more crushing than our ordinary feeling of everyday life or it has disappeared totally and in its place is something that makes us long for the absent solace of the tedious. Or just maybe we are shown that this is not the only scenario; perhaps we can be shocked into the realization that there is a need to find a way out of a numbing boredom of which we have been finally made aware. Given its ability to take on so many guises and disguises, the notion of boredom functions as a marker of a wide variety of social and psychological intricacies. These obstruct one another in the psyche of the modern consumer who has replaced the subject of history at the end of the twentieth century.[1]

So along with Foucault and Benjamin (an unlikely pair at that), we might also consider boredom as a positive force, as the opportunity to produce images, fictions, and discourses about this very state of affairs in which one feels entangled. It not only prevents and blocks a response, but also has the power to provoke one; anxiety is not the only product of an overwhelming sense of inertia. On the one hand, there is the fear that nothing could jolt us out of such an intensified feeling of timelessness—we are confounded by the impression that all extraordinary highs and lows are things of the past which have become subsumed under the bland, flattened routine of the everyday. Like an addict at the limit, we have reached an intoxicated saturation from which we no longer distinguish much variation—everything is reduced to a predictable state of presence vs. absence. Yet on the other hand, an anticipation of even the remotest possibility of something out of the ordinary or unfamiliar occurring at any moment in what now seems a continuum of uninterrupted waiting signals, for Benjamin, that in the very midst of the toxic routine of the everyday there lies that messianic hope for rupture and revelation. Among his notations for the monumental *Arcades Project*, Benjamin constantly and pointedly emphasizes this potential: "We are bored when we don't know what we are waiting for. . . . Boredom is the threshold to great deeds" (Buck-Morss 105). One must only conjure up the predicament underlying our tedium to have the passage of time become more than that. Thus the ceremonial aspects of repetitive routine may acquire a premonitory glow of expectation.

For Benjamin, the metaphors of dream and waking best capture the potential of this moment, especially in the realm of the cinema. The power to awaken the collective masses sleepwalking through history is tapped by means of the visual evocation of "the traumatic energy of everyday life through images" (Bolz and Van Reijen 46). It is through the shock value of the visual—first in Baudelaire's poetic evocations but subsequently flickering before our eyes on the silver screen—that technology intervenes in the intensified routine of daily life to pry open the eyes of the willing (or jolted) somnambulist to the hidden vitality of the now. This experience pierces the remoteness, the distance stretching between vision and object, "disintegra[ting] . . . the aura" (Benjamin, 1968 194) cast in the "protective eye" (191) to end the paralysis of a distracted gaze. Awakened from its enthrallment with the static moment that seems to go on without end, the eye witnesses the trauma of difference. Not unlike the tremendous visual impact of the opening scene of Spanish director Luis Buñuel's 1928 film *Un chien andalou*, Benjamin focuses on this orb as the site where the distraction of the subject may be broken with maximum force and intensity. A pierced eye brings into consciousness the act of looking and, one supposes, what is seen as well. If we symbolically cut through the organ of sight as we witness the razor blade slice through thick vitreous gel on screen, then we come to realize that we have been observing unreflexively along the lines of what Chris Jenks refers to as the false assumption of objectivity, an "immaculate perception" (5). As Petro concludes, along Benjamin's own lines of argumentation, boredom is fundamentally concerned with the sense of sight, and any resulting distraction or detachment (the visible sign of boredom) resides in a "fatigue of the eye" (272). Visual fixity constrains the observer to partial vision, perhaps as a refuge from the crush of satiation. Whether by absence (lack, invisibility) or by overload, distraction is the result of excess—we see too much or too little; we are exhausted by straining to see what may or may not be immediately accessible to us, or we withdraw altogether from the pervasiveness of visual stimuli. Either extreme yields the same result: given the difficulty of access to all or to nothing, we give ourselves up to the soothing forces of indifference. It is only in some tremendously optimistic, forward-looking scheme of things that the enthrallment of such a distracted subject could be held out as a potentiality for future revelation. And it is only in the consideration of time as both spent (meaningless, redundant, undifferentiated) and full of possibilities that waiting might be conceived as hopeful expectation and affirmation.

The temporal battleground on which we thus stand is the now, the present, which must be seized in order to "claim the territory between the future and the past, but [which] manages only to be devoured by them" (Lyotard 37). But rather than assign this present anticipation a negative value, it can be permeated with an ecstasy of insecurity—a veritable passion of waiting and indeterminacy. The eventual outcome, then, would not be relief but a state similar to Benjamin's image of awakening, of emerging from a foggy stupor with clearer, if more challenging, vision. As Lyotard confirms, "[s]hock is, *par excellence*, the evidence of (something) happening, rather than nothing at all" (40). When the apparatus of the cinema places our eyes on the line, as it were, to enable us to see that the real shock is that the secret behind the banal is our own state of being hypnotized by banality itself, then the power of boredom lies in its own narrative of implied escapability. Boredom is neither natural nor inevitable. The real revelation is the extraordinariness of distraction when it is brought to the level of consciousness. This is best accomplished for Benjamin in the flickering light of the darkened movie theater. As we move into a time of the unknown, looking back at the stunning achievements and dismal failures of the past century, I suggest that we may wish to once again look at films that address the "tedium and irritation of perceptual boredom, in other words, [ones that] enable an awareness of looking as a temporal process" (Petro 276). When we are confronted by our own anesthetized looking, when we confront ourselves on screen in forms we scarcely recognize at first, we can be jarred out of taking "the fatigue of the eye" for granted as a natural phenomenon. So the monotony of the sleepwalking subject—a dormant spectator moving through space, oblivious to his or her surroundings but set in motion—whose gaze is trained everywhere and nowhere at once, is assaulted by other ways of seeing when the film director finds in the camera lens a weapon for disturbance and intrusion. Even when focused on the same objects we pass by every day, and perhaps even more irritatingly so when aimed at them in particular, it renders materially present what we have become accustomed to viewing as nothing at all. Absence becomes presence. The camera, then, can fire up the desiring eye, which has until now for all intents and purposes become blind. Such blindness is the state of distraction we have been describing, when the push and pull of longing and its repression leave the gaze disconnected and distanced. No matter how close the object might intrude on our field of vision, we cannot seem to perceive it in any attentive way; we look but we do not see, for we have become accustomed to this static relationship with our surroundings.

But rather than take boredom as a phenomenon with some universal set of characteristics, we must set our sights on the specifics of history and culture. During the decade of the 1990s, in Europe and the Americas alike, a sense of waiting and anticipation intensified, both as one century drew to a close and as a new millennium was about to open before our very eyes. Anxiety was most certainly shaded by both melancholy and excruciating delight: we sat at the crossroads of a clean beginning and a sense of closure, a farewell to evils and horrors with new hopes for universal peace, a chance to use our knowledge of the past for the construction of a future, burying dead ideologies and liberating new ones. In both Mexico and Spain this decade embodied an intensification of the tediousness of the seemingly immeasurable time between historical events. In Mexico, the utopian visions of the 1910 revolution had waxed and waned over the events of succeeding decades, always accompanied by that seemingly eternal companion, the Partido Revolucionario Institucional (PRI or Institutional Revolutionary Party.) The congealed political institutionalization of a purportedly collective agenda froze historical images on the retina of the nation, keeping its citizens from registering the discrepancies between fact and fiction or, for that matter, distinguishing the ideological gap widening between them. These inconsistencies were out there, of course, but they were made invisible by official public discourse which promoted and maintained a thick interpretive veil between spectator and event. From 1929 to 2000, the cultural and political economies of the Mexican people revolved around the recognizable rhetoric of an official party whose promises turned into a litany of absences and whose end no one really believed they would witness in their lifetime. The narratives appealed to a mythic time, an undercurrent of continuity in which their own representation of events seemed to be imbedded quite effortlessly and "naturally." In point of fact, the majority of Mexico's twentieth century can be read as a "time without event" of frustrated collective distraction, punctuated only intermittently by uncanny moments of extraordinary violence. But this is the case when it is the middle class that does the reading of events. For those such as Subcomandante Marcos and the Ejército Zapatista de Liberación Nacional (EZLN or Zapatista Army of National Liberation) or other political groups and alliances dedicated to the task of pointing out the gaps between official rhetoric and actual social practice, the twentieth century has been one of constant violence by the government interrupted only by an intensification of its repression of alternative visions of history. Violence has only been officially visible when it is judged to be an enemy of the perception of "time without event."

Even those momentary horrors noted in public quickly ebbed back into the realm of the unseen: student revolts, massive earthquakes, peasant uprisings, natural disasters, political assassinations, and presidential frauds all were absorbed into the emptied signifiers of the ruling party's public discourses. The institutionalizing of the concept of revolution itself into official political structures has slowed down the perception of any event as significantly equal to the "original." The aura of that primal moment was unique and unrepeatable; everything else became part of the blur of post-revolutionary time. After the initial moment of rupture, things returned to what is conceived of as normal, a normalcy guaranteed by the numbing rhetoric of routine. From celebration (over international soccer victories, for instance, or finalists in the Miss Universe contest) to extreme suffering and violence, peaks and valleys are flattened into deserts of equal tediousness. Much has been made of those disturbances, especially by those observing them from a distance, but little has been said of the time in-between. PRI-time was forever, infinite, or so it seemed until Vicente Fox and the Partido de Acción Nacional (PAN or National Action Party) arrived on the scene to shake things up for real in the July 2000 presidential election. For the young in particular, this was the first time that the collective imaginary could conceive an image of change, of "event." And that image was focused on the tall, moustached man in the cowboy hat who used the media effectively to reach the distracted masses and seemingly spoke to them in their own vernacular language. Taunting them out of their boredom with politics, Fox publicly flouted some of the greatest cultural and political taboos which had been upheld over the years by the federal government: a promise to reveal the "truth" about his political and ideological adversaries in the PRI, the use of vulgar language as a sign of cutting through rhetorical stances, bullying the PRI to reveal its secret economic pacts and past repressive tactics, conjuring up the political power and fiscal rights of the Catholic Church, promoting the use of English in place of a traditional defense of Spanish as the only language for national representation, even threatening to flood the states along the United States-

Figure 1.1. The look of the new: Mexican multiplexes are the cornerstones of suburban shopping malls in the 1990s. (Photo collection of the author.)

Figure 1.2. The demise of the old: A popular downtown Mexico City movie theater from the 1950s. Now closed, it is a site for sorting garbage. (Photo collection of the author.)

Mexico border with faceless hordes of well-trained gardeners. On television and interspersed with movie trailers in commercial theaters, his face and party logo never left the public eye for long. Rather than merely operating a campaign of visual saturation, however, Fox's advisors shocked the public out of stupor and into believing a new time could be at hand by promoting the myth of change. The false security of an appeal to mythic origins evaporated into thin air; time itself became the trope of awakening rather than lethargy as Fox urged voters to look at the hands of the clock as they moved into the next century and the new millennium.

In Carlos Fuentes's book of essays entitled *A New Time for Mexico*, published in Spanish in 1994, this need for a sense of awakening is already encapsulated. Six years before the changing of the old guard begins to occur in "real time," Fuentes closes his discussion with a chapter entitled "Conclusion and Coda: Mexican Tempi." Not one but two threads of time are woven into his vision of end-of-the-century Mexico, permitting the dissolution of the trance of eternity and reconnecting time and event, the "chronotope" pegged by Bakhtin as the locus of the study of modern narrative and the axis of its generic conventions.[2] About this notion of "Mexican time" Fuentes writes: "Between the ruins of the past and the garbage of the future, Mexico tries to create a livable space in the present" (203). He seems to locate social space between the material vestiges of time—the decaying shards left over from days past and the accumulated detritus of today's consumption that will decompose in the dustbin of tomorrow. Time leaves behind the proof of its passage by filling the material spaces that surround us with traces of events; we are literally walking on layers of time as we move toward the "new times" of the title. In Bakhtin's words to describe a similar sense, albeit at a much earlier historical moment, "[t]ime, as it were, thickens, takes on flesh, becomes artistically visible" (84) through the narrative evocation of these ruins and waste products. Time moves forward at the pace of the production and consumption of such artifacts, or it is bogged down by their filling all the spaces that we inhabit and slowing our movements amid them.

It is the image of a hypnotic, dreamlike state of in-betweenness which has persisted across official discourses of power that has to be fractured before the events of the present can be perceived and critiqued with clarity. Until the Mexican elections of 2000, the appeal to a timeless national continuum by many politicians and intellectuals alike only served as a compensatory, "eventless" counterpoint to the realities of the North American Free Trade Agreement (NAFTA), drug cartels, and the relentless forces of globalization. Recognizable phrases and slogans used to pacify the populace into a state of tedious resignation just dull the senses until their empty words become "facts" that nothing can be done to change; all efforts against them are useless. But events do take place where and when we are made to think they don't; as in the urban shell game by the street-smart huckster, our eyes, confident of their ability to perceive where the moving object is hidden, are tricked into looking elsewhere and we are entrapped. Our response to such deception is first accusation and then resignation. One does not fall for the same scam twice; desperation, then boredom, set in, and one eventually learns to avoid the situation entirely. Our gaze is diverted elsewhere, distracted from the hypocrisy of an honest playing field gone awry; a lack of interest quickly turns into dispassionate distance. The spaces of individual distraction proposed and promoted by the forces of social stability bombard us with an alternative to "event": family, work, and home form the sacred triangle whose angles, in rotation and conjunction, mask the tedium of eventless time with the substitutes of leisure and prosperity.

A similar situation was taking place in Spain over roughly the same period of time, albeit long after the attempt for revolutionary change took place (during the Spanish Civil War of 1936–1939). Before the death of the dictator Francisco Franco on November 20, 1975, Spaniards anxiously awaited what would follow the demise of the recognizable leader (or enemy) whose countenance had stood in for so long as the public image of the nation and its politics. While the dictatorship per se had dragged on for close to forty years, changes within the structure of the government or the staff of its ministries had remained internal; the visible figurehead had stayed in place, uninterrupted and untouched by any event. While novelist Juan Goytisolo anticipated "el Día por antonomasia" ("that Day par excellence"; 11) that would divide time into Franco/post-Franco units, he counted on the comforting rhythm of obsessive repetition and methodically conjured-up hatred to carry him through. The pain of his everyday existence was so numbing for him that he no longer registered the hurt. It had become part of him, it was a dream-state to be counted on as being there each and every waking moment, like the invisible but omnipresent inspector of Jeremy Bentham's panopticon.[3] In a paradoxical equation of affect, numbness meant life (or at least survival by means of a lifesaving emotional anesthesia).

Yet even Goytisolo notes the figure of the sleepwalker as the perfect image for these generations of the so-called children of Franco. Having been forced to relinquish their innocence to the overwhelming and demanding patriarch, once they became adults they were unable to function as anything other than psychologically damaged and arrested children who had been ordered to close their eyes to the world. This

situation had persisted for so long that they were no longer aware of
their real surroundings; a state of what appeared to be permanent sleep
had taken the place of being awake. Situating himself in an in-between
state of psychological impairment that parallels his physical exile from
Spain, Goytisolo claims a life "sin rencor ni nostalgia" ("with neither
rancor nor nostalgia"; 18), an eventless time spent waiting for the
impending shock of Franco's demise. But even this anticipated pleasure, this rousing jolt of reckoning, is stolen from him: the brain-dead
Franco is kept alive artificially by technology so that the moment of
his death can coincide with the Nationalist day of mourning for one of
their fallen and martyred heroes. Rather than a "natural" occurrence,
history passes into the realm of artifice. So instead of an "event," the
dictator's death is reduced to a formulaic moment emptied of much of
its significance by its constant postponement. By the time death is
declared, it seems for many less a milestone than just another part of
the continuation of "time without event." Franco was no more dead in
death than he had been in life, when his image was mythified and sustained above and beyond a mere physical body. Of the agony of the
wait Goytisolo writes: "Hay hechos que a fuerza de ser esperados,
cuando ocurren al fin, pierden toda impresión de realidad" ("There are
events anticipated for so long that, when they finally come about, they
lose all impression of being real"; 11). The last registered event of the
Spanish chronotope, that conjunction of time and space, that the
nation had witnessed had been Franco's ascent to power; "nothing"
had happened since. And for exiles such as Goytisolo, time and space
shared a fundamental element of absence: both Spain and history were
perceived as existing elsewhere in space, or not at all "real" in temporality. The characters in his novels can peer across the Strait of
Gibraltar, but there is more than just a geographical distance at work.
The *neblina* ("morning fog") that they see is accompanied by an empty
haze of nonevents happening somewhere off on the horizon. As
Baudrillard sums up the decay of both reality and simulation,

> in contrast to the primitive rite, which foresees the official and sacrificial
> death of the king . . . , the modern political imaginary goes increasingly in
> the direction of delaying, of concealing for as long as possible, the death of
> the head of state. This obsession has accumulated since the era of revolu-
> tions and of charismatic leaders: Hitler, Franco, Mao . . . see themselves
> forced to perpetuate themselves indefinitely. . . . (25)

Time, which has become elastic and leaves no gaps in a never-
ending cultural and political horizon, precludes the interruption of
event: death cannot and therefore does not occur in the representation of

the collective imaginary. Death itself is merely imagined. Franco appears on the walls of post offices and government buildings, on all denominations of postage stamps, coins, and tax receipts. As Goytisolo puts it, the dictator is another Dorian Gray (15), never aging despite the passing of time in the outside world; the thirty-eight years of his dictatorship move without haste and weigh heavily on the material world as an eventless time patrolled by the infamous, gray-uniformed soldiers of the *guardia civil*. Such a temporal limbo leaves psychological scars.

In the twenty-five intervening years since the self-proclaimed Generalísimo's death, the enchantment with Felipismo (the government of charismatic leftist leader Felipe González) came and went, the Socialists rose to power and fell from it precipitously, the 1992 Barcelona Olympics sparkled for an instant in the eye of the international media, pacts here and there assured the monotony of less social and political disruption, and the advent of the millennium provided little for those distracted by the overwhelming consumer panorama of daily life. Isolation from the rest of the continent was replaced in short order by a nascent "Europhilia" (Ross 158) without so much as a missed step. After "la movida madrileña" ("the Madrid Movement"), an ephemeral social phenomenon whose celebratory intensity during the late 1970s and early 1980s flamed out in a blaze of visual glory, the tenor of historical time ebbed and slowed once again. Things "moved" no longer. As an emblem of youth and rebellion, of energy and tolerance, of the boundless spirit of creativity, "la movida" became just another blip in the whirling kaleidoscope of democracy on Spain's vast new cultural horizon. Emma Dent Coad summarizes this phenomenon in terms of the liberating power of economic capital and what it promised to provide the individual consumer:

> A combination of political and cultural freedom, increased personal income, and the desire to break with the past. . . . [This] created a market for new aesthetic ideas. . . . Painting, sculpture, fashion, jewellery, film, music, theatre, and dance blossomed overnight and were quickly hailed as the new hope of a new Spain. . . . Journalists and artists fed off each other in a mutual admiration society that had its own magazines, its own clubs, and its own galleries and shops. (376–77)

Having turned the mirror on itself and exhausted the eyes of the nation, what next for Spain? Once the newness of everything being new faded, where did one look next? The nation's eyes had been saturated and could no longer absorb more. Both the imaginary and the wallets of the nation had been assaulted and drained. When the intensity of the wait for liberation fizzled into the limbo of boring innovation—so much excess and spectacle after the endless years of dull grayness and drab routine—time again stretched out toward the infinite. The splendor of the present among the ruins of the past was overpowering only until the ever-new began to look like more-of-the-same. Nostalgia was out, it didn't sell; consumption was definitely in, but the tedium of choosing set in quickly (as did the unremarkable onset of economic overextension). Then the economic boom of the 1980s faded into the dark shadows of recession and high unemployment of the 1990s, part of the larger discourse of global disillusionment by those relegated to the far end of the banquet table. While Spain's conservative political ideologues had touted its "difference" for over thirty years, when Europe came courting at long last it brought with it the narratives of boredom and distraction. Spaniards were welcomed to the discourses of empty desire. Spain was no longer "different" in its eventual indifference to too much.

While movie theaters had been for so long the spaces in which leisure time could be filled, where one could escape from the routine of the workday into the promissory fantasies of the matinee, the double feature, or the midnight show, the 1990s came to challenge this venue. Home video, VCRs, and the demise of the commercial theater coincided with a retreat into that pre-eminent space of boredom: the home. Earlier in the century Franco had sent women back into the home to care for the family, from which future model citizens would emerge. This retreat later became evidence of economic success and the home a haven from the metropolis. Whereas the act of going out had always marked a separation between routine (domestic or workday) and a change of scene, late capitalism's striving for privatization and privileging its spaces turned this concept of time and space around. While the audience may claim valid economic and social reasons for such a withdrawal—ranging from the prohibitive cost of theater tickets for an entire family to a fear of the lower classes or immigrants invading the reclusive spaces of urban theaters—the factor of time itself enters into prime consideration. Rather than taking the time to reach the places where diversion and distraction from routine might be provided, one now prefers to arrange for the retrieval of videos and refreshments from the closest and easiest possible source. Routine absorbs both work *and* leisure, blending them together in a twenty-four hour schedule which is only truly measured by the limits placed on the return of the video rental and the economic penalty for ignoring them. Physically going to the cinema has been replaced by bringing the videocassette into the home, thereby extending the thickness of work time into the fanciful spaces of leisure.[4]

Contemporary films themselves frequently and insistently speak from within the mundane spaces which used to be the targets of escape.

Figure 1.3. Recovering audiences: Art theaters inaugurated by the Mexican government in the 1990s strive to lure spectators out of their homes and away from more commercial venues. (Photo collection of the author.)

Those discursive spaces of boredom and distraction—typically the workplace, home, neighborhood, bar or club, even an entire city—are displayed on living room screens for the members of the middle classes who fill their few empty hours with the images of characters longing to fill the time they have on their own hands. If the home viewers were to turn on the lights they would find themselves inhabiting a variant of what they gaze at through the filter of the lens. Yet so much of this activity to pass the time does just that—time passes indistinguishably as the viewer focuses without consciousness on the objects and stories of the marketplace brought into his or her own den or family room. Increasingly passive, the eye of the spectator looks unblinking at the flickering screen, fingers mechanically picking up snacks or raising a glass to the lips. What some have called "quality time," that is to say filling the fewer and fewer moments outside the workplace with intense schedules of endless diversions for family members to share, begins to take on the look of structured boredom at every turn. More space has to be covered in less time; overvalued activities must be crowded into a set number of hours set aside artificially by the individuals in the household in the fear that if these were to disappear the family unit would do so too. The chronotope of such life is a condensation of "event" or activity into the ongoing uneventful continuum of time which stretches into a lifetime.

How have film directors in Spain and Mexico in particular responded to or attempted to provoke such audiences whose remote, mechanical gaze does not appear to pierce through their own immediate surroundings? What are the figures, images, and techniques that stand in for those who wait for "something else," transfixed in some remote "time space" by the smorgasboard of media images that stretches out before their eyes? How might one invade the home or repackage the glut of objects that has overtaken our vision? Parent and child, neighbor and neighbor, old and young are held in rapture by the sublime moments of forgetfulness—what we sometimes refer to as "spacing out"—in front of the glare of the television set with remote control in hand. How might directors choose to provide an antidote to the prosaic dullness of events and consequent collective dulling of the senses? I propose that it is the cinematic genres of excess that some have mined which hold the potential to break through the distracted eye of the spectator and to disrupt the unbroken visual harmony of uninterrupted consumption.

In his discussion of postwar Spanish cinema, González Requena establishes an important distinction between two popular genres: the cinema of action and that of melodrama. He takes stock of the omnipotent presence of the forceful phallic hero in the first while remarking on a slippage into an overwhelming domestic "time space" of the feminine in the second. What he terms "the absolute kingdom of melodrama" is juxtaposed to the glorification of virility: "In a certain sense, melodrama can be understood as opposed to action narratives. If the latter is sustained by the virile gesture, by the test of the hero's power and audacity, the former is based on the lack, the loss, the suffering generated by the absence of the beloved" (91). By extension, rather than situating the generic codes of melodrama only within the realm of the family as their prime space, or in the "lens of misfortune" as Monsiváis sees them (117), I shall relocate them instead in the perceived "time without event" of boredom. The affect of "lack" and "loss," as González Requena summarizes these conventions, is visually condensed into the spaces of "self-renouncement and sacrifice" (91) inhabited by generations of women on screen. Within the walls of the domestic compound, passion has intruded and then withdrawn, leaving behind neither "virile gesture" nor paternal figure (except in the "traces" of previous action embodied in the children who are left behind, often nameless and unrecognized but material proof nevertheless of a time "with event"—or they would not be there). The Bakhtinian chronotope of melodrama, then, is found in "an ellipsis inscribed at the center of the film" (González Requena 94) which stands in for the missing, the former, or the lavishly celebrated-in-absentia. And what better to fill this emptied notion of time than the excess of emotion and fullness of visual display traditionally associated with the genre. That is to say I do not wish to alter the descriptive aspect of the melodramatic, but instead seek to place it within a different temporal scheme—a chronotope of timeless or eventless space loaded to capacity, or even overflow, with visible physical reminders of time past and now lost. Action is event-intensive; melodrama is between-events. By calling it "the passion machine" (García, 1995 153), Gustavo García emphasizes the melodramatic genre's encoding as feminine—the realm of pure, immovable passion—but also hints at its inhabiting a time of intense longing which is only measured by the previous event(s) or by the potential for future event(s). Melodrama posits a current rupture from both, one in which a plethora of objects surrounding the character(s) substitutes for historical connection. The "time space" of the melodramatic is, as Ana M. López points out, an intersection of "the three master narratives of Mexican [and Hispanic] society: religion, nationalism, and modernization" (1993 150). As the three discourses confront one another in a virtual stalemate of power, an overpowering sense of time without event is produced. Until the momentum shifts in one direction or another, the forces remain deadlocked. Nothing seems to move, but objects keep accumulating. It is in this arena of the visible that the master narratives meet up with their excesses.

If the masculinist action cinema embodies movement and commanding presence, implying its intimate connection with the historical, melodrama trains the eye on the juxtaposition between previous presence and a current stillness or absence. It dwells on loss, silence, lack, and missed desire, all of which are replaced by compensatorial stand-ins to relieve the boredom and monotony of the present. Each of the film narratives responds to a certain type of visionary excess that fills in the spaces of absence. One is concerned with a barrage of images that assault the eye and overflow the screen, dominating and overpowering the viewer. This belongs to what Jeffrey Sconce examines as "paracinema" (372), a series of hybrid genres dedicated to a merciless assault of the senses. The other condenses image and temporality into what Martin Meisel describes as "scattered chiaroscuro" or "punctured discontinuity" (65) which forces the eye to strain to decipher the presence of "something" out there. Insistence on too much (the cinema of action) or too little (scattered areas of clarity and darkness) forces the spectator to reconsider how the spaces of boredom have been filled with narratives so recognizable and accessible to the eye that we no longer pay much attention to them. The audience expects to find certain images in the center of focus; when that

focus changes, the gaze is displaced. I read both of these genres as potential sources of shock, as tapping into "deep anxieties . . . , [aiming to be]
stressful through suspense and disconcerting through surprise" (65).
Meisel's focus on the eye, as well as on overabundance and excruciating
illumination—as opposed to the sparse and the obscure—coincides with
what we have been examining as the axes for a discussion of the cinematic disruption of an enthralled sense of vision, what Benjamin emphasizes as that crucial "fleeting moment of recognition" (Gilloch 116). The
very atrophy of the power of sight, a decline of its potencial to decipher
and respond to the domain of the "real," is addressed by the cinemas of
excess. We are bombarded with constant reminders of the situation in
which we are placed: so many things keep appearing that we might
finally conclude we cannot sort them out, we cannot see how they make
sense. Even as we try to look away we retain the plethora of images
inside our eyelids like nightmares that are impossible to shake.

It is difficult to sort out pure examples of these generic conventions,
and it will prove obvious that hybrid forms are the rule of the 1990s. Just
as González Requena finds that melodrama has penetrated most other
genres "in an imperialist manner" (91), giving rise to a whole variety of
subcategories, including musical melodrama, religious melodrama (set in
cloisters and convents), Western-style melodrama (often combined with
the elements of the musical), gypsy melodrama, melodramas of immigration, and even wrestling melodrama, it would be difficult if not impossible to sort out all the crossovers among crime stories, thrillers, horror
films, film noir, sci-fi films, and the like. Previous formulas may survive
in these situations, but only as contradictory vestiges of supposedly
coherent narratives now recycled into formats whose concern is less the
audience's recognition of conventions or the pleasurable finding of repetition than with an invasion of the eye. The long-rejected style and editing techniques of commercial Hollywood films have been appropriated,
in some cases, as visual evidence of international appeal and production
values; but those same studio production systems that were identifiable
as foreign vestiges now force a nation to take another look at itself
"through other eyes." The economics of the European Union (EU) or of
NAFTA, both centerpieces of the globalizing world of the 1990s, may
reorient production in Spain and Mexico, but they also provoke a drive
to envision new identities in new contexts. The leaders of nations speak
for their constituencies, but the individual members that make up the
collective social group either accept what has become of their nation (in
a trance) or challenge how things are with how things might be (stay
awake). The dangers implied by waiting are obvious: one is placed at the
mercy of so many others and therefore misses the opportunity to speak

before one is spoken for. Modernity, as Graham and Labanyi point out in the subtitle of their anthology of studies related to the rise of modern Spanish culture, is not a fact but a "struggle." The antagonisms to be negotiated, the potential alternatives for civic culture, must be confronted not with the eyes of boredom but with true visual concentration. Blindness and amnesia—*desmemoria* or the casting into oblivion of "event" and the disengagement of the subject from the tedium of the everyday—go hand in hand with the hypnotic waves of consumerism that have washed over societies caught in the overlapping "time space" of nationalism/modernization. The spell must be broken by "an enhanced aptitude for recognition" (Meisel 65) produced through the readjustment of the angles of vigilance, the sharp edges of the everyday normally left hidden, the highlighting of unlikely images, and the conjuring up of "what is . . . even dreaded" (Meisel 66). We refer not only to the "even" dreaded, but to what is especially so even to the point of its repression (or to González Requena's sense of the *recusado* whose denial of "figurability" [Jameson, "Class and Allegory" 290] strikes a blow at the act of representation from the very beginning, since there is no image of what is dreaded among the myriad aspects of material or psychic life). Often, the most dreadful is what makes one react in a manner that is out of sync with the rhythms of a surrounding daydream and what forces the sleepwalker into awakening, perhaps to find him- or herself in the middle of a busy thoroughfare without any idea of how this life-threatening situation came about. As the runaway vehicle lurches toward the transfixed pedestrian, this can be a collision course. We find a perfect example in the car crash that opens *Amores perros*: no one escapes from this perilous position unscathed.

In place of capturing a moment photographically, stilling its action into the limbo of a snapshot's frame, such films can evoke randomness, immediacy, and fragmentation to disturb our line of sight. The random is time "scattered" (after Meisel); the fragmentary and immediate recuperate a sense of event-in-historical-process or the need for considering the now as part of something more. As James Lastra writes, using metaphors from sculpture and architecture,

> the random act of "framing" [implies] a disrupted continuity with something "beyond" the representation and therefore, crucially, that unity and coherence [lie] beyond the individual representational unit. While obviously indices of incompleteness and of absence, such disruptions also [come] to function as indices of an image's production. As the missing limbs of a Greek statue, the distorted form of the ruin, or the worn surface of a Gothic cathedral all signif[y] the passage of time, so newer forms of "lack" hint at historicity to fragmentary films. (273)

Calling attention to the passage of time through the intensified perception of nonevent may be effected through alterations in cinematic syntax, an overabundance of particulars and excruciating details, or even through a maddening lack of such specificity altogether. The chronotope of endlessness can only be comprehended through an appeal to its opposite: the marking of events; historicity. Legibility—how an audience attempts to make sense of the film's narrative and images—does not guarantee spectatorial awareness but often only the plugging into a series of recollections and ritualized patterns. The routine comfort of consumption must be rerouted to interfere with our expectations for both how we look at our world and what we see. As the various characters in the films we are about to discuss anxiously await the end of the workday, the arrival of the weekend, the return of a lost partner, the end of a political era, summer vacation, the love of their life, the appearance of the Antichrist, or the resolution of a crime—how might the spectator reread these symptoms of a "time without event"? And, to paraphrase a recent popular Spanish novel and film title, we might ask how we might manage to perform such a rereading and not die (of boredom) in the process?[5]

In the interval between the completion of this book's first draft and its going to press, much has intervened in the turn of world events. When I sent the manuscript to Albany for consideration on September 10, 2001, I could hardly have imagined the events that would occur in New York City and Washington, D.C., the very next day. Beyond the literal fallout of debris from the destruction of the World Trade Center towers, the subsequent psychological and cultural fallout are harder to calculate and perhaps are incalculable in any meaningful sense as yet. In the span of a few minutes, images of terror made their way around the globe and stirred citizens to evoke vivid scenes of John F. Kennedy at the Berlin Wall in the 1960s and Mexican rebels in the jungles of Chiapas in 1994: to paraphrase them both, on September 11 we were all New Yorkers.

In the aftermath of that use of common, everyday objects such as airliners as uncanny weapons of terror, we now live uneasily between historical deed and visual image. Yet another breach in time has opened up between fact and fiction, between action and the insecurity of what might, or might not, follow. An article published in the Spanish magazine *Cambio 16* on March 4, 2002, assesses this interlude in cultural terms for those whose job it is to represent ourselves and our times: "varios cineastas se han apresurado a asegurar que difícilmente ninguna producción sobre los atentados del 11-S podrá superar la realidad" ("a number of directors have hastened to assure [audiences] that any film made about the attacks of September 11 would only with great difficulty be able to surpass reality"; Márquez 64). To reconcile media reports at the scene that day with the fact that we were not witnessing just another superproduction with special effects has been difficult indeed; a sleepwalking city has been awakened, but it must figure out what to do next. In the meantime, as the more immediate memories of the "real" slip away, New Yorkers have begun to learn to live with terror. This is, without a doubt, a time of both "post" (September 11) and "pre" (the unknown), punctuated by moments of reawakening to threats of new terrors.

Rather than enter into a discussion of production, however, it is within the realm of consumption that we might discover pertinent and perhaps even surprising details about the relationship between post– September 11 Western culture and the bored movie-gazer. Since it is to theories of the popular that I looked to base my examination of films, it is to the same sources that I return to reconsider how the tedium of urban life was impacted by the excess of violence that has come to haunt us all through images that, at first, seemed to emanate from nowhere else but Hollywood (or the numerous regional cinemas inflected by it). Even as the dot.com generation's vision of easy and boundless prosperity had already begun to cloud over, as "Fox Fever" (Scoffield A9) had begun to die down and cool off after the Mexican elections of 2000, and as the realities of the new European economy had taken hold of the media in Spain, something new was added to the troubled mix. The daily fare of Basque terrorism, governmental corruption, and issues of immigration in an increasingly borderless (but tensely nationalistic) world suddenly united in a new vision of globalization based more on danger than on profit. Drawn together by both local experience and international communications, modern consumers have displayed something else in common: once again, it seems, we have turned to the artifacts of popular culture not just to escape from the horrors around us but to find a foothold amid the ruins.

Three scant weeks after the terrorist attacks, on the front page of the *New York Times* there appeared an article entitled "In Little Time: Pop Culture Is Almost Back to Normal." The dateline is Los Angeles and, in the opinion of network television executives, media focus groups, film distributors, and academics alike, "what's most striking is how unchanged the appetite for popular culture seems to be . . . people are probably clinging for consolation to old habits" (Lyman and Carter A1). Whether they actually satisfy our needs or not, films and television are where we imagine— we fantasize, perhaps—we will find solace and, just maybe, a recognizable semblance of ourselves. As the Twin Towers soon became a metaphor for insecurity and impermanence—what had seemed eternal in their imposing and excessively visible, material presence on the skyline was now merely several million tons of rubble—people scurried back to home and family in a newfound appreciation of daily routine and convention. Despite an invasion of our "home territory," one with both material and psychological dimensions, our cultural "appetites" experienced, the article assures us, a mere "hiccup" (B10) over the first few days. Videocassette rentals and movie theater attendance quickly returned to their "normal rhythm." Even if trade and economics took a beating in markets, one could hastily retreat from public disenchantment into private spaces reenchanted by the imagination. In this sense, the everyday has reverted to its role as haven, hiding place, camouflage and protective cover. In its assumed transparency—we all know what it looks like—the everyday is imbued with an aura of the normal and the natural, as if it were a found object located somehow outside society, culture, and, of course, history. As Ben Highmore proposes, "the everydayness of everyday life might be experienced as a sanctuary. . . . Or its special quality might be its lack of qualities. It might be, precisely, the unnoticed, the inconspicuous, the unobtrusive" (1). Faced with an epitome of intrusiveness, the everyday now signals a process of coping with and representing—yet not totally absorbing—such extreme and catastrophic disturbances. This transpires in the venue of the domestic, both within the home and on the screen (the latter being charged with contributing to "ordinary" life as we recall it). But Highmore calls such negotiations between familiarity and the unfamiliar "signs of failure" (2) when the landscapes of modernity cannot totally incorporate or domesticate interruptions and challenges into images of the mundane. And when these traces of dissonance are magnified and overstated—whether as excessive presence or exaggerated lack (somewhat like the skyward beams of blue light in New York harbor that stand in for what is no longer there)—the cultural products of which they form part become markers of social intrigue and fertile possibility.

So in the future we will need to undertake our rereading of the film codes of the 1990s under the rubric of even more intensified "signs of failure" of modernity uncovered by the events of September 11. Like the death of Franco and the fall of the PRI, one must consider the measure of the world before and the world after as two tenors of the "everyday." What might be salvaged from the debris of the previously mundane after the last truckload of twisted metal and solitary pillars have been trucked out of the metropolis? How do we recall now what the mundane was like before? The cinema's images of an acquired sense of boredom of everyday life that turned from silence into deafening explosion is where we might begin. If the lull of economic satiation is turned on its head, Highmore concludes, then we find that "[m]odern everyday life is 'sensational' (alive with desire)" (14). Maybe instead of "is" we need to look at the films of the 1990s to evoke how it "was" perhaps "alive with desire" but we were too bored to notice. The tumult of the spectacular, the extraordinary, and the excessive—the "sensational" in Highmore's assessment—is the din that accompanies Benjamin's awakening of modernity to both its promises and its paradoxes. The everyday may seem life-affirming in our most ardently held myths, but its darker side may also be fearful and life-threatening. We have come face-to-face with both.

JAIME HUMBERTO HERMOSILLO'S *LA TAREA*

Not Your Average Afterschool Special

The value attached to the visual across modern Western culture in the late twentieth century has as its emblems both photography and film as the media of choice for the collective transmission of cultural images. Visual reproduction has long served to certify events as "real." It is a token of their credibility, of their actually having happened "just the way we see them" before our very eyes. The resonance of traces of past events, often set in a minor key to evoke nostalgia, leave the spectator pondering the power of photography, first as "a key role as evidence" (Gunning 42), and then as an intrinsic aspect of the cinematic text which took its place in the domain of the mass media. As scientific processes, both forms of image production have been deemed nonintrusive, with the lens of the device serving as a neutral means of verification only, supposedly not influencing how events were cast into forceful cultural icons of national consequence and symbolic value. At the turn of the twenty-first century, however, such an innocence of representation is no longer able to hold an equivalent value in the mass-produced artifacts of the digital age.

As photography has been replaced by video and, subsequently, by digital technology as the everyday forms of media life, the link between image and so-called truth value has been eroded, and the privilege of a direct relationship with the "real" is no longer left unchallenged. This does not suggest, however, that Western culture's addiction to the easy satisfaction of linking event and representation has been cured by any means; our sleepwalking among images divided between the fantastic or uncanny and the purportedly true continues unabated. But, as Régis Durand writes regarding the powerful impact of both still and moving images, such a fundamental proposal is filled with impossibility from the outset, since such a partition is unfeasible. He spells out in no uncertain terms that: "a direct encounter with the real subject of photography is not possible, . . . we have to take the indirect path of the symbolic. Those who try to short-circuit it—by dreaming of a direct confrontation with the real (as in reportage)—expose themselves to violent returns of the repressed" (147). We are bombarded endlessly with constantly morphing faces and talking heads, with panoramas juxtaposed to closeups, and with the prelude to events alongside their aftermath, whether the images on screen are culled from the physical world around us or from the illusions in the minds of those who create those images. When one looks away from the moving picture, one is haunted not so much by the traces of the visible left on the retina but by those invisible afterimages that silently accompany our overt fascination with the "real." The encoding of truth in and around the filmed images of modern Latin American societies for so long has created a similar aura of veracity in those texts, shunting aside any hint of the lingering ghosts of the turmoil of inner political life in favor of the overtly real and political. When we find ourselves face-to-face with the material world we want to find what we have been exposed to on screen previously, what we expect to see. The discrepancy between the two—expectation or precondition and actuality—mires us in doubt and anxiety, and creates the need to break out of a sort of timeless time (Petro 265) into the realm of human history.

The reproduction of images from public—that is, collective—life exposed in what have been called the "early classics" (Rich, 1997 273) of the complex movement known as the New Latin American Cinema[1] has given way in many subsequent films to a focus on the inner workings of the social body rather than on the external mechanics of society in an effort to reconnect an audience with the increasingly elusive domain of the repressed. The jarring focus of hand-held movie cameras mobilized in the streets to document the epic political struggles of twentieth-century Latin America—from organized revolutionary masses, to civilian confrontations with the military, to the comings and goings of the inhabitants of the modern urban metropolis—more recently has been turned inward to gaze behind the closed doors that ostensibly separate the home from those other public spheres where all events have been taking place. Scenes of political confrontation in which shifting regimes of authority have managed to occupy center stage have ceased to startle us. Violence and suffering have changed from unusual acts to prosaic or mundane events. Crowds in the streets, riot gear, and casserole-thumping protesters no longer cause a ripple in the collective imaginary when the image of "Latin America" is conjured up. In fact, such groups of figures appear more like ghosts of the past than visions of the present; they occupy a time without chronology. To reach the audience in deeper and more indirect ways, filmmakers have moved the focus of their shots inward. As Rich writes, this alteration of the lens "marks a shift from 'exteriority' to 'interiority,' . . . redefin[ing] the site of political struggle as the sexual" (1997 281, 286) and thereby reconnecting the viewer with the political repressed.

Centering on emotional life and its ravaging by state agendas of modernization—especially through the experience and imagination of women—these films invest images represented on screen with a political charge equal to that of the public world previously foregrounded as collective document. At least the suggestion of such an aesthetic transition has appeared in films in which the portals to family dwellings and religious refuges have been cast as the thresholds into salvation for those trying to survive the risky business of the streets. Yet these very same spaces are often breached and overrun, in the end, by dark and frequently sinister alliances among the forces of politics, the military, and the market economy. At the end of the century, it goes without saying that emotional life is not free of the political; the home is the microcosm of the nation and its last bastion of defense. In it are reproduced the norms of the social world of which it forms an integral and frequently influential component. The enthrallment with the exterior tempered, the symbolic realm of homeliness (*Heimlich*) takes over, even if this too runs the risk of seeming to belong to just part of the daily routine. Some new element must be added to jolt spectators out of their lethargy or saturate them with so much excess—violence, emotion, language, visual detail— that they cannot help but see the contrast between the real and the representation rather than live beyond any overt reaction because of an oversaturation of the retina (and of all emotional response).

The genre of melodrama, identified by many film critics both north and south of the border as emblematic of Mexican cinema, provides the spectator privileged access to those interior spaces whose passions represent and intensify the contradictions of the processes of social modernization or their aftermath. In contrast to the prevailing tropes of that cinema's golden age (roughly between 1936 and 1956), which focused on masculinity in all of its extravagant post-revolutionary masks and disguises, beginning with the decade of the 1970s women have increasingly used the camera lens to rout out images of crisis in the passage from the old social order into the acclaimed New World Order. Many such films are still marked by a certain amount of ambiguity and indecision regarding possible alternate scenarios, but they retain these contradictions as pivotal elements of the production. As both directors and actors in "the production of the symbolic order" (Millán 11) in contemporary Mexican society, women may demonstrate a need to close the circle of the past, yet they often fail to provide the audience with convincing alternatives to traditional social structures and cultural values, despite their overt appeal to a gendered response to the masculinist order of the past. The latter is evoked as a continued presence—even when obviously going through moments of crisis, such as the presidential elections of 1988—against which women represent the capacity to fantasize possible opposition. Women briefly assume control over the apparatus of representation but subsequently often withdraw from open confrontation with the institutions of politics and culture, leaving the future impact of melodrama and its narrators open to interpretation. It is amid the accumulated debris of the masculine—language, attitude, power, manipulation, spectacle and display, euphemism, and the like—that directors and actors of the 1990s have taken a stand.

In Jaime Humberto Hermosillo's 1990 film *La tarea* (Homework), such a shift in point of view also integrates the economy of the nation squarely within the interior spaces of the middle-class family as a spectacle to be observed—and purchased on videotape—by an audience of avid consumers. The obstacles to the harmony of the nuclear family can therefore be witnessed by those same families on home ground, in the privacy of their living rooms and bedrooms. As director María Luisa Bemberg's 1986 film *Miss Mary* represented this inner space as a battleground between a symbolic economy of repression and the private forces of rebellion, with national events paralleling routine home life, so director Hermosillo posits a structural and cultural crossover on screen. Played by Julie Christie, the British governess of Bemberg's film's title encounters the forces of state brutality and female suffering cohabiting in the same family space. The film's characters display for the audience how "[the performance of] sexual acts involves psychic risk, [with the simultaneous seduction and rejection of] peronism [shown as] built in the bedrooms of the nation" (Rich, 1997 287). Defiance within the confines of domesticity disproves official public declarations of decency, order, and propriety as unifying structures of the nation while it reveals the chaos of desire and power underlying them. If we concur that these intertwined and suggestive narratives might be snapshots of occult political repression in Argentine society, I propose that the economic and cultural agendas of end-of-the-twentieth-century modernization (in the guise of a global neoliberal agenda) are constructed and deployed in the bathrooms, foyers, and private studies of Mexican households in films such as Hermosillo's *Intimidades en un cuarto de baño* (*Bathroom Intimacies;* 1989), *El aprendiz de pornógrafo* (*The Pornographer's Apprentice*; 1989), *La tarea* (Homework; 1990), and *La tarea prohibida* (*X-Rated Homework*; 1992).

Unlike the more-pronouncedly neorealist style of earlier Latin American cinematic works, which had underlying aspirations of editing jobs careful enough to obtain an unbroken visual continuity of story-telling, films of the 1980s and 1990s such as Paul Leduc's *Frida* (1984), Bemberg's *Camila* (1984), María Novaro's *Danzón* (1991), Guita Schyfter's *Novia que te vea (I Hope to See You as a Bride*; 1993), Tomás Gutiérrez Alea's *Fresa y chocolate (Strawberry and Chocolate*; 1994), and even Alfonso Arau and Laura Esquivel's *Como agua para chocolate (Like Water for Chocolate*; 1992) all shift our attention away from narrative scenes of collective commitment and social exposé. The spectator is transported instead to the darker realms of "banality, fantasy, and desire" (Rich, 1997 281) as other sites through which to explore issues of individual and national identity, sites less exhausted by the media but filled to the brim with traces of the conflicted realm of the mundane. It is through the characters Tita, Pedro, and Mamá Elena in *Como agua para chocolate*, for example, that we see the period between the turn of the century through the late 1920s in Mexico, and not through the hordes of savage revolutionaries who appear one night in the exemplary border town of Eagle Pass, Texas, to rape and pillage this community of women which has been seemingly immune to the ravages of history. Such figures emerge abruptly from the dark morass of political events but recede back into it just as quickly, marking chronological time with merely a traumatic trace of "event." Politics are relegated to intermittent—customarily violent—interruptions of the family saga, which is celebrated by means of saturnalian culinary feasts and sporadic social quarrels. The camera as a mechanical device capable of apprehending the "real" in the most accurate manner—perhaps a tribute as much to Kodak's marketing strategies as to the cult of modern technology—turns away from one (public) venue to scrutinize the less visible riches of another (private) one. As the movie camera tracks through the front door of sanctified home space, the panoramic social vision is left behind, but not the repercussions of the mental structures imposed on all those who inhabit both domains. Hence we become witnesses to the aesthetics of allegory in which the limits set by the greater scheme of the nation are implied by the constructs of the domestic. Larger-than-life revolutionary heroes of epic melodrama give way to the family unit as what Carlos Monsiváis calls the "real heroine" of modern society (118). This protagonist is haunted not by the treasonous phantoms of foreign invasion but by the ghosts of homegrown social disruption and civil discontent.

Through the everyday lives and private acts of individuals, the nation is portrayed as composed as much of invisible narratives as it is of visible ones. Films such as these recover an important aspect of the Latin American imaginary—the secret, hidden longings of men and women, and the underlying factors and ideologies that condition the formation of those desires. What was previously subsumed under the majestic tales of national movements and *grandes historias* (epic narratives) is foregrounded as the everyday stories of how individuals negotiate the private challenges of collective society. In the films mentioned above, the telling of history is up for grabs, although its official portrait has already been framed by the studios and production companies attached to the ruling party and has been sponsored by its fervent adherents and defenders. At this new juncture in representational alternatives, the vast space of the epic is replaced by those intimate pages of the diary and the chronicle; the sweeping dimension of myth is reduced to the chapters of private annals, personal stories, and homework assignments removed from the classroom and transported into the corners, cubbyholes, and closets of the domestic realm. The intrinsic validity of the act of storytelling remains intact, yet the vehicle for the transmission of the story now trains its lens on the details of the intimate and not the broader brushstrokes of the public. So-called private matters are cast into public domain for everyone to see; doors are flung open to all those interested in breaking through the superficial boredom of the home into the fertile and active imaginaries of those who inhabit its most obscure recesses.

Given the concentric structure of *La tarea*—it is visually and narratively made up of a film within a film—we might conclude that the classic (or traditional) documentary form and overt political content that audiences have been led to expect from Latin American cinema are critical parts of the implicit subtext or pre-text of the film's *mise-en-abîme*. Both what the spectator sees and the concept of how things are made visible—how one is led to identify and judge certain aspects of social surroundings, or separate the familiar from the uncanny, or perceive the nuances of the material world and its social and economic relations—are central to its workings. In this film, the director positions the audience as a voyeur on an equal footing with the ostensible object of seduction, the character Marcelo (played by José Alonso). Through strategies used by the filmmaker we are made aware of our own complicity in the making and interpretation of an image, much as international audiences have been led to construct an image of the Latin American "real" by means of previous cinematic projects. Just as Marcelo is impelled to decide what role he will assume in the film's production once he discovers the lens of the camera that has recorded the details of his erotic encounter with character Virginia (played by María Rojo), the spectator is placed in the position of self-conscious observer. What Ana López calls in earlier films "a naive belief in the camera's ability to record 'truths'" (1990, 407) as if they were preserved intact, unedited, and undisturbed by any mechanical means of transmission, is brought to light by Hermosillo through his focus on the process of cinematic composition. He has the camera lens narrow—both literally and figuratively—from exterior panoramic shot to interior close-up, drawing the audience into the realm of domestic melodrama for fun and profit. *La tarea* is the simultaneous creation of a product (the video narrative) and the marketing of it to an audience of consumers. He has us buy into the exaggerated promises of melodrama and then, through recourse to its codes of excess and masquerade, makes us an indispensable part of the text itself, for it depends on us for financial success. While we await the replenishment of our emotional reserves, we pay with our financial resources to find stimulation in the simulacrum of sexuality on screen.

For just whose fun and profit these cinematic images are intended may indeed be open to debate, but one possible response is provided by María Rojo's character in the last ten minutes of postproduction discussion with her costar. As it turns out, they are not the Virginia and her lover Marcelo we have come to recognize from scene one, but María and José, a married couple who have set us up to watch their enactment of a tryst. They are accomplices in the making of an artifact that addresses the intended audience's fantasies about women's sexuality, erotic secrets, and hidden anxieties (including AIDS); but, over time, we have joined in complicity with them to reach the end of the story and tie up its loose ends. María's *tarea*, the assignment she has just completed filming and we have witnessed being composed on screen, is given the following subtitle by its proud director: "Cómo la pornografía salvó del tedio y mejoró la economía de la familia Partida" ("How pornography saved the Partida family from boredom and filled its bank account at the same time"). In a sense, this half-jokingly made remark shared between them does indeed summarize the conditions on which the making of María's film is predicated. She has been inspired to make the film by two factors: the temptation of economic profit and an overdose of boring familial routine. In other words, her motivations are the fun and profit mentioned earlier, both of which are derived at the expense of the innocent spectator who has been preconditioned by a film industry whose representation of reality is sold without question. Financial need as well as the banality of everyday life are found linked together in the domain of what Marx and Engels called the "Holy Family," that structure held by Western tradition to be the natural foundation of society. It would indeed be a truly "heroic" institution (in Monsiváis's words again) if it managed to survive all the charges and attacks of modernity against its secure framing of collective tradition and personal salvation within the walls of home life. The director's interpretation of this rather fragile social edifice—how the struggle for power is acted out in a sexual encounter as well as in a set-up film scenario—impels us to focus on every gesture and every word. Is this a reference to the Mexican economic crisis and its effects on the home, to the bankruptcy of the institution of the family itself, or to the commodification of all human acts into economic exchange value? It is conceivably a way to imagine our times' greatest dreams and greatest fears—a loss of control over our lives, an exclusion from the raptures of the marketplace, a casting into oblivion of tradition, an accumulation of innumerable riches but nowhere to spend them—all rolled into one. Let us now examine in more detail how the image of the sacred turns into the icon of the profane, and how boredom becomes marketable.

A critical facet of this family scenario is its cultural context. In 1990s Mexico, in trends similar to those in the United States, the home video market began to replace the collective experience of the movie theater. With rental stores popping up as profitable cottage industries on every street corner, it became much easier to send a member of the family out to find a current release than to pack everyone up for an excursion to the movies. It is also less expensive to do so, even as the market simultaneously channels money into the film industry and keeps the production of new releases alive.[2] So the "tedium" of Marcelo and Virginia (the characters played by María and José) functions as a mirror of the privatized, middle-class boredom of the members of the audience who may be tempted to seek ways to escape the straight and narrow of daily life and line their pockets in the process. Video cameras and VCRs have become a staple of the middle classes for both recording special family events and for filling empty leisure hours documenting the mundane activities of parents and children. Home videos and the vast inventories of rental outlets have drawn the viewer out of the public life associated with a visit to the movies back into the realm of solitary pleasures behind the closed doors of home. To make a film about the very space in which the video is viewed is the perfect circle of metacommentary: those who appear on screen act out the same scenarios of life shared by those who are permitted to watch (via the hidden camera). It is like spying on yourself. Without an equally bored spectator who longs for—fantasizes about—excitement and entertainment, Virginia's "homework" is only of value as a narcissistic exercise for her own personal enjoyment, and it would have little or no impact on screen for other audiences. (Either that, or the project would merely fulfill the requirements of her night school class.) Its real market value is driven by those who are willing to pay for a personal experience that will enrich their own private lives in some new way. By watching the video, they buy into the mythical dream of a democracy in which equal access to personal satisfaction is announced as part and parcel of everyday life for all members of society without exception. The myth is an inclusive one; no one is left out, at least in public rhetoric. The entire self-conscious project presented in detail, from camera placement to postproduction wrap-up, presupposes the presence of an audience enraptured by the seduction of what is on screen to enliven their everyday routine. Spectators are an indispensable element of the process of production, as well as consumers of the final product. The predication of previous Latin American cinema on the unmediated eyewitness account of an historical moment lived before one's eyes opened up the continent to the eyes of the outside world. Hermosillo's film opens our eyes to the contradictory messages we receive from the media and how we interpret them: sometimes perceptively, often erroneously, but always ideologically. Not just the subject of the film is placed in question but the process (and value) of letting the outside in is as well.

From the very first sequence of images, the directors Hermosillo and Virginia place the cinematic process and the enticing but problematic relationship of spectator to image in clear focus. The two lowercase a's of the title word itself are composed of women's legs, encased in black stockings, jauntily kicking upward while dangling high-heeled red shoes from the tips of their toes. The entry has been framed, the doorway set, to the world of domestic melodrama. Women and *tarea*, work, albeit homework, are shown metonymically entwined into a single visible sign of the feminine and its implicit sexuality, inextricably linked together from the outset. Fragments of women's bodies are incorporated into the title credits, on display and available for visual consumption by the eyes of the marketplace. As the credits roll and then fade, the strains of the romantic *bolero* "Bonita" are heard on the soundtrack. This popular ballad extolling feminine beauty forms a bridge into the visual narrative and a link to the sequences later on in the film when Marcelo and Virginia, in the absence of the condoms she demands that he use, decide to dance instead of having sex. Alluding to the woman's physical presence—*bonita*—the music unites them in the erotic movements of the dance as a substitute for their original plan. Women, both audibly and visually, are encoded here as physically attractive by nature. A woman's place may still be in the home, but she had better look good after her chores are done. So the joyous calves and ankles of the credits show us, and the popular song lyrics reinforce her as the icon of sexual attractiveness but also as the seducer. The title's background stands in for the figure of the woman just as the fetishized fragments of faces, clothing, and makeup articles function behind the opening sequence of Spanish director Pedro Almodóvar's 1988 *Mujeres al borde de un ataque de nervios (Women on the Verge of a Nervous Breakdown)*. Celebrating women's space—both a penthouse apartment and a film-dubbing studio, to say nothing of the spaces women carve out in the lives of other men and women in Madrid—the Spanish film addresses some of the same gender-related issues addressed by Hermosillo. The unique perspective of each director, however, skews the respective films in different directions: one is a celebration of alternatives to the traditional family, the other a renewal of its recognizable structure. The concrete embodiment of femininity and desire is found here in the legs of María Rojo, an actress whose recent role in María Novaro's film *Danzón* (and, later, in Hermosillo's *De noche vienes, Esmeralda* [*Esmeralda Comes By Night*]) creates an instant recognition factor for audiences. While that cabaret film's establishing shot is an extreme closeup of a female dancer's legs and feet enclosed in ankle-strap high-heeled shoes, about to be set in motion to the rhythms of tropical music, *La tarea* offers sketched and stylized representations of the same appendages. The director then moves on to their inspiration of the entire cinematic narrative: these are the legs of the working woman as a seductress on her own turf.

The first scene opens with María Rojo seen in closeup, viewed by the audience through the lens of the very same video camera she is setting up on the floor of her dining room. Dressed in her working clothes—a practical vest, nondescript blue jeans, wire-rim glasses, and dark, flat, sensible shoes—her demeanor and appearance signal to us that she is in the process of production; she is a woman at work. She sings quietly to herself as she sets the stage for the action to follow. Crouched down, facing the audience, she is captured in the middle of the act of rigging up the mechanical device that we will have as our unblinking eye for the rest of the performance. From the beginning, we are not permitted to forget that there is a device mediating between us and the images we see on screen. We are not really there, but a camera stands in our place. As she casts off one set of work clothes and dons another, Virginia assumes the role of a woman on the job in a different sense. Disappearing from (our) view for a few minutes to effect her transition, she quickly reappears in the clingy, tomato-red dress, black stockings, and red high-heels that our eyes connect with another kind of work role, as suggested previously by the colors and images of the opening credits. Virgina works at luring us in through the icon of the spectacularly and flamboyantly feminine; she sets herself up as a figure to be desired through the bright shades and tight fit of the clothing. In other words, she sells her image to Marcelo and the film's premise—or what we think she intends to be the premise—to us. We are taken in by her rapid and radical transformation, and are set up by the camera to track her movements through the new situation suggested by her change in attire. No longer just another typical apartment in the big city, this becomes the space of adventure; the drabness and hypocrisy of everyday life are disguised behind the mask (of her red dress) of female sexuality on display. But we might ask ourselves why this appears on the domestic stage and not in public. Hermosillo offers us the amateur pornography of the suburban bedroom, or as close to suburbia as we can get in Mexico City.

As she hides the denim outfit of her first disguise, she also stows the tripod and other technical equipment under the furniture of the apartment in a very visible act of concealing the supports—the cinematic apparatus—on which all filmic texts must rely. Dependence on such devices is necessary for the shooting of the film, but for our participation in the potential pleasure of the shoot as well, as an ostensible scene of real life to which we are witness. We are aware that this technical machinery exists, even when disguised behind the mundane family furnishings of the room. Both Hermosillo and Virginia utilize this knowledge, since everything has been constructed with the purpose of allowing us, even inviting us, to look and to believe we are privy to the secrets and private life of the home's inhabitant. *La tarea*'s establishing shot is emblematic as it situates the spectator in a particular time and space, and it creates a certain complicity between director and spectator. What is condensed here is the conjunction of the visible and the invisible, the "real" and the repressed, the material and the phantasmatic. A camera takes our place inside this room and permits us entry into this closed space, but we are as yet unaware of how our own expectations and previous conditioning by images might mislead us into "seeing" things or viewing them from a particular perspective. The voyeur peeks inside these four walls, enticed by the images of the credits and the figure of the character Virginia into sticking around to find out what happens. Virginia's double performance is a staged contract with us—we are about to enter a zone of great promise, as signaled by the red dress on display to indicate the hidden attractions of domesticity and the flip side of the sensibleness of the traditional working woman. For once, it is she who sets the stage; the male voice we hear on the other side of the door is invited into her domain and the encounter takes place under her rules. Do we delight in her control, his attempt at manipulation, or both? Is this a game anyone can win, or just a game in and of itself? In the end, we are hardly witnesses to a remake of the traditional virgin-whore figure but instead to the end-of-century Mexican woman as full-fledged member of the labor force and as temptress exercising her will over another.

The audience has set in front of it not a finished product but what Susan Hayward calls the "reduplication of images" (219) of the film-within-a-film. Like Bentham's eye of the panopticon, we are lured into taking the position of the privileged and unobtrusive eye under the table, unsure as to what we might see but enticed to find out for ourselves. The homework that brings the act of composition into focus and the outside world into the home is the object of elaborate restagings and adjust-ments. The fairly obsessive attention of Virginia to the position of the camera, its access to the center of the room, and its angle of vision form a leitmotif of the entire narrative presentation. She checks and rechecks the precise tilt; she kneels (even when already attired in the blazing red dress) and peers intently into its lens; she resets it carefully after Marcelo knocks it out of line, almost as if she knows—by the end of the film shoot we realize she does know—that he will be back to take up per-forming again despite his rage at her duplicity. His consent is not verbal, but he does leave only to reappear, ostensibly to pick up something he has forgotten and, in the process, to open a discussion of filmmaking with Virginia. Virginia's fastidious preoccupation with the workings of the camera signifies for us the importance bestowed on the act of look-ing, and the privileged if problematic perspective of all forms of the visual. Between 1989 and 1992 Hermosillo himself returns in film after film to the same thematic and structural concern with representation, thereby enfolding Virginia's elaboration of cinematic restagings within his own. An intrinsic part of melodrama is such a compulsion to repeat, the steps of a daily routine made excruciatingly evident and detailed, as we shall see.

Such excesses in directorial presence, in planning and carrying out a shoot, in the constant reminders of the performative aspect of film, can be considered a response to what Martin Meisel has explored as "the dif-ficulty of seeing" (75) associated with the genre of melodrama. As corre-sponds to "interiority," the spectacle of the home is shrouded in shadow and filled with dark corners into whose recesses we may only peer by means of a strategically placed camera. Just as we think we comprehend what is coming into focus, the director reveals that perhaps we should not feel so certain since, after all, the order of the symbolic shadows what is most visible, leaving in the less-illuminated fringes the more deeply haunted facets of everyday life. Light and dark, revelation and secrecy, desire stimulated and desire thwarted all problematize both domestic space and the ambiguous cinematic language of intimacy or "interiority." What is diegetically represented as an intoxicating brew of seduction and manipulation is only the tip of the iceberg; the really tantalizing forces of eroticism and economics lie just offscreen where the light doesn't reach. The act of looking therefore requires of us more than we may have been accustomed to expect from previous cinematic experiences. Hand-held cameras bridge the distance between photographer and spectator, as well as between photographer and subject—or at least so it seems when we accompany a filmmaker on his or her journey through the melee of the streets. Now, however, the illusion of an unmediated image is ruptured and we are made to deal with our own reactions to the consequences. To paraphrase Ana López once again, the naive vision of the objective capacity of the camera is cast out along with the myth of the innocence of the spectatorial eye. Completing this homework assignment marks the deliberate invasion of one space by another, the casting of light into obscurity (depths both physical and psychological), the revelation that inside/outside are concepts that are mutually dependent to produce any sense of meaning, and the establishment of reciprocal information between the subject and the object of the gaze. Home turns into classroom, actress becomes director, man is seduced by woman, private acts are endowed with interest as public spectacles, and the often blinding glare of the outside world erupts into the shadows of domesticity. Among a variety of questions we are asked to consider are: how does one begin to look at scenes of the intimate life of the middle classes under klieg lights? Just what expectations do we bring with us? What does it mean for ourselves and for society when we are "caught looking"? And how do we project our own fantasies onto the actors caught in the blaze of the lights?

Such a visual intrusion or seepage of one space into another connects different sites of representation and different social roles. But it also indicates the conversion of intellectual activity (homework) into seduction which, in turn, is cast into the form of a marketable product. Here the film suggests an additional taboo subject, as risqué as other images we might encounter on the screen or read in the script if we search for a subject broader than sexuality. Current debates over what Dennis Allen writes of as "the overt commercialization of academic work" (282) open up the forum to questions of the value of intellectual property and rights over an artifact itself. Who discerns the production of a piece of work as

an original process or a response to the demands of the market? Place a
monetary value on intellectual activity? Sell a homework assignment?
Reap a profit from a film about the life of a typical middle-class family?
In the age of the Internet and all the services it offers us, these are not
inquiries but mere declaractions of fact, a series of rhetorical questions
whose answers we have assimilated into the unconscious life of everyday
routine. We are willing to pay for the visualizing of our "secrets" in concrete form, and subsequently validate them by saying they are available
in commercial release. The film as a "work of art" is no longer merely a
finished product devoid of an aura of authenticity and infinitely reproduced (in Benjamin's well-known phrase), but a visible and consumable
process which satisfies our craving for immediacy and revelatory observation. In a consumer culture, every facet of the imaginary is ultimately
up for sale; *La tarea* taps into this notion perfectly and flings it in our
faces for us to recognize as part of our daily cultural fare.

Human intervention into previously unseen and uncharted realms of
behavior—except, of course, in underground publications, imported
magazines, tabloids, or midnight film showings—takes us under the
table, both literally and metaphorically. We peek out and try to make
some sense of what crosses our line of sight, enraptured by the daring
project undertaken by Virginia (which, in reality, is even more than
meets the eye since it is María who sets the whole film in motion as she
assumes the identity of Virginia). To overtly document the sexual activities of a middle-aged, unmarried couple is an invitation to censorship,
unless of course, like Hermosillo, one only suggests what follows the
opening of the door to the home by leaving the audience at foot-level
and by turning off the lights of the foyer in the distance where all of the
erotics take place. Taking into account the proposal that the structure of
melodrama is "triangular" (Bratton, Cook, Gledhill 2), as hidden spectators we are suspended amid the conflicted spaces of virtuosity and vil-
lainy which are brought together in the territory of home. The family's
negotiation of the demands of the political imaginary is played out under
the scrutiny of the newly present camera. Challenges to unity—between
parents and children, between spouses—invade from outside to put to
the test the forces that keep this social edifice in one piece. As Mark
Szuchman writes, "[w]hen the challenge to familial integrity rises, a
female is presented as the foil. She represents the relentless force that will
have its way regardless of consequences, and she is the agent of blows to
the social conventions and the beliefs of her kin" (185–86). The figure of
the woman is pivotal in the triangle of relations: she deals with people
and forces which threaten to disrupt the needs of her particular group,
or which attempt to abscond with their sources of emotional and eco-

nomic sustenance. Yet she is also, at least in Hermosillo's interpretation, an agent of confrontation who staves off such attacks by pre-emptive plots and strategies. María, as Virginia, interprets her homework assignment as a chance to make money, killing two birds with one stone and replacing the tedium of the couple with the excitement of the chase. The sequential shot as an exercise does not demand placement in a room of their home; she decides that for herself. And when she chooses to film a couple engaged in the social foreplay prior to actual sexual activity, she treads on the fine line between the acceptable and the prohibited, the decent and the immoral, the light of sensuality and the darkness of sexuality. Playing on the chain of associations evoked by the title of Antonio Serrano's 1998 film *Sexo, pudor y lágrimas (Sex, Shame, and Tears)*, María already knows that taking this risk could make them a lot of money, and if she satirizes the whole process it may be even better. Then each spectator can be allowed to feel more comfortable with the act of spying because, after all, it may just turn out to be a joke and nothing more. Like a child hiding inside a cupboard, the spectator crouches down under the table, hoping against hope that Marcelo won't see the video cable running under the corner of the rug and blow the setup, intruding into the dark and problematic space of the "other" (ourselves) without whose presence the encounter of the two characters has little value. It is through the lens that we record our recognition (sight), repression (blindness, lack of comprehension), and liberation (sight restored) as we traverse the recesses of the room and of the situation orchestrated by María. What is brought out of the obscurity of the unconscious is the association between eroticism and economics, the economy which invests bodily functions and processes with value and meaning.

The sequence shot that forms the student's proposed course project is represented from the outset as a contradiction to the myth of the unedited text and as a reevaluation of the value of women's work. Not only is María adept at the art of directing, but she is accomplished at the more difficult task of capturing the audience in the thrall of the image. We are led to expect no interference by the agents of cinema, no interruption of narrative scenes, nothing but a flow of images whose coherence is consumed as unquestionably accurate and objective. But, like Marcelo, we get caught up by the story and are kept in the dark until Virginia provokes an explosion of our sense of security by Marcelo's spectacular onscreen discovery of the camera. She offers him two explanations for the narrative predicated on her rekindling a past romance with him: either it is the result of seeing a film with Marcelo Mastroianni and being reminded of his namesake, or it is the follow-up to an erotic dream she had had about her former lover. Marcelo is flattered by the second alternative but seems mystified by the first. Such metatextual references fall outside his comprehension, but to be cast in the starring role of her fantasies-come-to-life sounds good to him. Rather than fill in for a distant and remote icon of classic Italian cinema, he wants to star in his own feature film. This way he escapes any comparison, subconscious or otherwise, with a masculine theater idol but keeps his top billing in her amateur production. After an absence of four years—already quite a long interruption of desire's fulfillment—he returns to be recorded for future replay in some sort of private screenings by a potential audience of voyeurs. Possibly more accustomed to the cinema's mobile eyewitness camera, we are placed in a position to be intrigued by the notion that we will have firsthand access to the relevation of an intimate "secret" (Rich, 1997 283) so key to the cinema's move into interiors. We long to be in touch with what "really" occurs, or perhaps what we wish would occur, outside the center of focus. We dare not blink, even if we are relegated to the level of the floor, awaiting the outcome of our own longings projected onto the characters. As spectators, we have Virginia on our side. She assures us a clear view of what transpires as she orchestrates their scene within the space covered by the position of the camera, and even removes Marcelo's jacket from the back of a chair when it interferes with our line of sight. Two pieces of the triangle are in place: the camera (us) and Virginia (the storyteller); Marcelo is the last to be fully integrated into the configuration for the schema of melodrama to be complete. But for the contradictions to come into focus, we also have to admit our own delayed incorporation into the plot of María and José/Virginia and Marcelo. The woman has privileged knowledge of the double-layered plot from beginning to end, but the man has played along. The audience completes the third leg of the triangle.

Their chitchat and Virginia's constant interruptions in the staging of the final sexual encounter of the couple all delay the proof of a completed video. This postponed "sense of an ending" (93), as Linda Williams (following Frank Kermode) refers to it in tongue-in-cheek fashion, represents the narrative finale of the *mise-en-abîme*, though not that of Hermosillo's film. Rather than turn away in dismay at their chatter, however, we stay tuned, captivated by this titillation, accustomed as we are to serialized television melodramas and to postponed endings. Unlike pornographic films whose ultimate payoff for the spectator is the orgasmic "money shot" (see Williams 93), Virginia focuses on an image of sexuality that a middle-class audience might find easier to digest. A buildup to a cinematic closing is not the aim of the narrative; rather, we pay attention to the words and images that are woven around the whole scenario of the process of seduction by the woman and posturing by the man. All of the action in the film is meant to celebrate a relationship to which the audience might be able to relate, either as fact or as a shared fantasy. It must not be too hard-core but just seductive enough to challenge our patience and allow identification with one or both of the characters portrayed. Our pleasure in Virginia's film may emanate more from a feeling of anticipation than from a single, intense moment of ecstasy which, when it finally appears on screen, is riven by paradox, for in the throes of passion Virginia steps out of character and calls Marcelo by his real name, José. As we begin to find moments such as these that we did not anticipate, and to realize that something is going on of which we were not aware, we are caught between Virginia's actions and María's fantasies as they come together into one diegetic space.

In and of itself, the reuniting of two lovers may mean little to us as an innovative story line. This is an everyday occurrence, albeit one that usually takes place in the private environment of the family home or in the secret spaces of hotel rooms, remote hideaways, or other places of clandestine rendezvous. It is the third element of our melodrama, the camera lens, which permits us to acquire "sight" (in Brooks's sense of the melodramatic) and the pleasure of participation. The sequence shot and its repercussions on the audience form a metaphor for our own seduction by the camera into whose focus we are drawn by the tantalizing image it creates of the secrecy and privilege of the voyeur. As we settle down to watch, we are lulled into the comfort and security of the idea of the camera never lying or the truth on the other side of the lens being objective, but then we are knocked off balance by having to question what we see. The promissory enticement of exhibited flesh, whether in full view or peeking from behind a lace cloth draped enticingly over the lens, parallels the notion of having the camera turned on and in focus yet having the actors move out of (our) range of sight. As Virginia and Marcelo leave the arched space of the doorway, placed in direct center to frame them, we cannot follow to see for ourselves what transpires extradiegetically. Behind the walls or in the unlit hall to the right of the screen, they could be doing just about anything, but we can only speculate, using the little knowledge we have gleaned from the first few scenes. We cannot have our cake and eat it too; a sequence shot continues, steady and unmoveable, or it is no longer sequential. We agree to our limitations from the outset, perhaps without thinking, and cannot propose any alteration to the scheme of the film. We cannot trail behind the characters offscreen and are forced to fill in the missing parts ourselves, giving free rein to our imaginations and our own desires. We are made critically aware of our limits in addressing the "real," since we find gaps and spaces which, even with a camera present, are left open to interpretation. The tricks of the

cinematic gaze would seem to allow us free access—maybe something
like free trade—yet in all senses place us under the direct control of a
directorial and editorial hand. The camera both intrigues and unsettles us
for, like Marcelo, we willingly perform an act of amnesia once we know
it is there. Our tenuous position is only brought back to a conscious
level when we are shown how we have been taken in. José accuses María
of having tricked him, conning him into performing for her as Marcelo
(which, in reality, is impossible, since he would have noticed something
awry in her use of a name different from his own when she opened the
door to let him into his own house). With feigned disdain, he calls her
ploy "*tu truquillo*," a diminutive whose real force disappears behind the
fact that he knows about the entire game and only pretends to be an
innocent. Yet once he is publicly apprised of what is going on, he is
more than willing to play his assigned role in the spectacle. Part of her
truquillo includes allowing him to think he has forced her to ask for his
approval while she already counts on his being flattered into participating (or so they have previously agreed to stage the whole thing). The
audience, tricked by them both and by our own willingness to "forget"
the apparatus through which we are let in, stays outside until near the
end of the whole story. By that time we have been taken in completely
by our own misreading of the images, and it comes as a surprise to find
out how gullible spectators can be.

As an antidote to familial boredom—the waning of a sentiment of
connection between the subject and his or her social surroundings—the
mise-en-abîme of *La tarea* offers an ironic commentary on the promises
of an intimate portrait as well. If we comprehend a narrative of intimacy
as the exposure of human flesh to the camera or the consummation (or
performed consummation) of sexual acts, we are probably not disappointed. Boredom is the result of an excess of leisure time, possibly
accompanied by the anxiety or anguish that something else is or should
be going on but is not. It is perhaps a feeling of being out-of-sync with
society as one had always recognized it, or of loss at not being able to
reconnect. Jameson points out that the rise of modern society which has
witnessed the rapid growth of urban spaces and technological devices
"also witnessed a proliferation of . . . discourses on boredom, which
functioned to articulate the fading of subjectivity and the cure for its
relief" (cited in Petro 271). Such a social and aesthetic vision revels in the
passions and in a self-reflexive orgy. To observe oneself be bored gives
one both the subject and the object of the lens simultaneously: María
watches as José (alias Marcelo) and Virginia (her own alterego) go
through the motions of exposing their bodies and their repressed fears to
the camera. If we rethink the concept of the intimate as a revelation of

something more secret and hidden, as a unique access to the inner world not just of the sanctum sanctorum of the home but of its inhabitants' psyches, then perhaps the man and woman on display have performed both a physical function before our eyes and a psychological unburdening in addition. The tricks—or *truquillos*—of seduction as they are played on a consumer audience each and every day by the forces of the mass media are not as far removed from the scenes of *La tarea* as might first appear. Bait-and-switch advertising, the rapture of satisfaction followed by the downfall of expectations, promises of individual fulfillment to be gleaned from collective consumption, are all daily fare in the 1990s. Herein lies the true story of the middle classes and their seduction by the market economy.

Open discussions of the risk of contracting AIDS, the relative merits of different kinds of condoms, free sexual relations between unmarried partners, and women taking on the roles of sexual aggressors belong to the conjoined realms of acting and "pornography," as Marcelo is quick to point out. These are not topics "decent" folks talk about, at least according to the myths of the middle classes.[3] The cultural code word "pornography" opens up a variety of implications for the spectator: Mexico as a site of sexual tourism, conjecture about what type of porn film a female director would make, and a promise of unspecified pleasures to be found in the remainder of the film. All in all, it suggests in general terms a deviation from the norms of the expected. Marcelo spells this out in his version of such considerations to Virginia, who appears to listen intently: "No tengo nada contra la pornografía, pero el erotismo y el buen gusto sí que no se llevan" ("I've got nothing against pornography, but eroticism and good taste just don't go together"). The reference to pornography and eroticism in the same breath elides any hint of difference between the two. Signals of sensuality and prohibition slide over and across one another indistinguishably, for him, under the sign of economics as the overriding category under which any aesthetics must fall. Whether in good or bad taste, what sells sells, and giving it an enticing label undoubtedly helps promote it. Maybe even an appeal to being "modern" allows for such crossover judgments, with a certain amount of "erotic" content entering the hallowed halls of home as long as the audience agrees that we are not looking for signs of good taste (tradition) but for moments of enjoyment (innovation). If an equation of visually recognizable codes is set up—the private medium of video, closeups, nudity, a fetishizing of the woman's body and clothing, and the undeniable presence of the intrusive and spying lens of the camera—then perhaps the finished product can be classified under the heading of "soft porn." Rather than outrightly offending the middle classes, this general collection of products is popular in today's entertainment market. Meant for both male and female audiences, and not easily prohibited from family viewing given the take-home video format, watching soft porn at home is an acceptable leisure activity and a way to escape from the confines of boring routine. Such films are proof that one is sufficiently traditional to know that they are for home viewing, but simultaneously modern enough to choose to rent them for an afternoon of private diversion.

The image of a woman in one type of work clothing who obediently follows the guidelines set forth by her classroom instructor—who may or may not be a ruse, anyway—needs to be kept separate from her role as seductress. When María acts as Virginia, she seduces the man onscreen; when she returns to her blue jeans, she seduces us through the tantalizing presence of her camera firmly anchored on home turf. The character Virginia is a figure more complicated than immediately made legible to us, however, since the space of her two worlds overlaps briefly yet the long-term orchestration of the family structure must be kept in temporary abeyance.[4] The children cannot be allowed to intrude on our field of vision, and the real identities of the protagonists of the melodrama must not be revealed. She seems an integrated character, but in the end gives a double performance. The proof of the need for a division is the fact that the couple discusses how the children Teresita and Carlitos have been waiting just outside the front door for several hours while their parents have been shooting the film. They must keep that door closed while the fantasy plays out. The paradox, however, is that while the space of separation is maintained artificially, the economic glue that holds the family unit together is strengthened. María/Virginia cannot act the vamp with Marcelo at the same time the children are present; motherhood and sexuality are not allowed representation in the same diegetic space. The roles of director and seductress have something in common—an object, an audience, control—that the mother and actress do not. Under the "law of the father," the son and daughter are prohibited from entering until he gives the all clear. Virginia declares the shoot over; Marcelo exits with his briefcase, to return shortly thereafter, accompanied by the rest of his family. This is the truly emblematic finish—the return of the repressed from a space beyond representation, from beyond the closed door, from the darkness of the foyer. For us, the door is closing; for them, it has opened to reunite the familiar unit of parents and children. Dinner time is upon them and the camera will be turned off, the red outfit stowed away in anticipation of the next filmed "event."

The desires of the middle classes—to possess all the modern artifacts associated with success; to progress in economic terms through education, especially in the case of women; to earn higher salaries and afford luxury goods—can be satisfied, one is led to imagine, through the making of private-turned-public spectacles like *La tarea*. Marcelo and Virginia's initial staged reunion is filled with chatter that returns insistently to the subject of *"novedades"* ("what's new"), both in reference to the decor of the apartment and to their lives. What has she acquired since his last visit? She has added a rope hammock to the hall, and he is intrigued by it as a sign of the exotic (as opposed to the expected and the domestic). He is curious to know whether this change is connected to her interest in interior decorating (an acceptable type of women's work, after all) or to "something else." While she refuses to specify, Virginia hints that she has branched into what she calls *"otras cosas"* ("other things") since they last met. Among them, we assume, she includes the making of this film and her adventure into the world of directing. These are some of the strongest hints that something is indeed modifying home life, that other worlds are penetrating formerly private zones, including those of fantasy, and that images from those formerly closed spaces (*"las intimidades del cuarto de baño"*) are now part of the goods for sale in public venues. One of the best lines of the film, in fact, is delivered during the reconciliation scene between the two characters after Marcelo has stalked off the set, accusing Virginia of perpetrating *"un chantaje"* ("blackmail," "a trick," "a double-cross"). As he does earlier, in the fragment in which they discuss condoms (or their absence), Marcelo plays the role of victim once again. He charges her with entrapment after he spies the camera under the table and decries its invasion into home space. In response to her explanation of the "harmless" video as a class assignment, he wails: "¡Pero yo pensaba que esa clase te preparaba para reparar televisores!" ("But I thought that class of yours was training you to repair TV sets!"). Always practical, the man views the woman's incursion into the work force—or the space for an exchange of cultural ideas and cultural imaginaries—in concrete terms. How much will she bring into the family's economy? What is her "real" value, what she looks like or what she does? The screen stands as an icon for the pivotal importance of the media in modern society, with the reference to television repair service a nostalgic throwback to a less technological, more simple consumer past. Nowadays one aspires to bigger and better equipment, to keeping up with innovations, not to the maintenance of the old. Marcelo must be joking, we conclude. Moreover, manual labor and screen stars have little to do with one another: one type of work is a product of necessity; the other, a reflection of leisure time, disposable income, and consumer avarice.

At the end of the film, supposedly out of character now, José Partida (Marcelo) and María Navarro de Partida (Virginia), a married couple, look at the artifact we have just witnessed them produce. They see it as a joint venture and the camera as a dream machine, an investment of time and money which offers promises of opening new avenues of financial prosperity. If successful, they might both leave their real jobs of the nine-to-five variety. In a curious "reduplication of images" as Hayward notes of the *mise-en-abîme*, Marcelo's parting words (still in character) a few minutes earlier are echoed in the sentiments José addresses to his wife and director now. For both Marcelo and José, the camera both produces and records fantasy, in the first case as a performer and in the second as an investor. "Si te haces famosa," José begs María, "escríbeme un papel trágico, . . . mi sueño es ser actor" ("If you become famous, write me a tragic role, . . . my dream is to be an actor"). Of course, we know she has done this already and we have seen how it has played out. She has written him a part to play and cast him as the victim Marcelo. The film generally has not been considered a tragedy, however, but as something of a lighthearted comedy meant to entice the audience with the recognizable image of femme fatale María Rojo as the perpetrator of a seduction. But is it possible that there is a glint of the tragic in this "sophisticated and risqué comedy" (Torrents 227) whose theme of seduction is only the visible surface of the narrative?[5] Are we taken in—our curiosity piqued—by the idea that, as Virginia, María has inverted traditional gender roles as she has manipulated the spectator as well? Or are we (and her character) enticed by the idea that she plays at transgression, comforted by the fact that we can return to the banality of life having shared the secret of this little spectacle? Our collective subversion is not threatening beyond the realm of the home, and therefore the deepest secret of all. Even with the chance to challenge the rules of the domestic game, the woman director remains at the end to comfort us. It was just a movie, merely an act. Don't take it seriously because the whole story was meant for your enjoyment, nothing more.

The tedium of middle-class life finds its release in a cinematic narrative really not very far removed from those of the formerly disdained Hollywood dream factory. It is the attention drawn to the pretense of sequential shooting, a commentary on Hollywood's seamless editing and splicing, which orients and disconcerts the spectator rather than creating and maintaining the impression of an uncut visual story. By having the characters reunite in the domestic sphere, not as a sanctified couple but as a pair of former lovers coming together for the sole purpose of this erotic adventure, the focus of the melodrama on conflict and tension in the domain of the family is shifted somewhat. While preserving the setting of the microcosm, the allegorical connection to society's economic and cultural anxieties—mobility, class, gender roles, etc.—is fore-grounded with unusual clarity. Not a direct hit, *La tarea* is a glancing blow at the norms accepted as the glue of the social fabric. The family, after all, is absent; the space, uninhabited; the couple, a pretense. Whereas traditional melodrama would encode the man as an icon of power, and the woman as the target for the disruptive forces of the out-side world, in Hermosillo's film we find that the woman is the figure that copes with such challenges and makes them work to her benefit. At least for the length of this film, María is not just an apprentice in the art of cinematography but the director of all diegetic action. Cooperation from her costar is cajoled and prodded, allowing us to see her at work at putting together the entire project with a touch that could be described as "feminine" (dialogue, discussion, negotiation) rather than "masculine" (imposition, dictatorship, decree), minus any previous agreements to which we have not been witness, of course. If indeed Marcelo is brought into the "female sphere" of action as Hayward describes of this genre (203), the woman still orchestrates what goes on there even when she appears to give in to his fit of rage at being displaced. She smoothes over his protests at her audacity, and seeks some way to continue. Perhaps this is not that remote from the politics of challenge to the ruling PRI: make it all sound like a game, a play, an act you are being let in on, and if any questions arise say it was all an assignment, and a harmless one at that. When the technical apparatus is revealed to Marcelo, he is permit-ted by the director to parade before the screen, admiring his own semi-nude image as the camera rolls. Within the space of the shoot, the woman is in charge and she knows how to appear to cede to his demands to achieve the final product she desires. Is this sacrifice for the work of art's sake, or abdication of artistic control? Both Virginia and the female spectator can take some amount of pleasure from the contradictions embodied in the character Marcelo. In casting light on the home front, the camera shows that even under the careful direction of Virginia, Marcelo is given only one role to play: he is the preening male who must act out under any threat to his exercise of power. At least that is how he is scripted in María's film. If she has been allowed to overstep the boundaries of tradition, he retains the right to defend a return to status quo (after filming ends). He makes a big scene, criticizing her technical entrapment, but demands his place at center stage. The spectator becomes conscious that Marcelo knows an audience is in on their game; his change of heart is too immediate, too rehearsed, to be a sign of real (unscripted) innocence. All three parts of Brooks's melodramatic trian-gle are now in on the game: Marcelo, Virginia, and the camera as the eye

of the spectator. The last bastion of secrecy—the agreement reached
between Marcelo and Virginia before the film rolls—has to be breached
before the geometry is in balance.

When Marcelo accuses Virginia of letting her ego run amok, of using
him selfishly to her own advantage, this phrase is not completely out of
place in melodrama. But the lines would have been spoken in more typical circumstances by a woman to a man; he would have been the pro-
faner of the sacred institution of matrimony in exercising his right of
seduction. The voice of "good" (the woman, wronged or offended or
displaced) accuses the denizen of "evil" (the man) of having disrupted
the harmony of the home, one which has been predicated on secrecy and
misrepresentation to begin with. As Hayward concludes, "the melodrama focuses on the victim" (205), a figure driven by the nostalgia for a
lost, if artificial, paradise. Even in this representation, the domestic hangs
on the threads of that (by now) old cliché: sex, lies, and videotape. In *La
tarea*, their encounter does not allow forbidden hopes and longings to be
played out only to then be crushed by the weight of a masculinist reaf-
firmation of power. Here, all power has been corrupted by the force of
economics and is willing to compromise for the sake of profit margins.
Their fantasies dramatized on screen—they are filmed in front of our
very noses, after all, conveying the impression that nothing is hidden and
all of what we see is "true"—and the accused personification of evil
(Virginia) is revealed as just another type of good in disguise. Her longings—for money, for "art," for an antidote to the everyday whose meaning has been lost amid the tedium of earning a living—are clearly visible
to us all as the means to an end.

Despite having packed up and left the premises with a vow never to
return as part of so perverse a scenario, Marcelo meekly reappears just
after Virginia has apologized at length to the spectators through the
camera because what they expect to see—her *tarea*—will have to remain
inconclusa ("unfinished"). What might we miss, we wonder. She confesses to us, out loud, what motivated her to make this film: "me pro-
puse una venganza: usar al hombre como objeto y me salió el tiro por la
culata" ("I proposed to take revenge: to use the man as an object, and it
backfired on me"). It seems quite odd that in the domestic "female
sphere" a woman decides to apologize for trying to implement her fantasies unless, of course, this is also part and parcel of an orchestrated
game of cat and mouse. When Marcelo stands in the doorway once
again, he seems greatly interested in Virginia having chosen him, of all
people, as the protagonist of her project. When asked, she reassures him
that it is a decision made for two reasons: because he makes love with
the lights on (a practical consideration for a video director) and because

he is in good physical shape. The director certainly knows how to patronize her stars. "¿Sigue prendida?" ("Is it still on?") he asks, peeking out of the corner of his eye toward the camera on the floor. In a sequence shot it must be there and running, as the audience already knows. Among other situations, the video camera has now captured her asking for forgiveness. This act of contrition, a crucial aspect of the relationship between man and woman in the film, triggers his prancing and posing in front of the camera. But it also encourages his one admonition to her as director: when the scenes are done, he tells her, she should edit them "to put him in a good light," as it were. Her reminder that the rules of the shoot stipulate "*sin cortes*" ("no cuts") elicits one response from him only. He pleads: "Entonces, que no me califiquen" ("Well then, as long as they don't give *me* a grade"). If the evaluation of her performance is made evident—rendered legible or visible—in the form of a grade, then their collaboration will be judged, one concludes, by means of other than academic criteria. Does it pull off its stunt and convince us to watch? What financial rewards will they reap from this performance? The standard of value in consumer society is profitability—consumption by a paying audience. How hard one studies for the reward of a good grade, how much work is invested in an assignment for the approbation of the instructor, how much money people are willing to hand over for a product—all of these are indexes of social success or failure. To reach these goals constitutes María's real homework assignment.

Now we must return to Marcelo's earlier comment and ask to whom does his "que no me califiquen" refer. Who is it that should not judge him? Is this tape to be shown to María's instructor and the rest of her class? The possibility is intriguing, but it might prove academically problematic for the group to assign a grade to their performance. Is the video actually destined for some other spectators who will view the film at a later time in the privacy of their own homes, and it is they who should not try to place him on a professional scale of acting? Does he address those of us present, at least implicitly, since the original filming, making this a verbal wink at the *mise-en-abîme*? Marcelo's direct address to the eye of the camera closes the distance between audience and production, leaving the success of the entire endeavor in the hands of the spectator. We might concur with his request not to be judgmental since we know that his role in the production requires him to play into the hands of the director. Their video shoot is much less an uncut version of an erotic encounter than its parody.

If we consider the codes of melodrama in terms of sexual difference, as Laura Mulvey encourages us to do, we find before us yet another set of questions to be posed. Mulvey distinguishes between the "reconciliations" (Hayward 204) that package masculine melodrama into a neat artifact of resolution and harmony, and the fundamental conflicts left unresolved in what she calls "female melodrama." Equilibrium is the goal of the first, while the second aims to destabilize the masquerade of tranquility that serves as the basis of a masculine vision of social and sexual relations. If the genre is concerned in general with making sense of the family as an institution (either as *sub specie aeternitatis* or as flawed icon), what is the result of the conflicted encounters parodied in Hermosillo's vision of things? Are the ideological contradictions implicit in each character—director versus actor, wife versus movie star, spouse versus lover, homemaker versus worker, student versus mother, income versus artistry—bridged by any sort of sacrifice or accommodation on the part of either? One is led to wonder whether any of the pleasures we might derive from the negotiations between Virginia and Marcelo on screen produce more than a momentary respite from the way "real" things are. The enticement to form part of the triangular structure or web of intrigue may last only as long as the camera keeps rolling.

One of our considerations must be whether María's fantasies as projected through Virginia are so transgressive or disruptive that they never could be fulfilled, and therefore they exceed any attempt to negotiate a satisfactory conclusion to the narrative. Are the woman's fantasies any more visible by the end of the filming than they were at the beginning? Have they become so transparent as to find space in the collective unconscious after viewing *La tarea*? The dilemma of the task postponed casts aside the promise of a single, recognizable ending to the narrative plot even after Marcelo agrees to cooperate, for we realize that the film's completion entails more than meets the eye. Neither abandons the project, and our venture into their world of private quirks and adventures uncovers our own inner dramas. Virginia remains the focus of the project from the first shot to the last, with both the spectator and Marcelo (José) performing as she wishes; the visible eroticizing of her body is a means to an end, not something of value in and of itself. In the economy of her film (and Hermosillo's film) the woman is imbued with an exchange value adjudicated by the (implied) audience of spectators willing to invest in what they will see onscreen. None of us deserts her, thereby fortifying her dream of future success for their enterprise. Cottage industry has taken on a new profile here, a modern identity in the greater economic scheme of the modern nation under Free Trade.

So have we, as spectators, just participated in an exercise—a bit of homework—that in the end closes the family circle very neatly with the recovery of the children in the hall? Even if they stare at their parents and ask why their mother is dressed as she is, they don't interrupt a relatively normal schedule of routine events. If the "typically ascribed space" (Hayward 203) of the man is the work sphere, and the domestic arena is relegated (or delegated) to the woman, and if women—at least until fairly recently—have been identified more as actresses than directors, what have we really witnessed? What images have we been lured into constructing around the two characters in this frame? Hayward writes that "[i]n order to achieve a successful resolution to the conflict [in melodrama] the male has to function on terms that are appropriate to the domestic sphere. In this way he becomes less male and in the process more feminized" (203). José does not take all that seriously his wife's directorial debut, except as an economic incentive. He explains to his annoyed son and daughter who question why they have had to wait so long for dinner that he is merely indulging their mother's whim. He shrugs his shoulders and offers them an explanation: "es que a tu madre se le ocurrió hacer una tarea" ("it's just that your mother decided to do her homework"). Framed by this statement, María's film is an interruption of routine whose value is not intrinsic but to be set by the cultural marketplace. Under such conditions he has the role of the good guy, playing along and not making any waves. Our heroine Virginia is versatile; she has enough time to be director and actress, scriptwriter and camera person, and still have dinner on the table at a fairly reasonable hour. Any real sexual preoccupations of the middle classes have been torn from the private realm of the bedroom, reformulated into a "forbidden" liaison, and displayed on television screens across the country for the delight of all. The real "secret" (Rich, 1997 283) exposed through this film is that there are no longer any secrets. All aspects of life are up for sale. Privatization has ostensibly given citizens of the nation control over access to the means of producing films—even women can direct—and now the lens can focus on the images promising the most pleasure for the peso. The true work of *La tarea* is entertainment. It must compete for the consumer dollar with cable networks, satellite dishes, and movies from Hollywood. In this cutthroat arena, melodrama remains the most lucrative genre and the most easily recognizable road into the audience's wallet. We must keep in mind that the woman's purse—symbolic of the increased power of that sector of the population in the national economy at the end of the century—contains as many resources as the pockets of the men. To address the imaginaries of *all* spectators, to offer women a vehicle for looking at themselves in society, not just as objects of someone else's vision, entails the aesthetic (cinematic) and economic empowerment related to the production of the image. The camera's visibility stands in for the assumptions tied to cultural conditioning which come into play in all forms of representation and their deciphering by spectators or readers. The translation of the codes of melodrama into sources of real power for women—as embodied by the figures of María, Virginia, and even María Rojo herself offscreen—creates a potential weapon for those who have been denied agency over their own images. But in the process, the tedium of daily life can be exchanged for the experience of self-representation, as well as cashed in for the exchange value of a product made-to-order for the middle classes.

HOW I SPENT MY SUMMER VACATION

Danzón and the Myth of
Getting Away from It All

Even at first glance, María Novaro's 1991 film *Danzón* calls forth associations with other dance-genre films, such as Carlos Saura's *Tango* or his productions based on the plays of Spanish playwright Federico García Lorca and orchestrated around the culture of the flamenco. But upon closer scrutiny the Mexican film evokes, rather than the burning sensuality ascribed to gypsy or *payo* minorities, what Beryl Schlossman calls the "mourner's reading" (76) of a cultural vestige, a resurrection in images of that paradoxical moment when affirmation and denial coincide, when the spectator is confronted with the aporia of the real acquiring an aura of the unreal. In other words, we find before our eyes the conjuring up of a subculture fairly remote in time, and even more distant and estranged in manner, from 1990s Mexico (except among a small number of diehard and aging fans) for the purpose of affirming a national cultural image in the face of an encroaching (and somewhat fearful) globalization of culture. The aforementioned aporia or simultaneous sense of wonderment and stalemate centers on the fact that the rhythms and lyrics of the *danzón* refer back to an experience that would not have been shared by the majority of current middle-class spectators had they been around in the 1940s and 1950s, and to a regional subculture whose survival among immigrants to Mexico City was confined to popular, inner-city barrios. Chances are that the surviving members of the older generations which made up those groups are not today's audiences watching María Rojo on screen in renovated urban art deco–style theaters or in suburban plazas. This is an artificially created connection in which the unknowns of the past are foregrounded for a youth culture increasingly oriented toward images, language, and social values taken from the international media. One only need focus on Perla, the teenage daughter in Novaro's film, to recognize the boredom associated with this dance music for anyone not middle-aged. Perla dresses in jeans, changes boyfriends weekly, and has a somewhat secretive life apart from home and family. But Julia, her mother, does not give up on trying to recruit her daughter into the routine of the dance hall; to her credit, she is insistent, but, to her detriment, she is blinded by her own attachment to this charming but outdated custom for passing the time.

Upon offering up the dance hall for our consumption and then taking it away as a truly viable aspect of the present (other than as a Disney-style theme park attraction for the curiosity of the middle classes), the director "extrac[ts] the mourner's loss and experience of estrangement from the finding of History" (Schlossman 76) in what appears before our eyes but now as if from an unbridgeable distance. What first is introduced with the gloss of authenticity—in setting, dress, characterization, and musical rhythm—soon dissolves into a tropical night of timelessness. Much as Veracruz haunts the narrative stories of the films' characters as an optical device for some generic chronotope of historical recovery, so these same inhabitants of 1990s Mexico are stalked by a "time space" which they do not so much inhabit themselves as it inhabits them. Incapable of either return or advancement, of breaking through the stalemate of the present, Danzón's narrative remains stuck in a limbo of irretrievability, nostalgically attempting to provoke an illusion of experience in a spectator who is only temporarily lulled by the visual and auditory resonances of the untimely evocation of the danzón. Degraded but not entirely disappeared, both the musical tradition (an import from Cuba at the end of the nineteenth century) and the cabaretera-style film in which it appears may incite the audience into expecting either an eventful rememoration or an outright rejection. Instead they leave us in the arenas of artifice and forgetting, although Novaro's film seems to advocate this strategy for surviving the everyday as we engage with her vision of Julia's world.

Set in the now of the 1990s but tinged with the dingy gray remnants of other vague moments that can only be judged as past but not completely gone, Danzón has us focus on the social body of late-twentieth-century Mexico. We begin at the feet and work our way up to the face as we enter into a dialogue with the character, finding where our own experiences meld with hers. The style of the film can best be described as proceeding at the slow and rhythmic pace of the *danzón* itself: a repetitive and predictable cadence with no sudden shifts or changes to break the concentration of the dancers. With little chance for improvisation, the music becomes an allegory of history as an orchestrated series of events to which the dancers of the nation must adjust. The recognizable music of the soundtrack precedes any visuals and conjures up, for at least some of the audience familiar with its tradition in setting up conventional stories in conventional settings, expectations of recognizable narrative formulas and film codes. During the 1940s and 1950s, the *danzón* enjoyed great public popularity among the lower classes of Mexico City and also became an indispensable element of films such as *Maratón de baile (Dance Marathon)* and even Mario Moreno's (Cantinflas) *El bombero atómico (The Atomic Fireman)*. The 1948 production *Salón México* (the name of a dance hall akin to New York City's famous Roseland), directed by Emilio "El Indio" Fernández, set the atmosphere of an "original" against which all other films have been cast. *Danzón* is not a remake of the same story per se, but it certainly does employ the aura and conventions of the 1948 film to place the new middle-class working woman in the spaces previously occupied by and later associated with the working classes. In urban ballrooms and dance halls, epic encounters between public morality and private desires formerly played out against a backdrop of orchestrated musical themes and choreographed dance steps. But by 1991, these dance halls are proposed as spaces of social anticipation, mixed with nostalgia rather than moral decay. What better setting for a bewildering encounter with modernization than the space of tradition? And what more appropriate protagonist to embody this than a fortyish woman who is suspended between the broken promises of 1970s feminist rhetoric and the new promises of the PRI for a transition to economic democracy through the discourse of privatization? In his prologue to the filmscript for *Danzón*, critic González Rodríguez calls this time of transition and space of disenchantment the habitat of "un descreimiento de las transformaciones súbitas que deliró el credo feminista de los años sesenta y setenta" ("a loss of belief in the abrupt transformations that the feminist creed of the 1960s and 1970s raved about"; 9). These are the parameters of Julia's limbo.

Danzón opens with a double performance: the embodiment of the feminine and the choreography of a sensual melodic line ritually observed by two partners. We are made to look, not just hear the music

but watch as it envelops the scene of a social encounter. The close proximity of a heterosexual couple begs us to contemplate the dance as an
allegory of partnership in more than one sense. An extreme closeup of a
woman's feet encased in ankle-strap, high-heeled dress shoes, frozen and
motionless, anticipates their catching the next step of the dance. We
enter on a pause, between beats. The camera pans back slowly, but only
enough to give us a glimpse of a pair of somewhat thick ankles and mus-
cular calves poised for action in a medium shot. The filmscript directs:
"La cámara se desliza al ras del suelo y nos descubre otro par de piernas
y otro y otro. Todas las mujeres se preparan para el baile de la misma
manera: aflojando la pierna derecha. La cámara empieza a alejarse tan
lenta y suavemente como el danzón mismo" ("The camera tracks along
at floor level and reveals for us one pair of legs, then another and
another. All of the women get ready for the dance [to begin] in the same
way: loosening up their right foot. The camera begins to pull away as
slowly and gently as the *danzón* itself"; González Rodríguez 29). The
entire assembly of dancers shares certain information about procedure:
the woman waits for a signal, then joins the synchronized multitude.
The tango, the flamenco, the *danzón* all exact obedience to a set of rules
and protocol. As Carlos Monsiváis reminds us, such a cinematic closeup
pays tribute to the individual figure while a mid-length shot, by providing a broader context, relativizes the image on screen within a detailed
frame of reference (121). Novaro's opening shot pays tribute to the solid
legs on which Mexican women stand—literally and figuratively—and
their aesthetic appeal. The closeup instantly imbues these limbs with the
power of proximity to the real world of the *salón*, and it frames María
Rojo in the role of Julia Solórzano as the body on which time and space
come together in the aporia of modernity. The image of her legs functions as an "objective constellatio[n] around which the social represents
itself" (Adorno, cited in Mitchell 204), especially its irreconcilable elements, in condensed form. A synecdoche of the feminine, they hold a
material place in the layers of sediment of Mexican cultural history and
arouse a flood of possible associations: the liberatory power of popular
music, the rise of the middle classes since the first round of dance hall
fever, the enticement of a smoky venue, sublimated sexual desires, a
potential for social transgression, and the utopia of an escape from the
world of boredom and routine.

Once a haven for the lower classes recently arrived in the metropolis, in its second incarnation the dance hall has now become a "middle-
class diversion" for film audiences (Tierney 368). With the demise of the
structures themselves as a predictable result of urban renovation, the
spaces represented onscreen acquire an aura of the exotic, a look of the

familiar and the fantastic rolled into one. The third step in this progression was the recycling of the film's images into the ceremonies for the opening of a reconstructed copy of the original Salón México in central Mexico City in 1993. The film-inspired spectacle was attended by a horde of actors, celebrity writers such as Carlos Fuentes, and other intellectuals who reminisced about what they had missed out on the first time around, and was accompanied by the release of photographs and newspaper articles reporting on the opening of the original *salón*. *Danzón* lessons were the order of the day, inspired by Novaro's film, and María Rojo obliged the press by showing off her skill on the dance floor at center stage. She also gave numerous press interviews and described in detail the difficulty of learning the dance steps for her role in the film. A photo opportunity of the first magnitude, the premiere of the film and the dedication of the dance hall moved the time of the cabaret (and the cabaret film genre along with it) five decades into the present, and its cultural space into the eyes of those who would never have dared enter such proletarian haunts when they flourished. Unlike in the 1950s dance hall, where the *danzón* was a break from social routine and poverty, the cinematic version of the *danzón* has attained the status of "art."

The setting of the 1991 film is fairly mundane: a vaguely insinuated urban neighborhood with neon signs along its dark streets; the beckoning strains of a yet-unseen local orchestra emanate from a dingy doorway set in an old-fashioned façade in the old part of the city. Both aspects establish an overal look of time without event, as if it could be either 1948 or 1991. There are no indications of anything having transpired since 1948, with the exception of the advent of color photography. The dance hall appears both dissociated from the flow of historical time—it remains standing, even if run-down and worn—and a confirmation of the impossiblity of a cultural vestige surviving intact. This *looks* like Salón México, but at the same time we know it cannot be so since the real building was torn down and the neighborhood has become increasingly seedy. We are caught in that dilemma of the mourner when faced with the evidence of a demise: there is a body and it has been made to appear lifelike, but there is no movement and no heartbeat. It is brain dead, but we remain enthralled by the outward appearance of the cultural corpse. In the critical vision of Baudrillard, this is a simulacrum of the dance hall. Caught up by an apparition, we begin to make the assumption that some "secret" (as Rich has suggested regarding the First World's reading of the cultural products of the Third as exposé) is to be revealed behind the façade of routine and, at least in the beginning, so it appears when the happy dance couple is broken up by the unforeseen disappearance of one of its partners. The mysteries of the lower classes—previously based on crime and punishment, honor and retribution—have now been substituted by the more literal-minded middle classes. We need a new type of mystery to maintain the rapture of the moment, so we are made to ask: where is Carmelo?

A woman at mid-life, Julia Solórzano has found a fulfilling outlet in the dance hall to counteract the daily routines of home life and work. As Susan Hayward reminds us of the codes on which melodrama is posited: "it has to produce dramatic action whilst staying firmly in place. . . . Time is made to stand still, . . . objects function similarly to suffocate, entrap, and oppress" (220). Seemingly liberated by leaving the home, Julia would appear to find herself in a more rewarding setting; yet the motion that fills the dance hall is far from true action. As she explains to her eager student Susy later on in the film, the *danzón* consists of only four steps, and one covers little ground in its execution. While escaping from a cramped apartment and a life of repeated tasks, Julia falls into yet another trap. She knows the routine by heart: woman places hand on man's shoulder, man holds woman around the waist, at arm's length, using three fingers (and no more) to guide her steps. It is a formula that creates an illusion of social intercourse while maintaining a distance. After all, Julia insists, the two partners must never, ever look one another in the eye but instead focus on an imaginary point somewhere beyond the "real."

Julia is constantly reminded by the friends that accompany her that her daughter has grown up, that middle age is approaching, that time has passed despite the redundancy of their lives. The photos on her tabletop and framed certificates of past (dancing) glories covering the walls attest to her rapidly fading youth but continued physical prowess. While her job as a telephone operator reduces her to just another disembodied female voice on the line, one who connects other people's lives while remaining alone herself, Julia is sustained by the recognition and expectation of those who frequent the dance circuit with her. Through conversations with coworkers (all of whom are women) and the camera's constant focus on the contents of her middle-class apartment, the audience learns how often Julia goes dancing, how she comes and goes from the dance hall, and that she is the single mother of a teenage daughter, Perla. In the current phase of her life—after marriage and after the bloom and hopes of youth but before a definitive "old age"—she fills her free hours outside the structure of the workplace with dance sessions at the side of Carmelo Benítez (Daniel Rergis), "a man who is not really her man" (Jahiel 1). Between adolescence and old age, waiting for menopause to arrive and vehemently denying it is anywhere near that

Figure 3.1. María Rojo (Julia, left) and Daniel Rergis (Carmelo, right) in Danzón, a film by María Novaro. A Sony Pictures Classics Release. Reprinted by permission of Cinematográfica Macondo, S. A. de C. V.

time, trying to deal with her daughter's physical and emotional coming
of age, Julia marks time in the present. What film reviewer Leonard
Maltin sees as the "dreary" (1) job at the telephone company offers the
character little if anything to look forward to each day, except, of course,
for the companionship of other women in the same predicament and the
consolation of routine. The drab Teléfonos Mexicanos (Telmex) building
shelters the anonymous voices of the operators and the disenchanted
women who arrive without fail for work each day. Even Julia's dreams
for her daughter's future are limited to passing the torch—Perla will
inherit her place at the switchboard when she retires. The décor of the
apartment house, of the dance hall, and of the business office all confirm
the same timelessness, with "the desire for the unobtainable object or
other . . . just one final nail in the coffin of this claustrophobic atmosphere" (Hayward 220). While something may be going on outside, its
effects are slow to penetrate these walls. The audience awaits the demise
of the *danzón*, but it cannot fathom what will take its place. That step in
the direction of modernity belongs to Perla's generation.

Out of the blue, two occurrences change the normal sequence of
events and the strict linearity of the film's narrative. The first is a remote
echo of the privatizing binge the federal government entered into beginning with Salinas de Gortari, placing banks, airlines, and ultimately even
the Benito Juárez International Airport in Mexico City into the hands of
individual entrepreneurs and investors. In the film, this is reflected in the
buyout of the federally owned and operated Telmex by foreign enterprises—in particular, Spain and the United States—which have seen
Mexico as the perfect opportunity for new investment and potential
profit. The move requires Julia and all of her coworkers to attend special
retraining sessions, and it looms on the horizon as a disruption to the
customary work habits of many women. The second break with routine
is when Carmelo fails to appear at the usual time and the usual place for
his unwritten appointment to dance with Julia. There is never any direct
explanation given for this disappearance, no cause, just the result that
Carmelo can't be found. Conjecture by other women over his possible
philandering, then the rumor of his persecution by police, create a sense
of mystery. The same air of secrecy holds true for the restructuring of
the workplace—for the employees there is merely an announcement of
change; no one discusses the reasons.

Frantic over Carmelo (but, apparently, not over her job), Julia is
lured into searching for him after overhearing a conversation in which
her friends hint that he has returned to his hometown of Veracruz to
escape being arrested for some unspecified crime. Given the added
secrecy surrounding corporate takeovers and technological moderniza-

tion, at this juncture the only course left for Julia to pursue is to try and recover her loss. In an attempt to fill the void following an event that breaches everyday routine, Julia must follow the traces of Carmelo to see what is up, to try and piece together the fragments into some story-line, in her own words, for herself. The two sets of circumstances coincide in a single moment for this middle-class woman who must function on two fronts: work (the office) and leisure (the dance hall). Both her space of repetitive tedium and her place of physical release are now sites of frustration; the routine of her days of labor and nights of enjoyment ends abruptly and leaves her with loss. The fictions of workplace security, domestic tranquility, and personal pleasure are revealed to Julia, in an instant it seems, as just that: narrative stories and social performances. So she takes on the one thing remaining in a reduced repertoire of alternatives—she cashes in her retirement fund and takes a vacation to look for her lost Carmelo. Julia's daily worries, including nasty telephone callers, moody coworkers, and a troubled, rebellious daughter, condense into one overwhelming preoccupation that stands in for them all: the ghost of Carmelo. Held together by casual circumstances alone, and more than a little mystery as to his origins and current marital status, the characters Julia and Carmelo are used by the director to pose a fundamental question for the audience: how does one survive what appears to be a radical interruption of daily life without missing a step? If any sense of anxiety permeates the early scenes of the film, however, this has disappeared even before we are halfway through its narrative.

As Julia alights from the train at the station in Veracruz, a dreamlike display of mothers bathing children, porters in white uniforms, lazing young men on the platform fills the screen with the confirmation of a mythical portrait of the city. If spectators are familiar with this tropical city, they already know that the trains no longer run as they are shown onscreen, and that the Ferrocarriles Nacionales Mexicanos (Mexican National Railway) system is up for sale to the highest bidder. If this is Carmelo's hiding place, he inhabits a fantasy. A direct reflection of the faded bucolic painting hanging behind Julia in the railway car, this is a timeless Veracruz which is only reanimated by the reason for her arrival: Carmelo. As she descends from the train, the unfinished melody by Schubert that had accompanied her voyage changes abruptly into lively tropical rhythms. Julia's tight skirt, *danzón* shoes, and self-assured walk are highlighted by the catcalls and whistles of the men who witness her arrival and by the marimba on the soundtrack. There is much less of a sense of tragedy to the scene than a healthy reassurance of her powers of seduction, previously hidden by her role as a working mother. This woman is motivated; she knows what she is there for, even if she has to

learn how to go about finding it (him). Spectators might be heartened by
Julia's presence of mind that the dance (of the partners and of the nation)
will go on, whatever the outcome of this odyssey. By avoiding police
stations and missing persons reports, Julia gives the search for Carmelo
an air of summertime adventure and, frequently, of an afterthought. She
has gone to the tropics as much to find herself as to search for Carmelo.

So after more than a decade of marking time, spending her evenings
on the dance floor in the arms of the dark-haired, white-suited stranger
with whom she stresses she has had a close but only platonic relationship, Julia uncharacteristically takes a leave of absence from the phone
company. She places her daughter as an apprentice with her longtime
switchboard *compañeras*, and sets out by train for the coast. The story is
a road movie plus a version of *Cinderella* in reverse—the clock has
struck midnight and only Carmelo's white dancing shoes (figuratively,
of course) have been left behind. His disappearance, and Julia's decision
to take some time off just as new technology invades office routine, set
in motion the resolution of the contradictions of modernization in and
through the body of Julia. The same body that has served as part of the
national *mano de obra*, the embodiment of physical labor, is now used to
foreground desire (the impulse for a recovery of a lost object) and a
recovered sexuality. Julia has to come to terms with the three facets of
her daily life—work, leisure, and sex—if there is to be a resolution. As
markers of a kind of timelessness (a sense of things as they have always
been), Carmelo, the telephone company, and Julia's physical attractiveness have to be reaffirmed, especially in light of threats to their viability
in a New World Order.

In the few weeks that Julia roams the tropical port she is in endless
transition—seeking without finding, walking without destination, gazing
out at the sea—after leaving Mexico City and before finding Carmelo (or
deciding she cannot). The one constant is Julia's deferring a return to the
drabness and solitude of home and work in Mexico City until her funds
run out. After an initial attack of anxiety, smoothed away by the strong
but motherly woman (Doña Ti, played by Carmen Salinas of *fichera*-
film fame) who runs the aging hotel where she stays, Julia marks time
and postpones her departure. Hers is not the chronotope of rupture but
of circularity: she is bound to go back to the life she has left in abeyance,
to pick up where she left off, no worse for the wear, with a few new
experiences to tell friends about. She is secure in the fact that despite a
couple of changes here and there she can walk right back into the office
and the home. Seniority is wonderful; it guarantees Julia's place in the
system and a resumption of her everyday life. Even the brief sexual
escapade we witness onscreen is part and parcel of a licit mid-life crisis.

The *danzón* is a pressure valve for the chore of daily sacrifice and labor and a way to find recognition in another kind of family. The Mexican state, hardly a visible force at all in *Danzón*, is subtly portrayed as capable of weathering challenges without so much as a whimper. Long gone are the more overt strong-arm tactics of repression. Even as its traditional institutions confront the effects of technological modernization and a drive for private profits, the nation and its citizens can share moments of nostalgia that recharge their cultural myths. The transformation of the workplace to compete in a global economy does not impede a woman's voyage *out*, as well as her voyage *in* to find herself amid the haze of the social and economic challenges of the 1990s. Rather, such leisure activity benefits productivity upon her return because a "time out" lets workers catch their breath to begin the next round.

The invasion of the global is only background music to Novaro's story of the local, however. In a film lacking any master long shots, the director concentrates instead on the luxury of the isolated closeup. In the cracked and faded architectural façades, as well as the characters' countenance, the spectator must learn to seek out the telltale signs of "event:" crow's-feet, frown lines, black tresses fading to gray at the ends, the shadow of a moustache, a refusal to wear makeup to cover any traces of the passage of time.[1] The euphoria of the chase dissipates back into an understanding patriarchy which accepts its wayward children with open arms (and a mandatory retraining seminar). As Saragoza and Berkovich point out, the "resilience of the state" (30) appears almost menacingly confirmed in this film despite all of the enigmas and possibilities that pass across the screen in plain sight. Within the comfortable boundaries of the tedious and unremarkable cadences of everyday life, there is space for everyone. Julia is celebrated both in Veracruz (by those who admire her courage to seek out Carmelo) and upon her return (by friends and daughter alike). Measured strictly in historical time, Veracruz may be a port city ravaged by economic decay, governmental abandonment, toxic pollution, and a shift of shipping routes and tourist dollars to cities farther south, but for Julia its appearance in the shimmering mid-afternoon sun spells an entry into a new routine. Her money is not sufficient to make it a permanent one, and her roots still lie elsewhere; but for a few weeks she can create a parenthesis in an otherwise predictable life. The elliptical movements of the camera that track around Julia's body and her hotel room, around the tugboat captain Rubén (Víctor Carpinteiro) and the swaying of his craft on the waves as the two spend the night together, establish this sense of temporal circularity. Julia is outside Mexico City and outside Veracruz when she wanders the parks and the streets looking for Carmelo, just as she is outside the family and the workplace when she takes to the road. Where better to take refuge from routine than in the mythical tropics, against a backdrop of time without event, where all the ships come and go with overwhelming anonymity. This is where Julia can look for someone the audience might have already surmised she is not going to find. His details are sketchy, his past unknown; how could Carmelo be the real object of her pursuit? His very absence, paradoxically, fills her hours and helps her kill time. Even if she were to encounter him, they are almost strangers to one another, and the meeting would not offer much in terms of closing the narrative suspense for the audience. There is not much here for us to look forward to regarding Carmelo and Julia, just the future continuation of a melody whose notes have ceased for a bit, but whose haunting refrain serves to provoke interim tales.

Just as Julia's legs receive special pampering and cosmetic care, the rituals of the *danzón* and the city of Veracruz are presented as images needing cultivation to insure their timelessness will be preserved. The camera lingers on children bathing in colonial-era fountains, foreign sailors enjoying a night on the town, even the ceremonious preparations of local prostitutes getting ready for their weekend clientele. The narratives of routine are established by these repeated images into which Julia must inject her own interrogations about the lost cook. At first she can't quite catch the rhythm of port life, and she doesn't know to whom or where to make inquiries. But that is soon remedied and she manages to adapt her own discourse well enough so that she gets a response—not the one she wants, but a response after all—in return to her invented tale about a cousin who might have worked in the galley of a departed ship. As she must also do when she goes back to her place in Telmex, Julia has to learn to adjust to her surroundings. She has a role to play in a new economy, and this adventure has the blessings of the state. There is no husband to come after her, no father in pursuit. Julia may haunt the docks looking for her lost Carmelo amid the international freighters docked there, and she may change partners temporarily when she joins Rubén in the hammock on his tugboat, but these are signals of short-term diversions in a landscape of constancy. Despite all her lessons and careful guidance, Rubén can't master the *danzón* and she must return to the arms of tradition. Desire enters and departs the harbor daily but it never sails away with her, for that would signal a radical alteration of society. She can be distracted by the youth of the sailors, but it is middle age that has her in its grip. Julia is brought to her senses when she meets Rubén's family. One of many siblings, Rubén introduces Julia to his mother, a woman close to her own age, content in her maternal role. She is the mirror in which Julia, finally, sees herself.

In the closing scene of the film, the last dance we see shared by Julia and Carmelo upon her return is to the accompaniment of, not fortuitously, "Divina ilusión" ("Divine Illusion"). One illusion is, of course, that there is something out there for the middle classes of Mexican society other than what is already visible and at hand. There might be an antidote to the sameness found both at home and at work, but it is out of the hands of the individual to question its efficacy in relieving everyday tedium. A second illusion comes in the form of Rubén and the temptation to seek solace in a lost youth. Both lead Julia back to square one. (Leaving the audience to ask, perhaps, why this past is no longer recoverable but the *danzón* is.) So under the illusion that leisure time will bring a difference to life at some point down the road, women such as Julia can continue to do their jobs and wait. The impression of such a promise is not so much a misapprehension as an ideological feint joining two spaces: the illusion of participating in the production of the "new" and in the general accessibility of a reward for such work (time off). While marking time, one hopes to reap the benefits of not rocking the boat. In a real sense, then, Julia is not even "on vacation" in Veracruz but hard at work seeking to uncover a mystery to give meaning to her own life. The enigmatic Carmelo is the embodiment of this search, yet what she uncovers is that the real source of energy from which to draw lies within herself. Unfortunately, this discovery is tamed later on by Julia's insertion back into the realm of domesticity and wage earning.

After several weeks away from home and a couple of enticing encounters with the "extraordinary [and] the unusual" (Petro 265) in the shape of a one-night stand with a young lover and a growing friendship with a transvestite nightclub performer, Julia has managed to incorporate into the prosaic even these possibilities of interruption to the scheme of daily life. Rubén's youth—his mother is even slightly younger than Julia and mother and son are a constant reminder of the time measured by event, just as Perla is—and Susy's extravagantly feminine performance are tossed into the narratives of banality and assimilated by them. The first is told as a "classic roll in the hay and some stereotypical good loving" (Baumgarten 2); the second is almost matter-of-fact sisterly solidarity. As Julia tries to sort out just what sort of person she has just met in the Parroquia Café—someone who returned a pair of earrings she inadvertently left behind—the script tells us she ponders the situation in these terms: "Susy y Karla son mujeres—así lo siente—pero también son hombres. Y no es fácil acostumbrarse" ("Susy and Karla are women—she feels it to be so—but they are men, too. And it isn't easy to get used [to them]"; Novaro 65). But in the end that is exactly what happens; she tolerates them as she has accepted both the

Figure 3.2. *Víctor Carpinteiro (Rubén, left) and María Rojo (Julia, right) in* Danzón, *a film by María Novaro. A Sony Pictures Classics Release. Reprinted by permission of Cinematográfica Macondo, S. A. de C. V.*

Figure 3.3. María Rojo (Julia, right) in Danzón, a film by María Novaro. A Sony Pictures Classics Release. Reprinted by permission of Cinematográfica Macondo, S. A. de C. V.

presence and absence of Carmelo, with no questions asked. The script states categorically: "No sabe cómo juzgar a Susy. Claro, además no es cosa de juzgar" ("She doesn't know what to make of Susy/doesn't know how to judge her. Of course, though, it isn't something one should judge anyway"; Novaro 56). Postfeminist times and the advent of a liberal pose of indifference toward all difference have conflated distinction into democracy. Julia and Susy are just two working girls earning a living. The flattening of the narrative tone with which these encounters are portrayed, alongside Julia's fairly implausible offer to teach Susy to dance, contradicts the increasing social violence present in Mexican society against gays, lesbians, and transvestites even as the film was released in commercial theaters. The onscreen world of Veracruz is a grotesque artificial paradise whose peace is maintained by a leveling out of the economic distinctions that in real life would keep such individuals apart (or bring them together only under the sign of brutality, rage, or domestic violence against women).

Transvestites, prostitutes, hotel managers, and telephone switchboard operators are all merely women at work in the economy of *Danzón*. As they all seem to await something to interrupt the humdrum and predictable routine of their lives, whether in the capital or the provinces, they form a temporary sisterhood of women cast out to sea. Julia has lost her partner, Susy has been dumped by a man and is looking for someone more sensitive to take his place, Doña Ti seeks solace in the company of other women as she mourns the fact that her six children have gone off and left her alone. After a short period of time, each recognizes herself in the predicament of others. Doña Ti makes Julia a cup of coffee and shares household gossip as if they had known each other forever. Perhaps they do, after all, if we take Doña Ti as the image of Julia down the road after Perla has left home. Susy listens to Julia's troubles and identifies with her futile search for Carmelo. Both are victims—not of men but of the stories society weaves around the relationships between men and women. Together, they write their fantasies on a scrap of paper and cast them out to sea inside a bottle, hoping that they will be read by an understanding recipient somewhere out in the world. But this act is part of the routine of the search, just what women do day in and day out as they keep on marching in lockstep toward the future. They cast their fates to the wind. The world of Veracruz turns out to be only vaguely different from that of Mexico City. In each place, time emptied of work has been emptied of meaning (except for waiting to go back to work, whether at Telmex or in the tourist nightclubs). The anticipation of routine—Carmelo on the dance floor, coworkers at the office—and just pure anticipation of *something* happening in Veracruz both disappoint. Julia and Susy leave one another souvenirs of their brief time together, but they are merely ships passing in the night.

Figure 3.4. Tito Vasconcelos (Susy) in Danzón, a film by María Novaro. A Sony Pictures Classics Release. Reprinted by permission of Cinematográfica Macondo, S. A. de C. V

Now let us return to the concept of capital in Julia's life and its potential to create a new space for her, an alternate life narrative. Liquidating her only assets by cashing in the retirement fund set aside for all permanent workers by their employers as mandated by the federal government (at least so it was in 1991 before the advent of the AFORES or U.S.-style personal retirement accounts), Julia flees from a life of predictability and impersonal routine as just one among the millions of inhabitants of the capital who go to the sunshine and vague promises of the gulf coast. She is neither old nor young, her daughter is perched somewhere between childhood and adult responsibilities, she is not the lover of Carmelo nor his friend but "something else." Her flight to what was never a true tourist resort but instead a geography associated with naval vessels, foreign seamen, liberation, and sensuality in popular mythologies of the middle classes evokes the image of what has been marketed as an oasis emptied of time, a space disconnected from event in which tenuous and distant links to middle-class life may be drowned out by the rhythms of the *danzón*. As if it had just crossed the Caribbean yesterday, the dance is shown as continuing to unite people of all ages in ceremonies devoid of much enthusiasm but filled with determination. One only has to gaze at the emotionless performance of the repeated, stylized steps by older generations and their young grandchildren to witness its hollow cultural shell. The only one to imbue the dance with anticipatory pleasure is Julia. From Susy to Doña Ti, all of her acquaintances refer Julia to a public park here or there, a concert at some remote band shell, or a radio station that plays the old favorites for anyone out in the audience still listening to this music. But Susy performs to rock music or show tunes; Doña Ti sings *boleros* alone in the hotel. Julia has bought herself a trip to a past tinged with meaning only for her, one which she imposes on her surroundings. Otherwise, *veracruzanos* seem quite oblivious to either the survival or the demise of the *danzón*.

Any anxiety on the part of the spectator dissolves like just another fuzzy camera shot of the beach with its crashing waves or the stifling interiors of the cheap hotel where Julia takes refuge from the heat. She pays her bill day-to-day, investing in no extravagances except for the fan in her room. Despite the wad of money she pulls out on the first day, her retirement fund does not last long. Both money and dreams are more than slightly devalued here, and are limited from the outset by the restricted resources of a woman in her circumstances. This is not a Club Med getaway. Ordinary activities such as dining are reduced to the minimum; Julia indulges in cold drinks or ice cream to counteract the heat, but luxuries are few and far between. It is a far more monotonous life she leads in Veracruz than what one might expect while she is away from home. Light clothing, nocturnal pastimes, and seafood delicacies are part of a run-of-the-mill discourse of port life as she waits for something to happen. If Nissa Torrents finds the film "a pleasant reworking of a fairy tale" (226), perhaps this is the tone most indicative of *Danzón*'s chronotope: not quite past, yet not quite future, just a warm, lethargic present.

Like another curio to place on her shelf upon return, Veracruz's image is a collectible that assuages any apprehensions over Carmelo or over the *"actualizaciones"* (reorientation and preparation classes) for the Telmex staff. As long as she can still afford to buy a few days away from the nine-to-five of worktime, Julia can be transported to something like a theme park. The city of Veracruz is fragmented into digestible portions so as never to overwhelm her, but instead sweep her up in its warm atmosphere and assure her that despite a few unfortunate mishaps and near-misses the harbor is still a comforting place to be. Her *"mundo de aventuras"* ("world of adventure") (Novaro 71), as the script refers to it, is really just an extended family into which she moves effortlessly. As she is adopted by Doña Ti, whose suspicions of her are dispelled in a few minutes with the waving of a roll of large bills, so Julia adopts Susy and lets her in on the secret (feminine) world of the *danzón*. Her own daughter has rejected the rigidity of the dance patterns and formalities, but Susy is eager to learn for, after all, they hold something in common. They are women who wait—whether it is for the reappearance of Carmelo or for the arrival of true love, women's time is taken up by waiting. And in the greater scheme of things, the Mexican people wait. Three years after Salinas's presidential election victory of 1988, the nation anticipates change in forms as yet unpredictable and invisible, learning to roll with the punches but caught between the certainty of modernization and the uncertainty of its exact form. The same holds true for Julia, who inhabits the limbo between presence and absence (Carmelo), between past and present (wife and mother), between job security and the advent of technology (the phone company), and between visions of herself past and future.

In the meantime, both the body of the feminine and the space for the social body to reencounter tropical exuberance and sensuality are isolated and fetishized as images of a link to something "genuine" to be recovered. The port casts its spell over Julia and all of the other visitors, among them Russian sailors and Greek merchant seamen, to the rhythm of the marimba. We too are caught looking at objects and places overinvested with emotional significance but devoid of a greater sense of historical connection. Julia's combination of resolution and worry plays out through the camera's focus on her body, in particular the *"piernas de oro"* ("golden legs"), as the movie trailers and posters resoundingly and triumphantly promote them. Whether she is excited or discouraged by the day's events, her legs remain a solid foundation on which to move forward among the strollers on seaside boulevards or wade into the swirling waters of the gulf. Like the ready-cut dresses of the original dancers of the 1940s (Flores y Escalante 111), portside women adorned in flowered summer finery appear cut from the same pattern. Their resignation to the heat of the afternoon creates an atmosphere that is undatable, belonging to neither past nor present but to a time untouched by external occurrences. In the diegetic space of *Danzón*, women work as a confirmation of constancy and reliability. Travel may extend the range of routine to further geographic reaches, but not to events which might change the course of a singular grand narrative. Nothing extraordinary enough happens in Veracruz, not even her one-night stand, to make Julia's life take a radically new direction or to send up a warning signal to the nation at large. What Jahiel views as the "dullness" of the film's characters and action (2) is, in effect, a leisurely look for the audience at the faded glory of middle-class life romanticized onscreen. What we see is neither sad nor tragic, but even a bit comforting in its expansion of the promise of banality no matter where one might be tempted to stray. This only goes to prove that one can even take away the middle-classes' most prized possessions and they will learn to adapt. If and when Carmelo comes back into view, Julia will not be exactly the same but she will look pretty much so. Her changes are, at best, cosmetic. Her melodrama returns from the light of the sun to the dimness of the metropolis with only a changed look in her eyes to show for it.

Upon returning home, Julia unpacks her suitcase (and memories) to take stock of the material traces of her excursion. Like any other tourist, she appears to need some visible proof of her change of routine, of having been there in the flesh. She has to find a way to show the power of her investment in a vacation which, as it almost always does, allowed her to "get away from it all" without really doing so. The illusion of time off—perhaps the very same "divina ilusión" of the song title—permits Julia to pick up her previous life where she left off and the spectator to be sutured into the film's narrative. The camera sets the spectator up to peer over her shoulder into the recesses of her suitcase as she extracts gifts and souvenirs from her bag: a t-shirt, shell necklaces, a mask of Fidel Castro carved from a coconut shell,[2] dried and preserved frogs made into a group of musicians, a sun visor that sports the logo "I love Veracruz," an Italian silk scarf (a gift from Karla and the only non-Mexican object in her collection), a doll in regional dress and a bottle "with the ocean inside" (both from Rubén), and several jars of *concha nácar* (mother-of-pearl) cream for rejuvenating aging skin. (The last would obviously exemplify one of her cosmetic changes.) This collection of objects is her proof of a temporary hiatus that came to substitute for a real "event" in a boredom that found no means of representation until Carmelo's disappearing act. Her purchases, as well as the gifts from sympathetic acquaintances along the way, attest to her pursuit of, if not exactly happiness, at least recognizability and the comfort of repetition. What she eventually found was not what she was pursuing yet she makes her way back triumphantly to retake her place, revitalized by her search. The *real* challenge to Julia was not how to make her work more interesting, or how to earn more money, but how to learn to tolerate routine and even find distraction in it. Julia's journey has led to an encounter with the joys of being distracted rather than the woes of worrying about it. Besides, Julia exudes the air of reassurance of a woman who feels she has chosen to return, not been forced to.

A bright pink flower behind her ear, a new floral-patterned dress, and an enigmatic smile are the external signs of Julia's return to the dance floor with Carmelo. Her partner has, mysteriously, reappeared, no worse for *her* absence either. The bandleader personally welcomes her back, the couples take their usual places on the floor, and the music commences. The circle has closed. The celebration recognizes society's success at surviving her so-called rebellion even more than Julia's triumphant return to a humble but, obviously, satisfying routine. After all, she looks as surprised as the audience feels when we spot Carmelo emerge from the crowd of faces and walk toward her. It appears as if nothing has transpired; no words are exchanged. They glide into each other's arms and join the crowd of dancers. She didn't have to locate him; they merely knew where and when to find each other when things settled down in their private lives. She sticks with her admiring friends, her longtime job, and her *danzón*; he has been off on his own and what really only matters is that he is back. We hear no questions from her and he does not speak. As the leader, Carmelo holds out his arms for her to walk into and Julia obeys, a smile covering any other emotion. Impulse has been channeled into a reenchanted banality whose aura has been reestablished by a connection to the timeless *danzón*. The unspectacular becomes a spectacle.

Novaro locates Julia and the musical tradition within the cinematic frame but outside the narrative of history. In fact, the historical is extra-diegetic, lurking somewhere just outside our vision but never directly intruding upon the scene. As Schlossman reminds us of the power of the photograph for Barthes, the compelling nature of the image lies in its ability to "offe[r] and withdra[w] something that appears in visible form as an apparition of historical reality" (76). The rebellion of a woman and

the recovery of the *danzón* are only bits of a *petite histoire*; they do not
fit into any greater scheme. What didn't happen here was a break with
the system. What we find is a suspension of Julia being surrounded by
ordinary things and mundane people which have contributed to a
"fatigue of the eye" (after Petro). As if she had grown tired of seeing
people where they always seemed to be, Julia must learn to envision
them in a new light in order to create a renewed interest in life. Her
unbroken focus on family, work, and a domestic routine of relaxation
has been restored after a short respite elsewhere, and Julia can now look
at herself and her surroundings differently. She can admit to her age and
find in the narrative of a fortyish woman something to pacify any feelings of anxiety. She has been allowed to construct a "new" past for herself, one that includes characters on the order of Rubén and Susy. Even
if work goes on from here, she can take refuge in the fantasy of this
brief getaway.

The differences in Julia from pre-vacation time are commodified in
her purchases and her changed look. In her mind's eye, the decaying
port city where she spent a few weeks can appear as bright and gleaming
as the red-clad women who patrol its docks each night under the glare of
sodium lights. She has only to paint it so in the stories she tells her
friends. Julia herself has learned that she too can be made up to disguise
the effects of the passage of time just as easily, using makeup tricks and
the palate of colors recommended by New Age devotee Susy. The traces
of better times in the port and of youthful vitality in Julia can be brought
out with a fresh coat of paint. So works modernization on the culture of
the nation: the telltale evidence of daily encounters between tradition
and innovation is not to be feared but to be bejeweled as flashy and
provocative consumer goods. The same holds true for Julia: she can be
decked out in a luminous manner to distract our attention from the ravages of time. *Danzón* shows us that the expectation of job fatigue, added
to the terrifying anticipation of change, need not produce numbness but
rapture. Just as the open markets of free trade in the 1990s placed an
enticing array of merchandise before our eyes, so modernity itself can be
embodied in glitzy images, among them those of women as actors, directors, and scriptwriters. This is merely another cosmetic enhancement of
the nation's appearance on the new global stage. It is the spectacle everyone has been anticipating for a long time.

The extraordinariness of María Novaro joining María Rojo for this
production is the spectator's introduction, during the early nineties, to
what would become stock practice by the turn of the millennium. The
renovation of the Mexican cinema industry, its unofficial second golden
age for some, becomes fetishized in the bodies of women, both on- and

offscreen, as the messengers of modernity.[3] The "new" focus on female characters and a targeted interest in the purchasing power of women in the audience have not in and of themselves fulfilled their potential to provoke change in a social and cultural heritage that includes the post-revolutionary discourses of the PRI, resounding feminist promises, and the brief but intense flourishing of a fledgling gay-rights liberation movement. The insistent closeups of María Rojo's lower extremities, the overture to democratic inclusion through the use of seemingly accepted characters Susy and Karla, and the benign presentation of sexual adventure with a much younger man are all images that attest to the nation's readiness for becoming part of a global free-market economy. In a nod to cinema audiences beyond national borders, *Danzón*'s director goes a long way toward lowering anxiety levels among Mexico's present and future economic partners. In films such as this, economic modernization and social modernity go hand in hand; if a national society is portrayed as willing and able to absorb "difference" without violence, then foreign investment in its infrastructure is not far away. There is no harm, no foul in Julia Solórzano's coming-of-middle-age story. Neither she nor the institutions around her suffer permanent damage from her escapade with Rubén nor her reunion with Carmelo. Superimposed on the call to resuscitate an innocuous musical tradition is a triumphant hymn to modernity as an authentic component of Mexican life. Even what at first appears most difficult about grasping "reality" is, in the end, rendered in a form and an image. What made Carmelo go? What made him return? The entire episode in her life resonates only in the reaction of Julia and her ability to make it of relative importance in the greater scheme of things.

In place of a desperate struggle between tradition and modernity, *Danzón* constructs an intermediary space from which Julia emerges, reborn, to reclaim her place in the New World Order. Novaro's film does not erect a museum to house some set of symbolic cultural goods but allows Julia (and the spectator alike) to visit once again the sites where their fading traces may be celebrated quietly and harmlessly. What Néstor García Canclini calls the impossibility of construing "pure objects" (4) on either side—the traditional or the modern—leads each of the two strands of the film's discourse to fail on its own. For Julia's story to work out, we have to find the fantasy of universal progress set in specific, identifiable localities. As García Canclini contends, in modernity "what disappears [from the scene] is not so much the goods formerly known as cultured or popular, but rather the claim of some to be self-sufficient universes and that the works produced in each field are uniquely the 'expression' of their creators" (5). There is more than a hint of Benjamin's idea of the aura of the genuine in these words. The

Mexican (formerly Cuban) *danzón* now inhabits the space into which the global forces of modernization are pouring their resources and promises. Neither can deny its coexistence with the other and neither can claim exclusive rights to representing the nation. I would hasten to add that such goods or artifacts—*danzón* music or dance routines, tropical tourism, flowered clothing, and even the entire film itself—are, additionally, not the unique expression of one "time space" or another but of both simultaneously. While they hint at narrativity in a small sense, each with its own linguistic codes and references, even grander narratives of the 1990s are standing just off in the wings to encompass them. *Danzón*, then, is the site of cultural reconciliation into a new terrain of hybrid boredom. At the end of the film, Julia is not some independent figure lurking in the shadows of the nation. We need not worry that she will pounce without warning, either on Carmelo in accusation, on Rubén as the image of the future, or on the institutions to which she returns ready to work. Local memories and private dreams widen her personal horizons as the nation contemplates the turn of the millennium in the distance. But middle-class family values and habits remain intact, heterosexuality is reaffirmed as Susy and Karla are left behind without so much as a good-bye, and even middle-age sexuality is given a brief moment in the sun and then sublimated through the dance. The urban world of *Salón México* is not so much remade as refocused by Novaro away from *boleros* of passionate crime and punishment toward the softer songs of leisure. Traditions have yet to pass away, but they are being allowed to fade slowly in an atmosphere of little serious discomfort for anyone.

In his discussion of a past gilded era of Mexican cinema, Carlos Monsiváis proposes that "the arrabal [urban slum] was the thematic axis linking the public with its inevitable destiny—modernity" (125). Those caught between present poverty and the abyss of the future were located in a "time space" filled not with sweeping historical event but with "small episodes" (Monsiváis 125) to chronicle. Unable to grasp a vision of the world beyond the walls of the local, they were housed in neighborhoods, crowded cabarets, boxing rings, taverns, and dance halls. So it was that the *Salón México* story placed its characters on the cusp of a social morality about to be challenged by something that was not given a name but which appeared as the ghostly image of a brutal force that would sweep away the recognizable past. Modernity—in the realms of economics, culture, and morality—was the monstrous yet unformed creature lying in wait just outside the portals of home. In 1991—"*the year of Mexican cinema*," according to Nissa Torrents (222), as a result of privatization, jury prizes, and a renewed funding of projects—that axis has been moved from the arrabal to the middle-class apartment house, but it has retained the structure of the episode. Julia ventures further from home than the women of the 1940s, partially because she has more economic means than she would have had in previous times. But her journey is round trip. She proves that women can find something more within the home/work cycle if they just learn to look at it with new eyes. The spark of enchantment has been rekindled; one need only look at Julia back in Carmelo's arms to see its flame.

In the economic euphoria of Salinas's first three years in office (1988–91), the glory days of national radio and film stars were evoked by numerous new cinema productions, as well as by the inclusion of black-and-white portraits of yesterday's leading men and women on the walls of the dance halls. The star system and the lure of Hollywood-style icons beckoned to actors and actresses once again. In *Danzón*, studio promotional snapshots of XEW radio personalities fill the cracked plaster walls along the booths of the restaurant where Carmelo used to work, creating a link across time between the "new" and a celebration of the old. But as the camera focuses our attention on relics of another time imbedded in what is now in the process of change, we must consider to whom this film speaks. Is it one last, loving look backward? Or is it like the Angel of History atop the heap of cultural rubble, a figure tugged in two directions at once? We must place *Danzón* squarely on the threshold of NAFTA and its formalizing of the mass media as the vehicle for representing and mediating new relationships among the nations of North America. In this context, Pérez Turrent notes that "[it] is symptomatic that the success of this type of film has always coincided with periods in which there is talk of abundance, but which are in fact characterized by wealth, waste, and corruption" (107). He refers to the *cabaretera* genre on which *Danzón* is based, and therefore establishes a powerful connection between the times of Miguel Alemán (1946–52) and those of Carlos Salinas (1988–94). In each, the bodies of women made visible on the screen for mass audiences bear the brunt of cultural and social disturbances. While *Salón México* condemns the character Mercedes to death by inextricably linking sexuality, economics, morality, and crime within the stifling social spaces to which the lower classes are condemned, Novaro recognizes a new woman. The most marketable figure at the end of the twentieth century is that of the middle-class woman who has survived the politics of the 1960s, the economic crises of the 1970s, and the onslaught of militant feminism to find herself on the brink of yet another moment of change. Still unsure of "who she is," she is asked once more to become something else. For her, the one aspect of permanence in a landscape of change is the sentiment that all will be well by the time you get home. For Julia, home is still there when she makes the trip back.

While theirs is not exactly a love story, it is as close as we will get to it in the early 1990s. Julia and Carmelo form a new type of couple culled from the vestiges of the patriarchal older man (the one who leads in the dance) and the woman who matured during the 1960s and 1970s. As Julia Tuñón finds to be the case in the films of Emilio "El Indio" Fernández, the director of *Salón México*, "[h]is films told love stories because love was the most vulnerable element in the crisis of the original order" (189). So the audience might scour *Danzón* for the remnants of times and places in which one used to look for love and where we now find the characters ceremonially reenacting a fifty-year-old story in a new mode. By this time, however, the almost-incandescent light surrounding the female figures has lost some of its intrigue, and the sense of mystery or enigma has to be personified through different conventions. The state has to find a new place to hide; it cannot stand right out in the open. The relationship between man and woman no longer glows with anticipation as it might have in the lens of Gabriel Figueroa in 1948, but rather it has the aura of a comfortable old pair of dancing shoes ready to take off at the slightest sound of music. Such an aura is, in the words of Schlossman, "an illusion or a dream" (85) to be contemplated and reenchanted by a contemporary audience. This sensation can only be evoked by Julia's search for something not quite definable that has been lost, something she can recognize when she finds it but is at a loss to describe to those who join her in the hunt. The radiance of the ocean and the harbor are transferred to her change in expression when order has been restored, owing not to Carmelo at all but to some set of circumstances left in the realm of inexplicable mystery. What this is never called, however, is "love." Dolores Tierney quite rightly finds a changed moral tone in the atmosphere of this film when it is viewed within the codes of the *cabaretera* genre when she writes that "dance is no longer primarily a metaphor for sex. . . . [We witness] a desexualization of the *danzón*" (368). Sex and love have gone their separate ways by the end of the century.

While I must disagree with her identifying in this shift an overt sign of definitive independence for Julia Solórzano and a demarcation of a new avenue for the expression of female pleasures, I do think that *Danzón* repositions women to seek pleasure from within the spaces of home, work, and orchestrated leisure time and not from some outside sources. There *is* no love to be lost, for the only suggestion of loss other than that stand-in Carmelo who occupies the space of the love interest in previous films is that of work. Not only is Julia in potential danger of losing her job to technological innovation and automatization, but she has now spent her entire retirement savings and cannot leave work for the foreseeable future. The first is only a remote suggestion since she leaves before the big changes take place and we are not privy to what happens when she goes back on the job. There is always her daughter, one assumes, since she has stepped into her mother's shoes as an image of future generations of women ready to assume their rightful places in the work force. But the second aspect emptied from her life is the financial one, and this has immediate ramifications. She is in that precarious situation of many workers in the waning years of the twentieth century as the myths of union solidarity and government protection disappear. The safety net is gone, but Julia keeps her radiant smile. While in the last frames of the film she faces the camera without a visible trace of remorse or worry, and she picks up with Carmelo right where they left off in scene one, Julia gives us no hint of her dire straits. We must assume she is unaware of what is taking place, or she finds nothing to be concerned about. To keep from thinking about anything but a recuperation of her partner, Julia keeps on dancing, proud of her triumphant return to the space of banality and her conquest over the temptations of youth and rebellion. (Perhaps one benefit will be that she will better understand Perla if she keeps her own experience in mind.) To stop moving may indicate that the world of history and event has finally managed to encroach on the lull of the music which, across the closing credits, just prolongs the distraction of dance time. Like the weary musicians, Julia and Carmelo have just taken their equivalent of a time out; they have returned for the second set, refreshed and without missing a beat.

AMORES PERROS
Throwing Politics to the Dogs

For Hollywood film producers, the summer season at the movies generally represents big profits for the industry and little or no substance for the consumer. Sequels to successful action-packed blockbusters like *Mission: Impossible, 2,* with the guaranteed box-office draw of Tom Cruise, the Disney Studios' animated *Dinosaur* or *Shrek,* for instance, Eddie Murphy's return in *Dr. Dolittle 2,* or the updating of the Middle Ages with the music of the twenty-first century in *A Knight's Tale* are just selected recent examples of the fare international audiences have come to expect during the months when both work and critical thinking seem to be put on hold. As classes end and vacations are planned, light-hearted enjoyment and fast-paced entertainment outweigh any possible complexities of the plot, and innovative technology aims to captivate and enthrall those seeking relief from the heat of the dog days of summer in the city or those already jaded by endless weeks at the beach. Despite the best intentions of bookstore mega-chains in suggesting lists of the best summer reading for their customers on vacation, consumers flock to the movies to escape both the effects of the sun and the monotony of the days and months between Memorial Day and Labor Day. It would seem that even in the attempt to seek a distraction from a long series of summer days, audiences fall into the numbing repetition of sequels, prequels, and predictable blockbuster attractions.

This is not the case in Mexico, however. There, film production is experiencing what may turn out to be a long-overdue renaissance in the

areas of both quantity and quality, even as the time between the end of
the academic year (June or July) and the national holidays of September
looms large on the cultural horizon.[1] With the crucial presidential elections of July 2000 just around the corner and political campaigns running at full speed, the media took its place at the center of daily life for
the nation. In mid-June, 2000, *Amores perros* (ultimately not translated
into the proposed "Love's a Bitch" when the English version was finally
released in April 2001) enjoyed a thunderous opening. This, the first
full-length feature film for thirty-seven-year-old director Alejandro
González Iñárritu, has been heralded as the most recent example of what
promises to be entirely new cultural commentary for the next millennium by a new generation of filmmakers. Celebrated as one of the guid-
ing lights of so-called postmodern Mexican cinema, *Amores perros* was
released simultaneously in two hundred theaters across the country, and
it holds the aesthetic pedigree of international recognition as the winner
of the Film Critics' Week Grand Prize at the fifty-third annual Cannes
International Film Festival held earlier in the spring. The commercial
hype surrounding its premiere—first in Mexico and then in the United
States—goes a long way to prove that Mexican cinema also may be fast
catching up with its Hollywood counterpart as far as mass media publicity is concerned.[2] The pre-election atmosphere of combined exuberant
expectation and mortal dread—an exclamation point at the end of a particularly abysmal presidential *sexenio* ("six-year term") in which so
many fundamental issues and problems were never dealt with in any
substantive way and other dilemmas about widespread corruption surfaced—contributed to create the perfect end-of-the-century and end-of-
the-millennium national setting for this film.

No disappointment to the expectations of extreme cinema fans,
Amores perros is an unblinking look at a trilogy of situations and characters, interwoven across the class lines and geographies of contemporary
urban Mexican society. It turns neither to digital effects nor to simplistic
storylines to fill its extended time on screen (154 minutes to be exact),
but rather immerses the audience in an almost-unbroken stream of
intense emotional experiences that assault the eye, leading many reviewers in the United States to use language such as "harrowing" (Rainer
108) and "raw" (Rich, 2001 34) to refer to its relentlessly focused camera
work. By refusing to cut away when a shot begins to make the spectator
squirm, González Iñárritu accomplishes what Spanish director-in-exile
Luis Buñuel did so many decades ago in his visual assault on Spanish traditions: he returns over and over to the source of our discomfort, even as
we might try to deny its existence by looking away or wriggle in our
seats as we are shocked out of the lethargy of the everyday.[3] Simul-

taneously repulsed yet strangely tantalized at a very visceral level by the violence we witness visually and audibly—the soundtrack is filled with pulsating music, squealing automobile tires, and alternately whimpering and barking dogs—the spectator is trapped by this cinema of affect that uses the powers of such a generic form to address issues absent from many mainline films and images we have allowed to fade into the background of everyday life. Both the visual and auditory tracks unmask what decades of tedious social and political sameness have attempted to cover up. If Spacks finds "interest" (1) as boredom's antithesis, then this film sets out to occupy one hundred percent of our senses all of the time and to fill the void of time with interests and actions one after the other, and often even simultaneously. Its aesthetics could be deemed sheer overload as the excesses of daily life give way to blood, intense violence, barbarism, and paralyzing emotion in spaces we are accustomed to look away from rather than gaze at. We may lose "interest" in politics, in books, and in work routine; it is difficult to get lost at all in this film.

Jeffrey Sconce employs the term "paracinema" (372) when referring to similar films and videos whose aesthetics are based on the physical titillations and excesses of popular genres such as horror, porn, and skin flicks. Whether a true genre or a rich subgenre—or an even more complex hybrid crossover among several—such texts offer a vehicle for social commentary while grabbing the audience by the throat and shaking mercilessly. As Hawkins writes of these popular genres, what counts is "the ability of a film to thrill, frighten, gross out, arouse, or otherwise directly engage the spectator's body" (4). They do not allow us to stop looking because they are everywhere at once, creating an intensification of emotion reflected in our very physiology: nausea, sweating, trembling, and even flight. Sensations are evoked and mixed together in one spectacular package, one not always appreciated beyond the immediate realm of the senses since such intellectual processes require physical stamina. Like those audiences of the 1920s (and even those of today) who took the razor-slit eyeball scene of Buñuel's surrealist-inspired *Un chien andalou* literally and not as part of the realm of metaphor, more than a few spectators in the crowd had their hands over their eyes during the sequences involving prolonged scenes of dogfights and the blood lust of the humans who stage them. Ensconced in the lethargy and collective boredom of seemingly endless post-1968 Mexican politics, seventy-one years of government by a single ruling party, and an economic enervation following devaluation after devaluation of the peso, Mexican society gives the appearance of being seemingly unshockable. After all, what else could happen that would be worse than earthquakes, floods, hurricanes, mudslides, losing your entire life savings overnight, or waking up to another day of politics as usual and party-backed assassinations? González Inárritu has had to find a way to present images whose intensity will not fade, that do not become routine, that persist in our mind's eye long after the actual image on screen disappears from view. Like the pieces of human bodies and social worlds with which Buñuel contrives his films, *Amores perros* is filled with markers of "incomprehensible psychic catastrophe, obsessions, and eruptions" (Jameson "Culture and Finance Capital," 271) that never do coalesce into some great unified narrative of the city of today. Rather, they are indicative of the symptom and not the disease; their visible presence insinuates a need to overcome the invisible fog of boredom by provoking real, physiological agony in order to reach further into the dark recesses of the causes of such disturbing scenes. As Rainer concludes, "[t]he passion of those miseries gives the film its horrible grandeur" (108). By throwing the audience headlong into the seething life of the streets, we are made to walk side-by-side with the characters. Rather than provide a refuge for the fearful who wish to avoid crime by driving and not walking amid the crowds, automobiles offer the eye and the nervous system even more scenes of blood and gore. In fact, it is the violence of the modern machine—enormous, imported and luxurious—that precipitates the triptych of the film's narrative action.

The director hooks us into the diegetic world of the film by condensing into three interconnected stories the images of the general pain of daily life as well as those of the social, political, and economic "inheritance" of today's alienated youth and the elders who have prepared this crushing scenario for them. While critics have commented favorably, and at some length, about the commercial success of recent light comedies such as *Cilantro y perejil (Coriander and Parsley*; 1997), *Sexo, pudor y lágrimas (Sex, Shame, and Tears*; 1998), *Sólo con tu pareja (Love in the Time of Hysteria*; 1991), and even María del Carmen de Lara's *En el país de no pasa nada (In the Land Where Nothing Happens)* (which premiered in Mexico City on June 6, 2000, less than two weeks before *Amores perros*), González Iñárritu flips the coin to reveal the other, more sinister side of what it means to inhabit the D. F. (national capital) at the turn of the millennium. If J. G. Ballard's 1973 *Crash* was indeed "a novella of the last days" (Sinclair 57), a sign that the 1960s flower children and their communal pathos were indeed now part of the dustbin of history, this film contains the visuals and soundtrack to accompany a similar apocalypse. But is this a harbinger of a new era or "an elegy to boredom, loss, futility" (Sinclair 57) after the economic banquets of the early 1990s? Is this the twentieth century's climax or instead an anticlimax leaving nothing new to hope for and no affect left to tap except for the "tremor of excitement" (Ballard 12) resuscitated in a driver at the wheel of an automobile careening toward dogs, pedestrians, or open space? In a world dominated by technology, cars have become one with their drivers, who are searching for the erotic intensity missing from everyday life. As Ballard's narrator discovers after a gruesome collision, "I was surprised by how much, in my eyes, the image of the car had changed, almost as if its true nature had been exposed by my accident" (49). The exhilarated tone of this confession compares well with the hyperbolic images and sounds of *Amores perros*, which reveal the "true nature" of the modern beast.

No longer the "ciudad imaginaria" ("imaginary city") for the setting of Carlos Fuentes's early novels, nor the site for experiencing "el triunfalismo social" ("the triumphant attitude of society") of post-revolutionary politics, the capital city of the nation is shown instead as having "una modernidad que sólo ofrece la proliferación de la injusticia social, la corrupción política y . . . el dogma neoliberal" ("a modernity that only offers a proliferation of social injustice, political corruption, and . . . neoliberal dogma"; Bonfil, 2001 3). The film places individual characters' despair within an undeniably political setting. The director has stated, in fact, that it would be fairly impossible to separate the personal from the political since this is "a society where the chasm between the rich and poor is ever-growing and crime seems the only means of subsistence for millions of people" (Arroyo 29). And "crime" per se has an infinite variety of forms and countenances, from illegal dogfights in the slums to political assassinations in elite neighborhoods, and from murder-for-hire among bureaucrats (made worse by the fact that it is brother against brother) to the abandonment of children by their parents. All of these fall under what González Iñárritu calls "the legacy of 71 years of single-party rule" (Arroyo 29). This film, then, is a marker of the dying days of that rule and the possible opening onto an unknown, and perhaps even more horrifying for that very reason, social and political future.

Given the relentless free trade of images across the media of the Americas, perhaps it should come as no surprise that visual residues of violent "real-tv" programs, news footage of spectacular carnage such as Princess Diana's crumpled Mercedes, Quentin Tarantino films on the order of *Reservoir Dogs* and *Pulp Fiction*, and a fascination with the human body at its physical and emotional limits as portrayed by David Cronenberg in *Crash*, all abound in *Amores perros*. To this mix we might also add recent publications such as *Car Crashes and Other Sad Stories*. In this disturbing collection, the photographer Mell Kilpatrick presents us with documentary photos of horrific events, in particular spectacular and gruesome traffic accidents of the 1940s and 1950s at the beginning of

the postwar celebration of the American automobile, in order to stimulate us into creating verbal constructions of what these images represent
for us. As the reviewer Martin Levin concludes with all honesty, such
exercises in perception and narration are "brutally fascinating" (16), a
kind of therapeutic encounter with the uncensored and unexpurgated
parts of human conduct. They make us sit up and open our eyes. The
general orientation of contemporary television and videos toward the
documentation or, if needed, simulation of acts of cruelty committed in
everyday life finds an echo in the representation of relationships between
humans in González Iñárritu's film. At the same time, the director
brings out the affection with which those same human beings treat their
dogs: as sources of income, as companions, even as substitute families
and sympathetic listeners.[4] The grotesque juxtapositions might just make
us ask ourselves how we have reached such a historical point, what has
led us beyond the limits of the tolerable, and why these images perturb
us while others no longer do. Do they reflect a lack of interest, a simple
weariness, an internalized anger which has lost all outlets for expression
other than self-flagellation and the perpetual angst of the everyday?
Taking his eyes off the usual scenarios for a few moments, the director
casts us into a different world of excesses that bombards us with an
intensity of images we might not care to look at or to which we have
become immune. The Mexican government has used the sleight-of-hand
trick for so long, doing one thing while making a spectacle of another,
that it is difficult to gaze, unblinking, at one single image without getting
distracted by another. We lose attention; we don't connect events to one
another; we get lost in the repeated ceremonies of the everyday. But
rather than see their potential for liberating us from their monotony, we
are overpowered by the dull hum of their repetition that is the white
noise that accompanies, but does not interrupt, a vague sense of anxiety.

   A former student of communications and an obvious media buff,
González Iñárritu had subsequent experience in producing promotional
spots for WFM popular music radio that gave him a blueprint to follow
for the multiple layering and unceasing narrative patter of this text. The
need to string together endlessly diverse CDs and videoclips with narrative patter prepared him for what he saw as "cierto ritmo editorial . . .
donde sostener el interés del auditorio sólo podría lograrse a través de un
dominio del ritmo y de sus diferentes tonos" ("a certain rhythm of editing . . . where the only way to keep the interest of the audience is by
using an overpowering beat with a variety of tones"; León 16). Poised to
capture the visual rhythm of the urban jungle—from high-speed chase to
car crash, from stalking to kidnapping, from casing a venue to the actual
bank holdup—the director's camera never pauses to allow us to breathe

a sigh of relief. Rather than the predictable rhythms of labor and leisure, its speed is breakneck, the stories jump-cut into one another, any narrative closure is absent in favor of the immediacy of the audience's complete emotional engagement. A kind of visual Freudian repetition compulsion, *Amores perros* returns to unresolved traumas again and again. Its aim is not to overcome them but just the opposite: to make us unable to live without seeing them. The "cohabitation" (León 16) of three tales in one film recreates the pressures of urban life, the feeling that one is never alone but always exiting one scene to enter the next. The leftovers of previous scenarios and situations hang on, and we cling to what we have already experienced, perhaps with the hope of finally making sense of it all. But that ends up being a nostalgic throwback to a past we think we recognize. Actors and soundtrack (available separately in extended version on CD)[5] are not neatly isolated, divided, and packaged; they overflow in and around the crowds, of which each individual constantly and irremediably forms a part. The pedestrian-clogged avenues that have become routine news footage evidence of overcrowding and other ecological disasters, the faceless hordes that fill the subways and buses, reappear in this film with recognizable features. The impersonal city becomes repersonalized but, in the process, commits us to an emotional attachment to those whose countenances we find repeatedly framed in our angle of vision. Punks and skinheads reappear in the background of the lives of bourgeois characters; inside a television studio, a talk-show host interviews the latest blonde starlet imported from Spain to confirm the most recent gossip on her life and loves, while a horde of mongrel dogs surrounds a bearded street messiah just outside the building. What bonds them all together, in the words of the director, is their having to confront the ambiguities and contradictions in their lives, having to meet up face-to-face with "las consecuencias de su parte animal" ("the consequences of their animal nature"; León 16), intensified so as to take over the entire cinematic field of vision.

There is perhaps nothing harder to do than to accept the consequences of one's decisions, for better or for worse. It is easier to be swept up by the routine of a nine-to-five existence or another hard day at the stock exchange than to confront our ghosts face-to-face. We replace the tragedies of the past that haunt our personal lives with the bulging wallets of investments and business deals; we repress our failures and transfer our anxiety over them onto spectacular performances in other arenas (including those of crime and violence); we assuage our feelings of emptiness with houses full of commodities and luxuries. So it follows that for a nation to look at these interspersed stories as a collective history just intensifies what is reflected in them individually. The discomfort of the audience was evident, with almost one-quarter of those present walking out of the theater before the end of the film, shaking their heads in dismay. Whether it is physical repulsion that is evoked by these cinematic "body genres" (Hawkins 4–5 and Williams 144) that revel in the display of blood, or the involuntary conjuring up of something just as degraded but less articulated, *Amores perros* evokes a visceral reaction in the audience. Patrons of the theater are tempted by the publicity—there is no lack of enticing but unnerving stills used to promote the film—but then must confront the powerful images on screen. The film allows for no distancing from what is made overly visible, with an excessive physical response as the result. What knocks us off guard emotionally takes its toll physiologically, often making us flee to avoid the onslaught of even more of the same. Too sensational for many, González Iñárritu's film is grossing huge profits from word-of-mouth advertising as well. Newspaper ads in *La Jornada* announce "Si aún no sabes por qué 'Amores perros' es el nombre de esta película . . ." ("If you still don't know why 'Amores perros' is the name of this movie . . ."; 19 de junio de 2000 26) and reveal the participation of the director and his cast in a series of online chats at midnight during the week of the film's initial release to provide a sense of intimacy between those acting in the spectacle and those watching it. Just a few weeks before the Mexican presidential elections on July 2, 2000, maybe a confrontation with these violent episodes—allegorical premonitions of a society's encounter with its greatest fears?—is too much emotional overload for some to bear, producing a shutdown of the nervous system of some in the audience and their subsequent refusal to watch. Are they merely returning to the safe haven of boredom, having escaped the direct onslaught of "difference"? Or is their departure indicative of an affective rupture that cannot heal? The wounds of the animals, and those inflicted by characters upon one another, might provoke psychological wounds in the audience's visionary apparatus.

Despite the Hollywood-reminiscent promotional overkill accompanying the film's opening, an enormous difference remains between the works produced by the California Dream Factory and *Amores perros*. Here there are no happy endings, no neatly closed chapters in the lives of the characters, no nostalgic elegies of times past; but there is no apocalypse either. The momentum, the rhythm, of what we see onscreen appears to continue beyond the credits, whether we like it or not. The intensity of lived experience never falters, just as traffic noise crosses the opening credits and rock music pulses behind the closing credits, bridging the diegetic action and the extradiegetic. Things do not begin or end with our presence, and they neither get better nor go away—facts which lead the director to see this film as hopeful and not nihilistic. He leaves the audience off balance in a world that is already sufficiently difficult to inhabit even with two good legs to stand on, but he finds value in the learning experience culled from all the brutality (León 16). Physical and psychological mutilation, amputation, death, bloodshed, and cold-blooded killers-for-hire are not merely literal images, but metaphors for something even more disturbing that holds society as a whole together—our animal nature that we constantly (and sometimes successfully) try to domesticate and socialize into acceptable forms and channels. *Amores perros* is the conjunction of both the angels and the demons, of "los infiernos y las esperanzas de todos" ("everyone's heaven and hell"; León 16); and the visualization of how the *defeños* (inhabitants of the D. F., the Mexican capital)—or the rest of us for that matter—manage to survive it all. It also gives us an autopsy of what we are required to sacrifice in order to do so.

Three generations of Mexicans are linked by the geography of the capital city on whose streets the battles of their degraded lives are played out. The opening sequence places us inside an obviously lower-class housing project to reveal a family at war with itself and held together only by a slender thread of fear. Octavio (played by Gael García Bernal) is filled with wide-eyed desire for his brother's wife Susana (Vanessa Bauche)—a young woman abused and mistreated by her husband, with an infant in her arms and pregnant yet again—and this creates a tense melodramatic triangle which Rainer describes well as a closeness of "squalid intimacy" (108). To fill their meager coffers, Octavio decides to enter the family pet, a huge black Rottweiler named Cofi, in the local dogfights (illegal but unprosecuted by authorities who profit from bribes). So the two of them, man and dog, are launched into the underground world of blood, gambling, and macho posturing where life is cheap and death is a mundane, relatively unspectacular occurrence. They prove too successful too fast. Octavio's innocence in this arena, counterbalanced by Cofi's innate lust for the ring, sets up a rivalry with previous combatants who are jealous of their winnings. Cofi is shot mid-fight by the owner of a defeated rival. Cofi, bleeding profusely, is left for dead by the rest of the onlookers; Octavio and his partner pick up the dog's limp carcass and begin a desperate race to the veterinarian's office. A car chase ensues, with drawn guns and tires shrieking around tight corners in and out of the city's permanent rush-hour traffic. The losers refuse to allow Cofi to survive. It is at one of the downtown intersections where other drivers cautiously follow the green light across this vehicular no-man's-land—an uncommon and unexpected sight for those acquainted with real-life driving conditions in the D. F.—that we literally run into the second and third sets of characters in the film. The creep and crawl of everyday life meet the precipitous rush of unbridled youth into what looks like oblivion accompanied by horrific sound effects and splintering vehicles. The film is subsequently constructed around this vivid moment of a crash, fixing it in the mind of the audience with iconic value.

Valeria (Goya Toledo), the strikingly blonde daughter of the Spanish motherland, is on her way home from yet another routine interview to meet her lover Daniel (Alvaro Guerrero) when she is broadsided by Octavio and his friend on their way to the doctor. Wounded Cofi is dying on the backseat, as we are reminded with closeups of the exposed ribs where the bullet entered her side. Now we have another damaged body to balance out the canine-human equation of misery: Valeria's face, covered in blood, is pressed up against the glass of the window, which has been sealed shut by the force of the impact. Trapped inside her compact car, the actress is shown mouthing silent pleas for help. Meanwhile, the spectator watches raptly as a crowd gathers around the scene of the accident and a mangy vagrant approaches her car. The camera cuts back and forth between the boys' pickup and Valeria's red car, not showing us at first who will come to the rescue of whom (or if, in fact, anyone will do so). When the camera lingers on a narrative sequence of events, we see the vagrant open the driver's side door of Octavio's truck and reach across the front seat to coldheartedly pick the pockets of both young men, one of whom has died from the impact. There is no act of salvation here; in a dog-eat-dog world there is only survival. It is a fact of life that victims are fair game for those who arrive at the scene of the crime in this *"guerra civil subterránea"* ("underground civil war"; León 16). Only in a Hollywood film would we get to witness the fair-haired maiden being saved by the strong, handsome prince and living happily ever after. We never actually see Valeria rescued from the car, just a cut to the next scene in a hospital where Daniel and a doctor share whispered words about the possibility of her surviving. She does indeed make it at this point, only to fall victim to a serious case of gangrene later on. Deeply afraid of losing her future in the public eye and distraught over the disappearance of her pet dog, Valeria disobeys the doctor's orders to remain immobile and tries to save her dog, falling out of her wheelchair and causing herself permanent harm in the process. No human body is immune from being infected by society and history, hers included. She and those around her will suffer the consequences of her act for the remainder of the film. Like Buñuel's character Tristana (from the film of the same name) before her, Valeria will be left with no leg to stand on as she confronts the failings of herself and of the materialistic society around her. Each "whole" woman is the victim of unbridled male fascination at first, which is followed by the couple's descent into the complacency of routine and then the morality-bound dedication of the husband's responsibility at film's end. But while Tristana is bound by obligation to care for the elderly don Lope, the roles are now reversed and it is Daniel who looks after Valeria (at least as much as she allows him to do so).

Valeria's trajectory from sexy billboard promoter of commercial products to wheelchair-bound amputee follows a doubly tragic route, one bound to Octavio and his world by the split-second of the traffic accident. She loses her only source of income and public identity—a perfect body—and her terrier, all in the course of a few days. The prosaic activities of daily life, like walking and cooking and having sex, become extraordinary challenges. Her predicament intensifies when Richie, canine confidant and pampered companion, becomes trapped under the rotted floorboards of the suite her upwardly mobile promoter and the exemplary family man Daniel has rented for their new life together. Both are haunted by what they have lost: career, public recognition, security, and love (one in the form of wife and children, the other in the shape of the unquestioning affection of a pet). Heard more than seen, the rats that inhabit the hollow areas of the renovated building and threaten the lost dog which has wandered beyond his "normal" space are constant reminders of what happens to those who accede to their animal instincts: men lose their families, women sacrifice their beauty and appeal, faithful pets give up their lives. There appears to be no happiness for Valeria and Daniel, but there is no going back either. Like Richie, once they fall through the cracks into the dangerous realm of temptation and curiosity, they must confront the seemingly inevitable results. The same-shot repetition used by director González Iñárritu takes us down time and again into the dark architectural interstices to which Valeria has no access and which Daniel, to no avail, tries to reach to rescue the lost pet. The increasingly faint whimpers of Richie remind us of what is missing or absent. Yet despite their proximity to one another, there are always wooden planks between human desires and canine yelps (as there are between Valeria and Daniel). The floor is merely a physical representation of all the obstacles that keep emotionally tied couples apart. The implied danger—as seen in the quick shot of scurrying rodents—outweighs the graphic violence in this domestically centered sequence. There is no mutilated terrier, an image one might expect after seeing Cofi in the ring, but the audience is already disposed to be edgy after our overexposure in the first part of the film. The impact of Daniel and Valeria's story, one found by some to be "agüevante . . . y cursi" ("boring and trite"; Siever 3), lies in the transference of agony from pet to owner. The happy

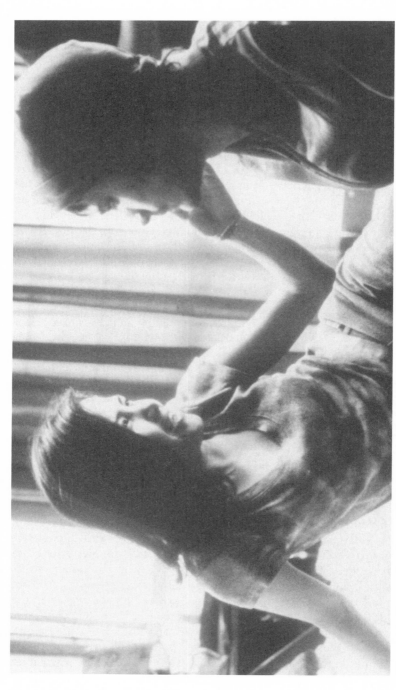

Figure 4.1. Vanessa Bauche and Gael García Bernal in Amores perros. Photo by Rodrigo Prieto. Reprinted by permission of Altavista Films and Zeta Films. Source: Photofest.

Figure 4.2. Gael García Bernal in Amores perros. Photo by Rodrigo Prieto. Reprinted by permission of Altavista Films and Zeta Films. Source: Photofest.

ending of the long-awaited return of Richie pales in comparison to the
gut-wrenching screams of the couple that replace their previously idyllic
giggles and coos. The menace to their happiness turns from something
substantially material—a terrible accident and its aftermath—to a psychological threat, a handicap that is both physical and mental. What is
put in question is Daniel's "love" for her: does he pry up the newly
polyurethaned floorboards in search of Richie, or does he give the dog
up for lost and just buy her a new one? His judgment is based fundamentally on the economics of the decision and its consequences, hers on
the sentiment of the moment. Both lose sight of the fact that by casting
their eyes on the plight of the dog they have closed their senses to what
makes human life truly human, and in the process they imbue other
species with more charitable and humanitarian characteristics than they
themselves possess. After all, dogs obey, they are loyal, and they do not
even protest inhumane treatment. They lick the hand of the owner to the
very end.

It is the third segment, however, that strikes me as the most
emblematic of the three, since the life of El Chivo ("Billy Goat," one
imagines as a reference to his unkempt beard; the actor is Emilio
Echevarría) spans the broadest social space and the most panoramic time
frame. Ex-academic intellectual, ex-Communist/political activist, ex-
guerrillero, former convict and current gun-for-hire, he is perhaps the
most tragic of all the inhabitants of this dog-eat-dog megalopolis, and he
is an icon of the disengaged and displaced. Taking a swipe at both the
character's history and any end-of-the-century political commitment, a
dirty cop who brings his client to El Chivo to engage his services
remarks that the loner is just like Subcomandante Marcos and the
Zapatistas, "pero de a de veras" ("but for real"). A force which in early
1994 took the country by surprise and continues to be a thorn in the side
of the federal government, the Ejército Zapatista de Liberación Nacional
(EZLN) is reduced in these few words to a bad copy, a simulacrum, of
something that once might have had real meaning. If such past events
survive in this film, however, it is only in the memory of those who were
there at the time, and who now "know better" than to get involved and
suffer the consequences of involvement. Otherwise, history is reduced to
a haunting figure that young people prefer to avoid completely and for
which the new bourgeoisie sees little use. References to previous times
and places are made by thugs, scam artists, and middlemen who profit
from society's escalating violence—or by figures whose only place is on
the extreme margins of society. In this society of survivalists, El Chivo is
caught between the teary contemplation of his wife and his daughter
Maru (Lourdes Echevarría), whom he left behind twenty years earlier to

Figure 4.3. Goya Toledo and Alvaro Guerrero in Amores perros. *Photo by Rodrigo Prieto. Reprinted by permission of Altavista Films and Zeta Films. Source: Photofest.*

fight the good fight, and a profound disillusionment with the post-1968 Mexican political system. His aging body bears witness to the wearing down and selling out of all hope to the forces of the market economy at the end of the twentieth century. He is neither worker nor consumer, although he contributes to the stability of the system by fulfilling the needs of those who frequent the underground economy, consumed by envy and greed, to preserve their own social and economic status. He makes a living from the deaths of others.

Like the dogs from hell that fight to the death in the previous scenes, once El Chivo has tasted blood he can't seem to give it up. He vacilates between emotional extremes but, in the last scene, is shown walking away from it all as if, with that gesture, things will start anew somewhere else. He steals a dead man's wallet but faithfully attends his mother-in-law's funeral; he tapes a picture of his daughter to the ceiling above his bed but doesn't hesitate to bargain over the fee to kidnap and murder a corporate executive; he adopts Cofi, the wounded Rottweiler, only to find that her killer instincts cannot be subdued, yet he cannot pull the trigger against an animal who is only obeying her previous owner; he breaks into Maru's home to glue a picture of himself into her photo album (and her life) but sets up a confrontation between two jealous brothers and places a pistol between them to have them end the dispute once and for all. He is the intermediary force between Cain and Abel, furnishing the weapon that might terminate the rivalry by violence rather than by mediation. Contradictory to the core, El Chivo inhabits a Mexico that has moved on since he was in his prime during the decade of the sixties; it is a nation that now only sees fit for him to play the role of assassin, despite the director's avowal that "He may be a killer, but he's not immune to love" (Arroyo 30). Of course, over the past twenty years that same society was steered by the PRI into full participation in the economic projects of the new technocrats (what some refer to as neoliberals), and the nation is nothing if not the result of such programs. Given its premiere only weeks before the general elections of July 2, 2000, which had been touted as the opening of a door into the new millennium, one cannot but see in this film a reflection of the Mexican public, fed up with the longest-running political machine/party in the hemisphere. Young people have seen little point to joining political groups or movements, since their votes have never meant anything in rigged and stolen elections; the wealthy worry only about the continuation of the policies guaranteeing their financial success; and those who thought they could effect change found out the hard way that it just wasn't going to happen in their lifetime. The PRI has been dethroned since the release of this film, but the other alternatives (such as the Partido Revolucionario

Democrático [PRD], the Democratic Revolucionary Party) met with equal failure on the national level. As some political analysts have concluded about Cuauhtémoc Cárdenas's loss in the last presidential elections, his party simply failed to respond to the times. Instead, the Mexican left held to a stagnant social and political concept of Mexico's (nationalist) future as "una izquierda que no ha sabido renovarse y que insiste en bailar cansada los ritmos del siglo pasado" ("a left which has not figured out how to bring itself up to date and which insists on dancing the same tired old rhythms of the past century"; Loaeza 1). Of course, this now refers to the decades of the twentieth century when Mexico had several flirtations with the parties of the left and put its faith in nationalist interests. When faced with the blindness of ideologues on any part of the political spectrum, the director of a film such as *Amores perros* blinds us with the shocking scenes of everyday hyperreality in what a young film critic has termed "este país tan mágico y surrealista" ("this magical, surrealist country"; Siever 3). From official blindness we have moved to cinematic insight, and from the internal workings of the nation to a preoccupation with an international media image. Internal boredom has only been broken through by the intrusion of the external and the global, which bring a new optics to the images of national identity.

The shrugging of shoulders at the sellout of this figure of the former political romantic, the naturalness with which he just strolls into view from the outset, drifting across the edge of the screen and then disappearing again, is to this spectator much more chilling than the sensationally filmed battles between the sort of canines that roam the back alleys of any urban metropolis. Although the director and his crew offer the obligatory testimonial that no animals were harmed during the production of the film, the real-looking blood and gore are the kind of fare many of us are used to seeing onscreen ever since *Reservoir Dogs, Pulp Fiction*, and the assorted Freddy Krueger films were released. What Romney calls, quite accurately, a portrait of "the dog beneath the human skin" (3) reveals a much crueler nature in the human owner than in the canine counterpart. We must not forget that our pets are reflections of ourselves, that they are rewarded or punished for obeying our commands, and not for living down to their basest level of behavior unless it is exploited for our (social or economic) benefit. As humans, we should be able to reason, of course, and hold in check those dark forces that threaten to surface when the temptations of revenge, greed, or personal gain of any sort lead one to resort to violence. Dogs sense the need to survive, even if they are normally passive and dependent on the care of kindhearted human beings; people who yearn to go beyond the basic necessities of life and the "now" fall under the hypnotic spell of urges,

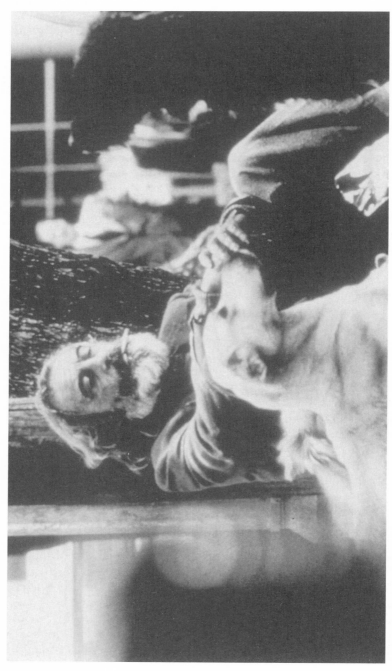

Figure 4.4. Emilio Echevarría in Amores perros. *Photo by Rodrigo Prieto. Reprinted by permission of Altavista Films and Zeta Films. Source: Photofest.*

desires, and dreams (or nightmares, of course) and just may be enticed into the realm of excess. This is the prohibited territory of *Amores perros*, where love moves from infatuation (with Susana, with Valeria, with the guerrillas) to obsession (with money, with beauty, with power) and where the end always seems to justify the means. Nowadays, humdrum lives are not the stuff of cinema unless they are launched into the realms of excess and used as an artificial counterpoint to the intensity of the real. The cinema, or paracinema, of extremes has as its goal "the right and duty to offend" (Hawkins 214), and if it makes a profit at the same time, so much the better. One is led to surmise that such financial success would not be a subvention of tedium but of its antidote. In her concluding remarks about the "horrific avant garde," Hawkins sums up society's need for such a counteraesthetic by referring to Mark Edmundson's exciting work on the expanding and adaptive role of what is known as the Gothic in contemporary culture. On the mainstreaming of "trash aesthetics" such as Milos Forman's 1997 film *The People* vs. *Larry Flynt*, Edmundson writes: "Rather than leave it to the politicians, the social scientists and the now beloved market forces to shape the future, we need the visions of our artists to give form to our hopes and terrors" (28). These are the same hopes and terrors that were abandoned to the boredom of daily life, of political rhetoric, and of economic expansion. But some of them might also be the anticipation of change once the audience is startled out of its inaction in the face of a political system whose demise, like Francisco Franco's death, seems a mythical scenario to the very end. Hal Foster reminds us that the "supreme fictions" (xv) of political systems, social scientists, and market economists require the counternarratives of opposition to emancipate both dreams and nightmares. And what if those very same conjurers of the anti-aesthetic managed to combine images of terror with the forces of the marketplace to produce an artifact that sold beyond one's wildest dreams? What if the market promoted terror, fright, and fear as sensations we all needed to experience, as if in a collective catharsis? Could this not be the greatest terror of them all, a political vision driven by the marketplace of fear? Would it lead to envisioning an alternative in the nation's imaginary or create a panic back into the realms of banality and redundancy?

By presenting us with representatives of Generation X, the Generation of 1968, and a petty bourgeois pretender-to-the-throne of social power, we have three sorts of despair and dystopia in González Iñárritu's film. The first is that of institutionalized disadvantage, rebellion, and youth. The second is a utopian thinker gone terribly awry, and a voyeur of his own daughter's success as a participant in the building of the new nation under the order of the PRI. The third is a portrait of the traditional myth of the bourgeoisie, which always thinks it has all of society under control but lives in fear of finding the barbarians at the gate. Octavio is too young to have lived any glory—aside from the winnings of the dogfights—but is already cynical about his chances to succeed in life. This fact is confirmed for him when he finds out that Susana absconds with his money and rejects his pleas to run away with him to start over again. This prospect of yet another family tragedy never takes root, but it shadows their every move for much of the film, and is an obsession Octavio refuses to give up. Daniel never thinks he will fall victim to any disasters because he is certain he has sufficient financial resources to keep the evil forces in society at bay and that beauty is the key to open the door to the magic kingdom of wealth and fame. But El Chivo—a nickname only, without any family name or social connection—has had it all: wife, daughter, career, social cause, and then rejection and loss. We eagerly scan the old photographs with him as the camera places the spectator alongside the character to peruse albums filled with images. The albums recreate a life history that omits him abruptly from the family epic, and then ends in the dismal present of absence. As a street person he is physically and materially present among us, yet in other ways he is almost invisible. Everyone looks the other way as he passes by, just another dirty face in the crowd. Now you see him, now you don't. As Jameson notes, in language reminiscent of Baudrillard's discussions of simulation and simulacra, the industry dedicated to the recuperation of historical detail removes figures from their immediate context and presents them in isolated fashion, they "are not the outcome of anything, nor are they the [overt] antecedents of our present; they are simply images" (1986 318). El Chivo is not this or that without linguistic footnotes or commentaries by another character to clarify where he fits in the broadest of terms; he merely *is*. The killings he carries out are reported in the daily newspapers as anonymous acts committed by unknown assailants for mysterious reasons. Like a dog bred to attack, the revolutionary has made the transition from guerrilla fighter to paid killer without a hitch.

And this is where the spectator might just be tempted to think twice about his story. Do the thirty-somethings of Mexico 2000 view their parents, teachers, and national politicians (those whose age approximates that of El Chivo) as burnt-out old strays willing to do anything for a dollar (or, in this case, 150,000 pesos)? The students who took over the campus of the Universidad Nacional Autónoma de México (UNAM) in 1968 might have been colleagues and/or peers of El Chivo, so what of the ongoing student takeover of the same campus begun in 1999, as this film was in production? Just where does the director situate politics in

his moral judgments on these characters? The cheating husband is nothing new to film or literature, and the marginal punks seem to be heirs
apparent to the *teporochos* (street kids addicted to sniffing glue) of earlier
decades. El Chivo, however, belongs to a smaller body of characters that
have surfaced in works of literature over recent years. Among these
works we might include Héctor Aguilar Camín's *La guerra de Galio*
(Galio's War) or Jorge Castañeda's demythifying biography of Ché
Guevara, or perhaps even José Rafael Calva's groundbreaking novel
Utopía gay (*Gay Utopia*; 1983) with its alienated college professor
Carlos. In each of these cases, characters throw political utopias by the
wayside and leave them behind in favor of "personal lifestyle choices" as
we say nowadays, or a commitment to "*salir adelante*" ("get ahead") on
one's own. So what of the politically committed man who, as he tells
Maru, just wanted a better world for everyone? González Iñárritu's
character El Chivo is far and away the most disturbing of the film, perhaps owing first of all to his larger-than-life visibility onscreen. Given
far greater access to this type of character than readers of the literary
texts mentioned previously, film audiences are confronted with the
Angel of History in the form of a bearded teacher/prophet/killer. The
subtitle "El Chivo and Maru" comes on well over an hour and a half into
the two-hour-and-thirty-three-minute film, so those who have left the
theater miss this critical piece of the puzzle. The repulsion toward dogfights has taken precedence over waiting out the whole story, with the
last narrative fragment offering the most subtle social condemnation.
Spectators who remain for the film's entirety see before them a powerful
iconic figure of the nation's recent past, one which connects disgruntled
youth (revolutionaries in potential) and disillusioned middle age (whose
past and present are both configured as nightmares) in a solitary image
of loneliness, poverty, and remorse.

Pining for a way to recover some sort of relationship with his
daughter Maru, the glint of tears in his eyes an indication of his awareness that this will never be possible because any meaningful connection
between the past and the present has been permanently disconnected, El
Chivo lives in an eternal today in which each knock at the door of his
shack in the slums holds new potential for financial reward. But what on
earth will he do with the money? Does he leave it in secret for Maru,
whose home is definitely upper middle class? Does he give it away
anonymously to "worthwhile causes"? Is there still a clandestine link to
some political group or other on the margins, as unlikely as this would
seem for such a loner? Is the act of taking the money an end in itself, a
symbolic gesture of defiance against a system of which he no longer feels
a part, except to exploit its barbaric internal conflicts? Is El Chivo a

parody of those who do belong who are always on the take? It is certainly difficult to say, but the character leaves the audience many issues to ponder. In the very last sequence of shots, El Chivo is shown in extreme closeup cutting his long, scraggly gray hair, shaving his beard and moustache, donning his professorial glasses whose broken frames have been taped together, and clipping his Howard Hughes-like fingernails into more acceptable shape. Is his new appearance—a civilized-looking armed warrior of the streets—just another disguise, since it is so obviously a threadbare pastiche of his earlier life? Are we witnesses to a real change of heart and a new beginning? If so, his conversion is precipitated and mysteriously motivated, to say the least, after all this time. One cannot just walk away from the past and declare it dead and gone nor, by extension, can an entire nation feel compelled to do so along with him. As he ambles into the distance across the parched, cracked earth of the Desierto de los Leones just outside Mexico City, El Chivo is a figure that doesn't quite fade into the sunset. Instead he becomes another gray shadow picking his way aimlessly among the clods of dry ground. He is a residue of the past which cannot disappear totally but which continues to resurface, unexpectedly, in different times and different guises. Like a spectre haunting the urban landscape, El Chivo is reminiscent of Ixca Cienfuegos, that mythic remnant of previous cultures and societies who inhabits Mexico City in Carlos Fuentes's 1959 novel *La región más transparente* (*Where the Air Is Clear*).[6] Yet Cienfuegos is the quintessential archetype of cultural continuity, despite the bloody combat of everyday life, while El Chivo is just another animal in the urban jungle, changing his stripes to blend into the natural habitat without leaving behind any trace of his passage except for a pile of dead bodies. Like the killer instinct that flares up in Cofi when placed in the ring for the first time, El Chivo is the materialization of a nation's hidden urge to devour its own. He appears out of nowhere and fades away in the same manner. His presence does not explain a thing about the past or his role in it—that is left on the level of gossip and innuendo among ex-cops on the take and other underworld characters. Society does not come to terms with him, nor does it attempt to listen to his tale of woe: his family has disavowed any contact with the man who abandoned them for something he saw as more ethereal and utopian but who ended up in the clutches of the law.

As the curtain closes slowly over the twentieth century and, today, as the Partido de Acción Nacional (PAN) rejoices in its triumph over the PRI, seen as an outdated emissary of yesteryear, *Amores perros* seems to propose shutting our eyes to the debris of the immediate national past as the story of what produced today's legacy of violence. Taken as a cultural marker, this film represents, without a doubt, the end of a mythos, in a manner similar to J. G. Ballard's novel *Crash*, which served as the basis for Cronenberg's film of the same name. To encapsulate the residues of the twentieth century, González Iñárritu relies, as did Cronenberg, on "rapidly-cut high angle drifts across previously under-imagined territory and savagely implicated close-shots" (Sinclair 8). So we are shown that in the nuclear social unit, Octavio has little or no loyalty to family ties but instead lives in a cocoon of instincts and drives which compel him to pursue his sister-in-law and the lure of lucrative dogfights. On the other hand, Susana clings to the memory of her dead husband and rejects once and for all Octavio's invitation; she is trapped by her fears and cannot step out of the tiny space of confinement she now occupies as a single mother and young widow. In other words, Susana inhabits a social cage of her own construction, owing to the choices she made previously and to the consequences to which they have led her. Daniel is left to care for a handicapped woman whose vestiges of beauty lie only in the memory of their once-passionate affair. He is shown, toward the end of the second segment, calling home just to hang up the phone when his wife answers. She is the phantom that haunts him, just as Maru is indelibly burned into the conscience of El Chivo. Like it or not, Daniel is bound to Valeria by her current physical needs, not by the powerful emotional attraction that originally brought them together. Plagued by their past, neither can exorcise the pain of memories which, with each passing day, become more and more remote images carried around internally like a life sentence.

Preceded in the theater by campaign trailers promoting a utopian future for the nation by presidential candidates Labastida and Fox, *Amores perros* is hounded by the cultural climate that produces and informs it. Rather than the monsters of sci-fi epics, or the splatter-and-gore of slasher flicks, or even the seductive titillation of melodrama, this cinematic debut situates monstrosity on the city streets inhabited by almost twenty million people. If that is not a scenario for violence and brutality, it is hard to imagine what is. As the upper economic echelons of the population spread out from the capital into the state of Mexico in search of breathing room for their social fantasies, so many more still walk the asphyxiating streets of the metropolis with nowhere else to go. (The pace of this daily pounding of the pavement is captured mimetically in the throbbing beat of the soundtrack and the fast cutting between shots.) Is this where they will usher in the millennium, amid a decaying infrastructure, with criminality out of control, little or no prospects of meaningful employment, limited educational resources, and institutionalized corruption? Or is this where new hope lies because,

despite it all, one learns to survive? A traffic accident serves as the catalyst to let us hear the stories of Octavio, Susana, Daniel, Valeria, Maru,
and El Chivo which, in isolation, are tragedies and in conjunction are
evidence of a national catastrophe. Whether the elections of July 2, still a
couple of weeks off as this film opens in theaters around the republic, are
the spark that ignites the mix, or the imagined panacea for so many ills
and regrets, remains to be seen. In its spectacular portrayal of the frustration of those who inhabit hell on earth, *Amores perros* clearly signals a
moment of transition—not just from one historical time to the next millennium, but from one political moment to something else. What that
might be has yet to be seen, but this film opens up the space for a
plethora of possibilities that might follow on the heels of the orchestrated accidental encounters of the lives onscreen. As the backdrop of a
horror film, the city is an inferno whose gates are guarded by a twenty-
million-headed Cerberus baring its teeth at every turn.

At the beginning of the film, the ultimate result of the narrative—
traditionally the last unit in chronological terms—is exposed to the
viewer. Things are set in motion with a resounding crash of steel and
glass, the director's embodiment of a leap toward the future. From this
there begins a staccato pattern of return shots to the account of events
which lead up to what has already been revealed to us as the final
tragedy. The future has been displaced, in temporal terms if not spatial
ones since our stage has been set long before we reach the final act. As
Moretti writes of the modern version of the epic, this presents the audience with "[a] present pursued by the future, which drives it toward the
past. A 'strange' present: unstable, overdetermined" (242). To paraphrase
Moretti's words, *Amores perros* is the portrait of a present—the *último
sol* ("last sun," "sun of the last days") in the historical cycles of the
indigenous legend—dogged by the notion of a future as catastrophe.
Like Ixca Cienfuegos, each day for these inhabitants of the great city is a
"salto mortal hacia mañana" without the luxury or security of a bungee.
Framed by a world obsessed with millennial thoughts and fears, with the
terror of crossing into unexplored and uncharted social, cultural, and
economic territories, and with a desperate longing not to be left out of
what is "new," González Iñárritu's film brings together onscreen an
everyday life that is "strange, . . . unstable, overdetermined," with the
need for society to recognize itself in those very same estranged images.
While the totalizing dream of the traditional epic identified collective
desires in the exploits of the individual hero, modern narratives offer a
delinking of individual and state in favor of pitting one against the other.
What Moretti examines as the "savage," "barbaric," and "primitive"
reading (13) of the modern individual's struggle against being subsumed

by the nation might reflect the exploits of Octavio, Susana, Daniel, Valeria, and El Chivo as well. Each is still alive, not as a result of the safety net of social programs and agendas but because of his or her individual stance against the brutality of society in the New World Order. Individual histories are constantly intersected and deflected off course by other histories, emphasizing digression in storytelling and in a recurrent appeal to emotional overload. While pointing a finger at the conclusion from the outset, the director estranges the present and past from an easy transparency of interpretation. One might feel the events that unfold, but they are not always explicable in rational terms. The horror of the car wreck—what is seen as much as what is heard—never quite lets the spectator recover from being left off guard. What seemed to be the apex of human suffering turns out to be just one part of so much more: dogs fight to the death, men rob terrified bank customers at gunpoint, thugs are paid to beat up "enemies," all in the dawn-to-dusk course of a normal day's work. *Amores perros* is a prime example of the accumulation of images of terror and despair found by Hawkins in "low Euro-horror" (112) films whose cultural debris piles up at the expense of the sublimely maintained affect of the spectator. While this may not be the only way to get the attention of a society in the throes of cultural and political transition, it is undoubtedly the most direct. This is a legacy the twentieth-century mass media has left us: overkill sells. Hollywood's productions are prime examples that fill screens around the world, whether they be films of narrative excess, verbal or gestural profusion, or the stylized abundance of the films of Pedro Almodóvar. But extravagance and exaggeration also just might make a culture's greatest fears become a visible part of the collective imaginary rather than the phantoms of individual insomniacs.

5

STILL JUST A
DRESS REHEARSAL?
From Archibaldo de la Cruz
to Penélope Cruz

The general social atmosphere pervading the decade of the 1990s in Europe is represented by the structural collapse of inherited political and economic systems, their downfall most acutely and vividly visible in the broken monuments and dismantled icons bulldozed from public squares to become either part of the dustbin of history or, alternatively, marketable souvenirs. So why is it that in 1997, in the midst of such a spectacular display of cleaning up the debris of the past, Spanish director Pedro Almodóvar turns not only to established British mystery writer Ruth Rendell for cinematic inspiration, but to that iconic pillar of cinematic history, filmmaker Luis Buñuel? Throughout his directorial career Almodóvar has consistently and vehemently denied any backward glances, any and all connections between historical sources and new productions. We might conceive of this act as a token gesture of reconciliation with the past, now reduced to a pale shadow of history by the late 1990s. Perhaps it is a nod to the recent international celebration of the Buñuel centennial. Or might there be some other forces at work at this turn in the path leading triumphantly down the new cultural and economic road of the twenty-first century?

Perched on the edge of the millennial precipice, as spectators we had before us an intriguing array of artifacts representing the entire twentieth century, many of them part of the highly touted "cultural recuperation industry" (Labanyi 402) or "cultural transvestism" (Jordan and Morgan-Tamosunas 114) rampant in contemporary Spain. As Almodóvar positions himself beside Walter Benjamin's Angel of History, looking back at the route that led to the triumphalist post–Cold War rhetoric of 1990s capitalist globalization, on what might this self-professed king of *pasotismo* ("political apathy") focus? If not training his eyes on the shards of fascism, the discards of socialism, or the storms of nihilism—what Rosalind Krauss has called "so many ontological cave-ins" (290)—then on what? The positioning of Buñuel within the culture of what we might call Spain's second transition from democracy into the world of global consumption of the twenty-first century, and the spectator's facing the convergence of two sets of images—taken from the films of each of the Spanish directors—places in question both "[t]he burgeoning of the copy" (Krauss 290) in the form of visual quotations at the end of the century, and an ideological acceptance of the coherent vision of an original. Indeed, Western society on the cusp of the millennium was so enthralled by the spectacle of the infinitely multiplied artifact that representations of both history and aesthetics splinter into innumerable fragments, providing Baudrillard with the source for his theory of the simulacra in which the commodity is divested of all but the form of the sign itself. The commerce of these cultural citations is posited on an emptied signifier, a placeholder for an absence, a substitute for "event." In Bakhtin's formula of analysis, the commodity is produced in the "time space" that reaffirms place and disavows history.[1] In commodity culture, the artifacts of the twentieth century are merely pre-texts for recombinant couplings by a horde of *bricoleurs* who swarm about them, extracting what they desire and then moving on. Yet in the case of Almodóvar, any question of a seamless unification of past and present is put to rest by the subsistence of unassimilable traces, of survivals which may just catch the consumer's eye as signs of difference, even if their historical origins are less than clear. What is out of sight is not necessarily out of mind and, conversely, what is placed in plain sight is not guaranteed automatic visibility or, for that matter, legibility.

Aside from an overt return to the traditional codes of melodrama (which was welcomed by many critics), *Carne trémula*'s diegetic dialogue with Buñuel is charged with tensions that operate on a variety of different levels and give material form to Benjamin's concept of film as "mak[ing] history from the debris of history" (Bolz and Van Reijen vi). Such historical remnants materialize the space occupied by society but, in this particular case, they do not necessarily reinscribe events within perceivable relationships of temporality. By reinserting the cinematic subject—if not the truly historical agent—into an aesthetic continuum, Almodóvar thereby places the representation of criminality—from Archibaldo's "rehearsal of a crime" to Víctor's felony conviction for one he has supposedly committed—on center stage for our millennial reconsideration. Articulated as a visual synecdoche for the absent, we might even say exiled, Buñuel, Archibaldo de la Cruz stands in for a whole realm of possibilities that haunt the subsequent text yet are truncated by the erasure of the social and political connections of their original source. As an icon of cinematic forefathers, Buñuel is coincidentally and paradoxically divested of his emblematic power as a *Spanish* director but reinvested with a generic aura of some genuine expression of the transgressive. The recovery of Luis/Archibaldo signals Almodóvar's recuperation of the two media which dominated storytelling in the twentieth century: photography and film, as encapsulated in the 1955 cinematic text. Whether overtly or more surreptitiously offering the audience images of history, movies and photographs have placed the power of the image at the center of our world-in-progress, and Buñuel has seen fit to juxtapose their potential for bringing events back into our line of sight. What force these media retain in the face of digital culture and virtual reality, how much the spectator has come to rely on them for comprehension or so-called truth value, and the naturalization of a sense of confidence in the reliability (dare we say objectivity?) of the lens are all pieces of *Carne trémula*'s story.

The technique of montage, so fundamental to the rupture of the image's spellbinding power over the spectator, is deployed by Almodóvar to incorporate things past as historical schism rather than as a return to a recovered instant or spark of authenticity. Wrested out of context, previous shots and scenes stand sequentially disrupted and reorganized. Any guise of immediacy and exact reproduction is revealed instead as technology and artifice, and interest is revived in the relativity of their power and in the questionability of logical sequence. We need not acquiesce to the anticipated boredom of a twice-told tale but can instead visualize how storytelling has lulled an audience into a false sense of comfort or a false image of identification. If these fragments were previously part of a narrative story, they are now invested with the potential to address aspects of difference and discontinuity in its retelling. Montage editing, a technique inherited from director Sergei Eisenstein and the Soviet experimental cinema of the 1920s, puts into practice the concept that "collision or conflict must be inherent to all visual signs in film . . . ; it is from the collision that meaning is produced" (Hayward

79). The first principle of such a mechanism is that the rapid alternation between shots creates moments of new insight at their intersections, making classic narrative cinema less natural and its privileging of a coherent storyline predicated on a different chronotope. Yet rather than demythify storytelling altogether, Almodóvar offers us the fossilized remnants of tales and images with which we may constantly and continually produce new versions of narratives and revise our experience of events. In *Carne trémula*, the director does not sacrifice story altogether but makes us reconsider how it is told and who allows us to see it from which point of view. The montage serves, then, to distance the spectator from the suggested time and space of an original, a more comfortable notion tied to some intrinsic moment in the historical past when, it is supposed, a charge of meaning was placed on the image once and for all. The spectator is now required to hear the tale and listen to how it is told. When it is no longer seen as a completed sign but merely a visible, contingent vestige of "time space," the symbolic encounter is made relative to an endless number of new collisions fraught with significance for each new spectator. A singular sense of story becomes a multiplicity of stories, all of which respond to the experiences and pleasures of perception through the condensed chronotope of the present.

By turning backward to something already there (a sort of readymade object), we may insinuate an appeal by the director to the myth of tradition; but the fragmentation of the artifact's contextual shell breaks any such nostalgic notion. The aesthetics of montage, Benjamin reminds us, is of necessity one of violence since "a true quotation does not affirm, it destroys" (Bolz and Van Reijen 53). The recovery industry, then, is based on a simultaneous rupture with the historical past and a freemarket recycling of its imaginary remainders. In short, Almodóvar's quotation of the visible symptoms of irreconcilable contradictions—be they related to gender, sexuality, or national identity—makes the audience reread Buñuel's reading of culture. The title of the 1997 film itself— *Carne trémula* (*Live Flesh*) with its indirect reference to chorea or a series of involuntary, spasmodic movements of the human body—pulsates with the contingencies of melodrama's triangular structure, one held in delicate balance by the tensions of the images on which the narrative turns. The triangular structure of this genre constitutes within itself the patterns of frustration and fulfillment on whose tensions the narrative plot is based. How long can such an artificial equilibrium be held in check? Eduardo Subirats refers to Almodóvar's films as containing an "ecstatic fascination with the dissolution of the subject" (218); his characters inhabit physical bodies which are violently and tempestuously "seized by meaning" in the words of Peter Brooks (12), embodying in the flesh what the structures of society attempt to mask. How Almodóvar appropriates from Buñuel the tics that make them twitch uncontrollably—the true significance of the *carne trémula* of human flesh—enables us to examine why it might be that Tom Conley is led to the conclusion that "Buñuel displays the model of perversion that recent film has tried to revive since the demise of Franco" (xxiv). I would propose that perverting the linearity of a singular narrative argument, and perverting visual identification, are cases of cinematic interruption. But they are, as well, two obvious cases of cultural haunting by the ghost in the machine. Against the passivity of an audience's generalized boredom with assumed narrative continuity, the filmmakers retell the tale through the lens of aggression (against the spectator as much as against the formal order of the cinematic structure). In a broader sense, the more general figure of criminality and evil is conjured up by an absence and addressed through the scenes from the confessions of the human body which is present: Archibaldo himself.

In Buñuel's 1955 film *Ensayo de un crimen (The Criminal Life of Archibaldo de la Cruz)*, the opening shots situate the Mexican Revolution squarely within the spaces of still photography and the frozen images of the photo album, which is the space for recording historical actors and events. Relegated to such a static mode of representation, historical events are fragmented and aestheticized; they are placed under visual control and captioned by the collector or by the photojournalist for the consumption of the masses. By 1955 the revolutionary photograph is merely what Rosalind Krauss calls "a curio" (296), functioning to preserve a moment now past and, four decades after the revolution, no longer imbued with the spark of history. The traditional role assigned to this medium, to portray "the real," is a convention now placed in question for an audience of the 1950s. The relationship between medium and event began its decay at the very moment when the original shots were taken; when the spectator is exposed to what Archibaldo (Ernesto Alonso) experiences, the process of rupture between spectator and image is set in motion. It is only when events erupt outside young Archi's own window that historical reality intrudes on the comfortable snapshot of elegant domestic space which the family inhabits and threatens to render their previously boring and routine relationships illegible. In the absence of the guardians of the law—the figures of either mother or father, who have gone to see the opening of a theatrical presentation at the local playhouse (before they are turned back by the arrival of the revolutionaries in town)—the adolescent boy's social and physical impotence, followed by a whole range of compensatory fantasies, is transferred onto the only other body materially present, that of his governess (played by Leonor Llausas). As she falls to the ground, mortally wounded by the real bullets that have crossed the threshold of family space and serenity, bridging the gap between desire and crime, the body and the law are permanently and indelibly emblazoned as one in the imaginary of Archibaldo. His subsequent dress rehearsal of a crime, one which never transpires under *his* authority at least, is an obsessively ritualistic act that leads to his own erasure as subject. He can never occupy the social space of an adult if he is not found guilty of an act of transgression —that singular, iconic representation of symbolic masculine power over the cultural environment. In marking the feminine as the only possible site of such transgression— the nanny's demise at the hands of the adolescent male, at least as he concludes it has transpired—Buñuel frames the masculine, not much differently from how Almodóvar will in 1997.

Desperately seeking to be held accountable and punished for the inscription of his youthful desires on the body of his governess, Archi cannot accept the recurring verdict of innocence from the agents of the law. Through the use of an eyeline-match shot, the spectator sees that the governess is actually the victim of a stray bullet fired in the heat of battle during the revolution. Archi, however, is blind to this fact, and he composes a narrative to fill in for what he does not see. While acting as a voyeur of the world outside this bourgeois home, the governess gazes toward the unseen source of the tumultuous noise drifting up from the street below. The events of history occur outside; the uneventful "time space" of melodrama is confined to the domestic sphere inhabited by the woman and the boy. But the connection between the two realms is explicity revealed as the audience is given a glimpse of both through the windowpane. We connect what Archibaldo does not, for he is unable to see from both angles; his vision is limited to the reassuring routine of the everyday. Other than as a masculine agent acting on a passive feminine object—the "crime" he connects to a self in need of validation and a coherent sense of identity—Archi is blind to what actually has occurred. As an adult whose voice-over confession we hear from the very first scene, Archi is haunted by the traces of the feminine burned into his memory. Committed to a hospital ward after the death of his wife (so he tells us, but we have to wait to see for ourselves), Archi recreates the events that have led him to this place. He constantly flashes back to the details of the fallen, supine figure of the nanny: her exposed and vulnerable throat, the blood oozing from the wound, her legs encased in black silk stockings. These condense his desire and guilt (and simultaneous longing for both) at critical stages of his life, as they embody the traces of authority he has tried to appropriate for himself. His rehearsal of the crime recreates each detail of this original scene, plotted carefully so as to make certain that this time around he will not fail to be indicted. Yet this act is revealed by Buñuel as more masquerade than anything empowering, for Archibaldo takes on a series of roles which, in the end, lead only to a conclusion filled with artifice and performance. Following this, he feels he must annihilate what he cannot become, so he desires the death of the feminine personified in the body of the woman. But each time a woman dies, she has fallen victim to a force other than Archibaldo: a jealous lover, a neighborhood strangler, a criminal who fortuitously arrives on the scene to steal his place. There is always someone who comes between Archi and the bodies on which he longs to act, constantly altering the convention of the melodramatic triangle while perpetuating scenarios for the male protagonist's fantasies of power over women and over society's prohibitions. In a curious forking of the paths, however, as Archi establishes his economic identity in Mexican society as an eligible bachelor chosen for an arranged marriage, his sexual identity remains frozen in the primal scene of the nanny's death. His visible symptoms of psychic distress bespeak an individual in crisis. But they also hint at the rupture of the boredom of the bourgeoisie which has counted on uninterrupted social and economic continuity but has awakened one morning to the blood of revolutionary change in their own living rooms. Archi has been rehearsing the life he expects to inherit, only to find that he no longer recognizes it. The death of the governess creates a desire he longs to fulfill, but it is one which he is condemned to miss out on.

The female figures in this film—his mother, for whom the governess is an obvious surrogate; a nun in the hospital ward; a tourist guide; an innocent daughter offered by her mother to Archi—are all foils for a male gaze motivated by fear and anxiety. While Archibaldo's hands never actually commit murder, women are punished again and again at the hands of male violence. A nun is chased until she falls down an elevator shaft, a bride is shot at the altar in cold blood by a jilted suitor, an obliging young woman who brings Archi a glass of milk on a velvet pillow is found strangled in her ransacked apartment. Each time he tries to implicate himself, however, Archi is found to be materially innocent. In Buñuel's cinematic universe, Archi's crimes of perversion are not real crimes at all, but merely theatrical stagings. In fact, the director subtitled this film a "comedy" whose true crime, we might be led to surmise, has yet to be committed. Perhaps after the camera stops rolling, or when Archi gets what he wants (the woman of his dreams), then his impulse to act out his fantasies could place him in the role he desires. But such gratification is constantly and insistently postponed. The bourgeoisie, that great object of fascination for Buñuel, reestablishes order after the intrusion and disruption of revolution (a civil war, we must remember) by absorbing Archibaldo back into a narrative with a happy ending. But the film's last scene is seemingly grafted onto the rest of the story. In an emblematic closure of events, Archi reunites with a woman whom he thought he had lost to another man. They stroll away from the camera down a park lane at sunset, but not without one last closeup look straight into the lens as Archi glances over his shoulder, perhaps to see if we are still there. Has it all been a joke, or have we just been given a glimpse into a society incapable of seeing its most psychotic members as criminals? Or perhaps psychosis is just a dress rehearsal for something more, that is to say something other than what we can see before our eyes.

In his biography of Buñuel, Baxter writes of the liberties taken by the director with the script whose characters had been garnered from a novel by Mexican writer Rodolfo Usigli. What interested Buñuel, as had been the case in some of his previous productions such as *El*, were the internal fears and machinations of the psychopathic mind and how the imaginary feeds off and twists to its own ends what are apparently routine, everyday objects and occurrences. What leads a man to think of committing murder is a process through which events are invested with special significance: nothing is as it first seems but instead part of a personal repertoire of iconic images constellated around a trauma or fear. And what spectators might anticipate seeing becomes something quite different, changing in front of their very eyes from the mundane to the spectacular or the grotesque. Usigli's original protagonist was an upstanding member of the nation from a socially prominent bourgeois family driven to crime by a distortion in his perception of the world around him. As Baxter notes, this scenario of psychic transformation fascinated Buñuel and he could not help but think of it in terms of specific cultural contexts. So once again Buñuel "made an instant connection with the sort of men who had kept Franco in power" (Baxter 240) as he pondered the result when the tedium of normality is affected by the intrusion of the pathological. Old money, small-time bureaucrats, military and religious figures, and other social embodiments of prosperity despite the longtime dictatorship would populate Buñuel's films during his entire career: all those individuals whose private vices were sustained by public gestures of virtue and absolute support for a strongman (Franco). "[A] bourgeois marked for life by a random childhood event" (Baxter 241), Archibaldo accommodates what he sees to the condensed vision of the dead nanny he carries in his head. The lilting melody of his mother's music box revives these images and the myth of power over life and death associated with the box.

Buñuel's own intrigue with such notions of accommodation play out through the film, as Archi attempts to mold and manipulate women into the only scenario he is capable of imagining: that primal scene he faced when politics (gunshots, war, bandits) and sexuality (legs, blood, death) converged on the governess's body. Is Archi no more than a well-meaning bourgeois whose contradictions seem like just so many images from the surrealist absurd? Or is he a monster whose criminal subconscious is set free each time he hears the tune on the music box that he carries as a vestige from his childhood past? Is he liberated when he relives the traumatic events of the past, or is he a slave to what has come before in order to maintain the constant rhythm of routine? Like a photographic still, the image of the past haunts Archi into adulthood. As he moves on both biologically and socially, his image of human sexuality is frozen. The narrative does not drive forward but loops around to recover the past in a series of ellipses, telling the same story again and again. As a counternarrative to the official tales of the revolution, however, the evocation of the dead governess "throws the forward drive of diegesis into reverse as it were, scattering the coherence of the narrative into a disseminatory set of permutations" (Krauss 298). Each appearance of a woman's body, each replay of the sweet and catchy music-box melody, differs from the one before since it is framed in a new context, becoming a mere vestige of a past moment. The same holds true for Buñuel's pathological character reframed in the film by Almodóvar.

The repression of erotic desire, as well as the desire to suppress history (the entire past of this character to which we have been witness) are tools that have been mobilized in the name of social stability. No matter how artificial the last shot of Buñuel's film might appear, it serves to reestablish the couple only because we have all made a pact to ignore what we have seen. This is, after all, the overt fulfillment of the character's deepest longing. Only a trace of doubt lingers to break the spell: Archi's final glance at the camera. Eliding the two parts of what González Requena describes as the "thematics of guilt . . . within a psychotic economy" (92–93), the elements of Buñuel's filmic universe compose a melodrama in which unresolved tensions get housed behind firmly closed doors, ones still impenetrable, otherwise we would have access to the darkest recesses of his new family. Life goes on outside; we are left with the anxiety of the invisible. We already have been given the privileged sight of the original crime that set everything in motion. Now, as Archi gets ready to take on his new relationship at the end of the film, how might we imagine it to be articulated? The spontaneous curing of his obsessive behavior is unconvincing. From the opening shot of wartime testimonial photographs to the closing sequence of spectacular bliss, we have witnessed a change of venue from outside to inside, from the public narrative of historical events to the private world of timeless domestic illusion. How to reconcile the two, if at all?

While the sustaining force in melodrama is certainly mystery—a dark secret constantly threatening the stable symmetry of social structures and personal relationships—this either may appear diegetically or temporarily be relegated to a space outside our vision until it directly threatens the story. The triangle that complicates balance and symmetry produces an agitation it had attempted to hold in check, much as Archi's re-imagined adolescent scene provokes in him excitement and anxiety at the same time. Mystery in some form drives the narrative sequences of both Buñuel's and Almodóvar's films. The various physical or psychological restraints to which the characters are subjected are transferred from the subject's frustrated search for a female body on which to ritually reenact the crime in Buñuel's film to the discovery of the corpus delicti—a body of criminal evidence—in *Carne trémula*. Interestingly enough, however, Almodóvar shifts the eye of the camera from the phantasmatic woman (the assassinated nanny; the absent mother Isabel Plaza, played by Penélope Cruz before her character's tragic but perhaps predictable demise) to the wounded man (wheelchair-bound David, played by Javier Bardem), returning to the masculine framing of Buñuel even as we close a millennium that has touted Almodóvar as the quintessential "woman's director" (Jordan and Morgan-Tamosunas 115).

In his film, Almodóvar recovers Archibaldo's narrative, but now intercut with another, updated crime scene. This time around, Buñuel's film appears as a late-night rerun on cable television. The secret fantasies and anxieties of the sleepless middle classes are now easily visible and accessible, playing on their own living-room television screens. Our domestic triangle is composed of two men and a woman, and it is Elena (Francesca Neri) who acts as the pivotal figure of the story which, ultimately, will deal with the elimination of one of the two competing male forces (one a rehabilitated criminal, the other an impotent officer of the law). What Buñuel left open as Archi's possible future—after the wink of complicity—is now the present, as the camera intrudes on the private spaces of contemporary Madrid. But because the lens functions to cut the world of images into pieces, the illusion of its unmediated power of representation is made visible through Almodóvar's cross cutting citations of Buñuel's film. Any stable notion of Archibaldo's masculine identity in a seamlessly edited story of happy endings and clean beginnings here becomes a fiction interspersed amid the conflicting narratives of other characters. Consuming Buñuel's cinematic fictions as fodder for his own work, using Archi as *carne de cañón* as it were (a reference to "cannon fodder," the original title of Almodóvar's text), the director not only quotes two scenes from the previous film but uses as an invisible pre-text Buñuel's establishing shots of the concept of vision from his groundbreaking film of 1928, *Un chien andalou*.

If we recall the famous razor-slit eyeball/moon-cut-by-cloud shots of that much earlier text, we may fill in the gaps in the crime scene one fateful night in a typical Madrid apartment, although at first glance there may appear to be no such slips of sight. Almodóvar's characters fall victim to what they think they see, just as Buñuel's spectator was tricked into looking at connections between razor blades and clouds by cinematic images placed in rapid juxtaposition. Now, the director's cross cutting of shots deters the eye from matching up an action and its agent, thereby removing the automatic assignment of an identity to an individual. Who shoots whom, and why? Just who really pulls the trigger? Even if we see fingers grasping the handle of a gun, to whom do they belong and to what impulses do they respond? Who is the criminal and who the victim? Is guilt so easily assignable as it might seem, or are all the actions we witness somehow justified? Two consecutive scenes linking Buñuel's and Almodóvar's films will mirror one another: the first I will return to shortly. The second, sealed in a look between policeman and supposed criminal, between desire and the official agent of the law, brings together the junkie Elena and good cop David across the intrusive body of Víctor (Liberto Rabal), whose adolescent crush on Elena precipitates the actions leading to their violent encounter in *Carne trémula*. Like Archi's governess before her, Elena is the elusive figure of desire for purported pizza delivery man Víctor. She is accessible to him only through ritualistic reenactments with other women which serve as rehearsals for the real thing. Just as Archi thought he could control his governess, Víctor thinks he has captured the heart of Elena after a single encounter. We must recall, however, that this is the stuff of melodrama and that the scenes respond to a set of codes bound by suspense and mystery; they are a "matter of seeing" (Meisel 75) what lurks in the dark recesses of the mind, in the dark streets of Madrid, in the hearts of the three characters, and in the nervous tics of all human flesh. For the genre to succeed, a fit must be made between how the spectator's eye and the human mind are equipped to deal with the images whose ghostly traces inhabit the frames. The puzzles and anxieties this genre presents allow us to reconstruct the scene of the crime, but not until we have cast some light on the preconceived notions we bring with us and which many times prevent us from the "sight" of resolution.

An establishing shot, accompanied by a screen title, situates the observer in 1970s Madrid at the opening of Almodóvar's film. The constitutional rights of citizens have just been suspended (so we read onscreen) and a figurative darkness falls over Spanish society to accompany the literal darkness of the night. In this shadowy setting, the piercing scream of an unseen woman accompanies the somber lighting of dusty bulbs on a holiday star adorning the façade of a rundown city building. Her screams form a bridge between inner and outer life as the camera, now inside, tracks down a long, dark hall to stop at a closed door. Behind it, at home, Isabel, played by Penélope Cruz, lies curled up on a bed, about to give birth. This lone woman is the source of the noise that breaks the stillness of what is truly a "silent night." With the help of Doña Centro (Pilar Bardem), Isabel manages to make it from her sordid room in a brothel to a city bus, where her son is born before she is able to receive medical attention. As panoramic shots of the city scroll across the windows behind her, but the camera continues focused on the vehicle's interior, one cannot help but recall the images of the manger and the icon of another child represented as born on what is called Christmas Eve. Closeups of mother and son condense the intimacy of the first few moments of an excessively tender relationship between the two,[2] before real life intercedes in the form of a fatal illness, a complication which will tear asunder any hope of happiness in this initial family scene. Knowing from the opening credits that the Ruth Rendell novel *Live Flesh* served as an inspiration for Almodóvar's tale, we might being to wonder whether this is the first "crime" of our story. Is the portrait of domestic happiness in the gray days near the end of the dictatorship criminal for its failure, allowed only to exist among the faint traces of maternal love that are doomed to fade away with time? It is of note that Rendell, Buñuel, and Almodóvar all predicate their narratives on such an absence from daily life: the criminal who has returned home after being paroled in the first instance; Archi, whose mother left him alone with his governess to experience the horrors of death and desire in the second; and Víctor, who lives through difficult times before he is sent to prison where he will learn of his mother's death by means of one last letter from her in the third. Each character—Victor, Archibaldo, and Víctor—is separated from his family and surroundings, and later attempts to integrate himself back into them after time has elapsed. Meanwhile, events have occurred elsewhere—outside the walls of the prison, outside the bourgeois home, outside the jail cell—but tedium reigns for each character.

Isabel's relationship with Víctor, the son born in such inauspicious circumstances, contains the first two pieces of our melodramatic triangle in *Carne trémula*. The third piece of the puzzle turns out to be money—the 150,000 pesetas she leaves behind as her legacy from prostitution

Figure 5.1. Víctor (Liberto Rabal) visits his mother's grave after being released from prison. Reprinted by permission of El Deseo, S. A. Source: Filmoteca Española.

after dying of cancer. The mediator between mother and son is capital in all three texts. For Almodóvar's character, a roll of bills represents in material form the selling of his absent mother's body and makes Víctor wonder out loud, in a matter-of-fact tone (except for a short interjection of amazement as he calculates), how many tricks she had to turn to earn that much. For Archi, life is an uninterrupted stream of material comforts, with a guarantee of plenty of food even during the revolution, and the company of a beautiful young governess. For Rendell's Víctor, the home furnishings he sells off to an antique dealer upon his release from prison do not remind him of happier and more innocent times, but finance his future in the dismal world of economic necessity. The setting, after all, is England after Thatcher. Each time, money is the only mark of individual identity in a consumer society such as the one taking shape before our eyes by the end of the Almodóvar film (whose actions close out the 1990s). Víctor survives incarceration, wins over Elena, and is present to usher in a "new" Spain. The triangulation of maternal love–son–economics is mirrored in the closing shots of Víctor and Elena, twenty-six years later, rushing to the hospital because she, too, is about to give birth to a son. This time, the trip is taken in a minivan and not on public transportation, and they reach the clinic in time. Speaking to the unborn child as they race through city streets crowded with Christmas

revelers and shoppers laden with gifts on the eve of the holiday once
again, Víctor shouts: "¡Qué suerte tienes tú, cabrón! ¡No sabes cómo ha
cambiado todo esto! ¡Hace mucho tiempo que España ha perdido el
miedo!" ("You're so lucky, you little bugger! You don't know how all
this has changed! Spain lost its fears long ago!") Grafted on at the end of
this cinematic narrative, like Archibaldo's gesture toward the camera
four decades earlier, the punchline could not seem more spectacularly
artificial. Is it out of place, or not? Have Víctor, David, Elena, and the
culture around them really worked through all of their fears and anxieties, or have these tensions just changed shape once again and allowed
them to settle back into time without event? Franco is dead and all fear
has disappeared. Is Víctor the last bearer of an historical conscience at
the moment of declaring an imminent happy ending? His articulation of
the phrase *no sabes* posits the closing of one narrative and the opening
of another, disconnected in time and tradition from what has now been
made to disappear from the urban horizon: poverty, prostitution, single
mothers, and tenement housing have made way for images of "progress"
and purchasing power. 1990s Spain has proclaimed itself the "Gateway
to Europe." Slums have been bulldozed, the dingy buildings and tor-
mented human relationships made to disappear behind a façade of the
New Family and the New Nation.

Like Archibaldo de la Cruz before him, it takes Víctor Plaza the
entire film to conquer his elusive object of desire. But while women represent punishment along with reward for Archi, Elena is Víctor's ticket
into the establishment. If Elena overcame her habit, and Víctor found
religion (as he does in prison), they would be the perfect couple. Unlike
his cinematic predecessor, he accomplishes this through a process of triumphant integration and not a search for society's condemnation of his
actions. During a stint in jail for shooting a policeman, Víctor reads the
Bible and he joins the ranks of the employed and successful in the end;
Archi remains a loner amid the women for whom he longs, although
they barely recognize his existence. Both characters embody some sense
of innocence, but only Víctor finds a way to make this acceptable and
profitable as he plays the dual role of naive adolescent wronged by the
system and sexually adept lover. Vowing to catch Elena by becoming "el
mejor follador del mundo" ("the best fuck in the whole world"), Víctor
apprentices with Clara (Angela Molina), the wife of David's police partner Sancho (José Sancho). Víctor constantly calls attention to himself as
the perfect embodiment of powerful masculinity, while Archi's impotence and innocence are maintained despite his yearning for criminality
and power. Their anguish over invisibility is resolved in two different
ways: one is handed what he wants out of the blue in the last scene (the

blonde Lavinia—played by Miroslava Stern—reappears in the park and reaches out to Archi, making him smile with glee, perhaps at society's own innocent view of him); one has eliminated all obstacles and claims Elena as his well-earned trophy. Víctor Plaza is a self-made man.

In *Carne trémula*, Víctor's aggressive courting of Elena precipitates police intervention and the commission of a real crime. In the end, Víctor and Elena embrace across the wounded law enforcement officer David, no innocent at all since it turns out he is sleeping with his partner's wife, Clara. As we retrace our visual steps back to the scene in which David, Sancho, and Víctor take aim at one another in Elena's apartment where an attempted rape reportedly is being committed, we are made to see that it is not a lovestruck adolescent who has gunned down the cop, but Sancho who forces Víctor, against his will, to fire his gun. Our melodramatic triangle is renegotiated when Elena marries David, now a paraplegic, and closes the door on Víctor. Later on, however, David is expelled from the domestic sphere into exile in the United States and Víctor triumphs. Less than "whole" flesh, David becomes first a physical reminder of their encounter, then an eyewitness to Víctor and Clara's trysts, then an absence. Archi's flashbacks to the body of the governess which he never manages to purge from his psyche disappear in this narrative, a convention altered by Almodóvar to remove the agent of disruption from our line of sight and leave any lingering doubt as the mystery to be solved. Keeping in mind the audience's expectation for closure, the need for equilibrium and banality to be restored, the director addresses what Paul Sandro calls our "residues of desire for a [clean] ending" (45).[3] David is eliminated from the frame, his voice-over telling us that for the first time in six years he and Elena are spending Christmas apart; he is in Miami with friends. Onscreen we see a tropical postcard with David's holiday greeting; this dissolves into a shot of the minivan racing to the maternity ward. Elena's screams echo those of Isabel so long before, and bridge the transition from postcard to traffic jam. There is no visible wink to the audience, but the agent of the law has become crippled, then phantasmatic. The only traces left of David for Elena and Víctor are lingering words written on the card and recited over the soundtrack. His story has ended; his flesh is stilled along with his narrative voice, which has faded to the written word. If this represents the model of cinematic "perversion" to which Conley refers, it does so in the sense that it overturns expectations, it betrays any remnant of the "thematics of guilt" perceived in the actions of Archibaldo de la Cruz. In the process of moving from the stricter codes of crime fiction to the aesthetics of melodrama, Almodóvar retains Rendell's fascination with the "collision between society and the individual, particularly where circumstances drive the individual to behaviour that society regards as somehow abnormal" (McDermid 1). The economy has passed from psychosis to the open market; crime not only pays—it sells. The question is whether it disrupts the drudgery of the everyday or just confirms the notion that everything can be assimilated into a narrative used to fill an audience's leisure hours.

Figure 5.2. Head shot of Elena (Francesca Neri): the woman caught in the middle. Reprinted by permission of El Deseo, S. A. Source: Filmoteca Española.

So how exactly does Almodóvar work with the vestiges of Buñuel's film? He extracts from them a series of shots from two specific scenes, which I return to now in more detail. These images are intercut with the first meeting of Víctor and Elena onscreen since their (for him) memorable evening in the nightclub. It takes little time for both Víctor and the audience to realize that it was memorable for the young man, but less so for the woman strung out on drugs. The two stand face-to-face on her turf; they are seen by us from both below and outside the building (the phone booth across the street) and then from inside the door. When we invade Elena's territory along with Víctor—she buzzes him in, thinking he is her drug dealer—we must be prepared to pay the consequences. We have to look, and look carefully, at what transpires. This is the point at which Buñuel/Archi enters our line of vision (but not Víctor and Elena's). The death of Archi's governess is sutured into the narrative sequence at the moment when Elena rejects Víctor's continued sexual advances, crosscutting between the couple's struggles and Archi's wide-eyed astonishment at what he views as his unmediated power over

women. Elena is a woman bound to her chemical addictions as much as
Víctor is addicted to his memory of her; she only expresses interest in his
presence if he is the *camello* or drug dealer who will supply her with what
she so desperately needs. Their obsessions bring them together since,
without her passion for drugs, access to the apartment might not be
accorded this young man, who is not even a faded ghost among her memories of a night at the bars. Through the mechanism of the shots/reverse-
angle shots used in this sequence, the spectator is stitched into two
different but parallel discourses. The viewer is alternately positioned to
adopt the gaze of each of the characters in turn, and therefore each
becomes both the subject and the object of our look. The montage of
images forces us to reread the scenes: those on the television screen meet
the actions of the film to destabilize the certainty with which we might be
tempted to solve—or think we can solve—the crimes committed.

Elena and Víctor struggle over her father's gun, which she draws to
protect herself from this unwelcome intruder who has come to declare
his love. The weapon is dropped in the scuffle, but not before Elena fires
a single shot. She misses Víctor and ends up wounding herself. The
camera follows not Elena as she falls or the stunned observer Víctor, but
the course of the bullet as it ricochets off the baroque iron grillwork of
the balcony, finally grazing Elena's head. Cut to the television screen. As
we see the governess fall to the ground in Buñuel's film, we must recall
that the bullet which strikes her is not in Archi's line of sight; in his eyes,
she succumbs to a force other than the extradiegetic revolver: he has
willed her dead. Cut to Archi's face in closeup on the TV as he is fascinated by the death that has just occurred before his eyes. This is followed immediately by his lingering gaze on her bloody, trickling wound
and lifeless legs. We overhear the end of the adult Archibaldo's voice-
over monologue recounting his version of what happened, but only the
very last word—*"placer"* ("pleasure")—is audible, the rest just fades into
indistinguishable background noise. Almodóvar then has the camera cut
to a police car, summoned by neighbors suspicious of the noises coming
from Elena's apartment. The sound of a shot has emanated simultaneously from the television and from Elena's home in a double performance that unites the two films, as well as the two realities. The
characters are coincidentally recreating a cinematic encounter between
Archi and Lavinia and producing the new circumstances of its potential
rereading through Elena and Víctor. Together, the crosscut events interrupt the diegetic action, which cannot be resolved until the end of the
film when the guise of innocence (David, Sancho) is revealed as guilt,
just the opposite of Archibaldo's case. Here, Elena is the victim of her
own act, of her own overdetermined (melodramatic) reading of events.

She is not an innocent bystander gazing out the window at the unfolding of the mysterious forces of a revolution as the governess did. As Elena lies unconscious, the blood oozing from her head in an image reminiscent of the other woman whose lifeless body transfixes the stare of her young pupil, Víctor merely sits passively on the couch, holding the gun. His physical presence has precipitated the act, but he is, for all intents and purposes, innocent. Like Archi, however, he will return later to the scene of his crime through his relentless pursuit of Elena. Events have intruded on a chronotope without historical referent, and the characters are left unable to respond to the causality implied by history.

Figure 5.3. Partners David (Javier Bardem) and Sancho (José Sancho) take aim. Reprinted by permission of El Deseo, S. A. Source: Filmoteca Española.

Archibaldo misreads what he thinks he sees. But the narrative disruption created by the montage now produces, paradoxically, a more "orderly telling" of the tale (Sandro 89). We have been permitted clear access to the trajectory of the bullet, and we share this secret with Víctor. (Archi never understood his nanny's death, even if the cause was clear to the audience.) Stunningly, we are now part of a triangle ourselves: Víctor, Elena, and the spectator are linked into a community of presence through a shared image. Cut back once again to the Buñuel film on the TV screen: Archi drags a mannequin toward a roaring furnace.

He has dressed this wax look-alike of his dear Lavinia in some of her own clothes he has stolen, and ceremoniously proceeds to destroy the visible evidence of his recreation. Holding the mannequin tightly by the neck, Archi stares in awe at the vision of the fire before him and, through it, directly at us. He seems to hesitate, but then proceeds with "Lavinia's" immolation. As the camera tracks in a for an extreme closeup of one of the legs tearing apart from the torso, Archi bends to pick up all the pieces, then tosses them into the flames. We see his face framed by the dancing flickers of light as the parrafin melts and any trace of individual human identification disappears into the inferno. In a stunning reference back to his own previous film *Un chien andalou*, Buñuel has the mannequin's eyes liquefy and disappear first. In Lavinia's material absence, after her departure from the scene of what he had hoped would be the perfect crime, he has been driven to recreate the figure of this woman with his own two hands. In the wax figure, she is both herself (a representation of herself, of course) and *his*; she is the object of his desire and the visible embodiment of it as well that he longs for and attempts to reconstruct. His ritual reenactment of the destruction of the feminine which both attracts and repulses him is not repeated verbatim by Víctor, who instead comes to the rescue of Elena by saving her from herself and, later on, from David, for whom she sacrifices her freedom under a feeling of guilt over the shooting.

But Buñuel's meltdown does not show the destruction of the object of desire but rather that of its representation. Through this action, and then for Almodóvar through Buñuel, we are reminded that cinema is also only representation and that the immolation on screen melts parrafin but not flesh. The objects we consume with our—often passive—gaze return with a vengeance to set up an awakening of the senses. The "scene of the crime" has shifted, then, from objective reality to the cinema and it is by means of this last medium that the victim(s) may work out a form of representation for the unrepresentable. What Jameson proposes as the "figurability" of a concept ("Class and Allegory" 290) points to the link between the perception of "real" social forms and configurations (such as class, for instance) and their tangible representation in the imaginary and/or onscreen. Inserting Buñuel's images of Lavinia and Archibaldo into the narrative of his film, Almodóvar jars our memories and our consciousness out of sleep and into a moment of awakening. We see (become excessively aware) that we are looking and, as Benjamin observes, "the camera introduces us to unconscious optics as does psychoanalysis to unconscious impulses" (1985, 237). Our experience of death—whether through the sacrifice of Lavinia or through the uncanny power of Archi's gaze over the fate of his governess—is placed in the center of focus and the visual and psychological detachment and refusal of the *recusado* is reconnected with the "real." As González Requena proposes, in postwar Spain the only possible actualization or articulation of a recognizable image of the nation's recent past is the generic act of violence. It embodies "the impossible restoration of a symbolic reference [to civil war which] leads, finally, to a confrontation in the imaginary: to war, in its most lethal form" (85). There is no image of war per se in Buñuel's film, but there does appear a conversion of what was not "settled with bullets" (González Requena 85) in the excesses of fury, rage, and brutality displaced onto the woman's body. Archibaldo, in essence, has declared war on Lavinia's effigy since it is through her manufactured double that the texture of civil society can be attacked in the most malignant form. The economy of *Ensayo de un crimen* is the laboratory of the perverse in which Archibaldo seeks to inscribe in the symbolic order what has remained, if anywhere at all, solely in the imaginary. Given the lack of symbolizing the social and personal trauma of civil war (revolution), Archibaldo turns his gaze toward women. The unexpressed returns in the heat not of passion but of fire itself; the scene of Lavinia's symbolic extinction is a symptom of Archi's psychosis. He does not deny what has occurred to set things in motion—the death of the governess and the advent of revolutionary change—and in fact he constantly attempts to claim the absence as something belonging to him, the result of an action taken on his part. His reiterated confessions to the crime are intended to produce a discourse about just this absence and to provoke his own inscription in the symbolic universe. But Archi is doomed to failure on all fronts: no agent of the law believes his narratives and he cannot even carry with him the recognizable (or "figurable" as Jameson would have it) tag of "criminal." (Víctor is just the opposite: an accused criminal who has committed no crime.)

In *Carne trémula*, then, an opposition is set up regarding Buñuel's original crime scenario. As Archi watches intently, the flames die down and the television image fades to snow. Then the camera pulls back to frame Víctor sitting calmly beside Elena. Slowly coming to, she shares the space of the couch in close proximity to the intruder. The gunshots of the earlier film shatter the psychic world of Archibaldo into numerous pieces of a larger puzzle, one both social and sexual in nature. In Almodóvar's later version, the grazing wound to the head darkens the relationship between man and woman, but it is also the spark that ignites their passion. The moralistic ideals that might motivate Elena, Víctor, or David all narratively unravel into the survival and dominance of this singular emotion: excessive passion.[4]

The scene inside Elena's apartment, witnessed from an external vantage point, is deciphered by neighbors and police alike as a rape. All events proceed from this presupposition. In Archibaldo's case, he is never accused of such a violent act in spite of his desire for just that—the pleasure of breaking rules and breaking through the orchestrated boredom of life. The spectator has seen no crime committed by either Víctor or Archi, yet the films pit them against one another through images in juxtaposition. The conclusions we might reach within the diegetically presented crime scenes are in total opposition: one man appears innocent (of all but plotting a crime) and the other is made to look guilty (of something he did not do). Archibaldo inhabits the timeless spaces of bourgeois comfort and protection, substantially removed from the world of history and politics and insulated by unlimited family finances. Víctor is not a violent delinquent but the adoptive son of Madrid, a child of the streets who must adapt to the changing demands of a city in the brutal throes of progress and modernization. His birth on a bus is rewarded by a free pass to travel public spaces at will, as a witness to all the expanding and modernizing metropolis has to offer. Archi inhabits the timeless; Víctor is pure event. Archi is melodrama; Víctor is action film. Yet both characters are united across time and space by and through the figure of a recumbent woman. Their bodies—the quivering flesh of life—confront what is for all intents and purposes dead or absent: the victim of a crime who continues to fascinate by means of the traces left behind. The two films montaged as one demand we revisit this scene to reconnect them.

Almodóvar's audience is positioned repeatedly just outside the window: outside Elena's flat, alongside David's car as he shoots pictures of Víctor and Clara together, peering into the dark interior of Isabel's (later Víctor's) shack on the impoverished outskirts of the city. Can we use the photographs, as David does, as evidence to prove some sort of indisputable truth? And what if there is no visual documentation? The tensions acted out in the domestic realm of Elena's apartment—replete with childhood photos and mementos of her diplomat father—implicate encounters between private desire and public legality, between passion and repression. As Peter Brooks concludes of this genre, "Melodrama refuses repression or, rather, repeatedly strives towards moments where repression is broken through" (19). The onset of boredom having occurred in the past, only recourse to the extremes and excesses of passion can now disturb the inertia of the middle classes. The agents of the law destabilize the home, but at the same time they provoke a reconsideration of what incited their entry in the first place. It takes Elena years rather than days to accept Víctor and to see him as he is, but the moment of recognition does occur. It has taken a shootout on home turf to bring out what might hold the couple together.

After Víctor's release from prison, and his reencounter with David and Elena, who have clung to one another since the shooting, a triangle is once again set up. David's departure for a wheelchair basketball tournament leaves the door open, both literally and figuratively, for the meeting of live flesh. Víctor and Elena cast out any last vestiges of guilt over the details of this encounter as Víctor confesses to both her and the audience that their tryst has been his plot to take revenge on David and Elena for the miscarriage of justice that sent him to jail and for her refusal to accept him. While Archibaldo remains consumed with a guilt that he wishes to make public, Almodóvar's characters are released from its grip because they have been accorded a way to get over the past. Elena and Víctor may be addicted to one another, but what happened between them earlier is merely the catalytic spark, the originary big bang, of what follows. Desire is no longer a crime but the stuff of romance; passions may lie dormant but they are never truly paralyzed. If we reread the film in an allegorical sense, eventless time resides in the body of the paraplegic David, while Víctor and Elena are only temporarily removed from the course of events—they rejoin the flow of history at the end of the film as they race down the highway toward the future.

If Almodóvar does not start from scratch but instead participates fully in the Spanish economy of cultural recovery, he does so with no sense of nostalgia whatsoever. There are no long camera shots and no fades; closeups abound until the last scene, when Víctor's van hurtles at breakneck speed toward the medical center. Buñuel is a pre-text that informs this film, but he is used as a catalyst to rupture the static bleakness of a chronotope of monotony. The past is a business, an investment, a hot commodity, and not something inherently more authentic than the present. The director's crystal-clear closeups and medium shots frame the bodies in question—from Archibaldo onscreen in the flat through Víctor, David, and Elena—within their immediate surroundings, focusing on a layering of contradictions and conflictual situations. As befits the melodrama in particular, these shots and sequences allow for the establishment of relationships between individuals and for an intimacy to be created which, like the "scattered chiaroscuro" Meisel emphasizes as the visual trope of melodrama, makes us work to fill in the dark spots and celebrate the excesses of luminosity. The inheritors of the world of Buñuel/Archibaldo are forced to confront such violent overthrows of routine as representations of the tensions amassed just behind the unbroken horizon of the modern. The cultural baggage of the past, having accumulated with each passing day, forms a mountain of debris from which the director may scavenge the discarded images to form marketable products, but it requires a violation of visual serenity to encode them as capable of reaching a distracted eye. The recycling of clothing items and other visible artifacts of other times and other tales does not recover the moments that produced them, but it does afford a digression in the narratives of today. The authority of the male voice—Archi's confession in voice over—disappears from *Carne trémula*, replaced by a narrative stuttering. Like the mystery of David's wounded body (who pulled the trigger?), our story tells us how he got to be in such a state by tracing the narrative clues of a cultural mystery, one which we must piece together for ourselves from what the director offers. Hardly conventional in the codes of classic narrative cinema, but most certainly indicative of a lingering enchantment with the mysteries of masculinity, the director has the camera focus much more frequently on the details of Víctor's body, and even on David's, rather than Elena's. This contrasts with the domination of so many scenes by the overpowering image of Archibaldo's governess, and it produces the effect of a wounded narrative. The triumphant rhetoric of progress is not the fiery discourse of the passions. Almodóvar has shifted the scene of the crime in *Carne trémula*.

This film, then, is about looking back, but only implicitly so because it is all about looking.[5] If Buñuel's creation of Archibaldo placed in question the social price of the individual getting what he (Archi) wants, or the collective price of the survival of the bourgeoisie in a post-revolutionary society, then Almodóvar has superimposed another layer on these images. The tremendous social and personal cost of Víctor and Elena's triumph over all adversity, but especially over the mundane, is easily outweighed by the happy ending. But if Buñuel already gave us ample warning about taking the last wink at the audience too seriously, then we cannot read Almodóvar's film with any less sense of irony or "perversion." The extremes of the criminal acts framed by these narratives—acts committed under the sign of passion—are not the stuff of a gray history legitimized by serious-sounding discourse. Instead, they represent the dark, intriguing spaces of the human psyche which have been brought into the light of the celebratory words of progress and modernity and are left for us to gaze upon with no little sense of paradox. As such, the audience can consume the images of these acts as another set of objects to be enjoyed—perhaps even intentionally and consciously as perversions, as Conley reminds us, if we were to identify with Elena and/or Víctor, both of whom end up being incapable of living within the boundaries and limits of a life of moderation. But then again, moderation is not the order of the day; gloss, style and retro-chic fashion are all signs of excess, not temperance. The invention of euphoria as the icon of post-Franco Spain is part and parcel of the linkage of political, social, and economic freedom under a single banner of melodramatic excess. Indulgence and celebration close *Carne trémula* as if they were an antidote to the stigma of the gray pre-history of the 1970s; Penélope Cruz/Isabel has to disappear from view. Even in her life of prostitution, she is too drab, too afflicted, her life too uneventful to form part of the "new." The intensification of emotion, the buildup of passion from the shadowy street scenes of the emblematic beginning to the noisy, crowded, overflowing downtown of the closing visually condense what is occurring between the characters. Part of the pleasure for the spectator is a possible sense of identification with the couple Elena-Víctor who have risen above the bonds and restrictions of social morality and guilt to cast off these restraints, then gone on to reap the full benefits of the 1990s marketplace with no remorse whatsoever. After all, remorse signals regret for having caused a disruption of some sort, and in this film such acts are celebrated, not condemned. In the free-flowing cultural and economic exchange of the new Europe, Spain can no longer afford to be "different" in any sense of the word. Spanish culture can be spectacular, exaggerated, more; its fragmentation must be made visible, and its performance of daily ritual holds the key to its international recognizability. It can never prove to be too much but must always avoid appearing too little. Obsession—with goods, with appearance, with being an active member of the consumer crowd—is not a crime; it is the lifeblood of consumption. Authority is out, opportunity is in. Passion rules.

If the nation has "changed," as Víctor so euphemistically if enthusiastically puts it in his monologue on the way to the maternity ward, the clamor for social progress has been at the expense of sacrifice. Melodrama has long shown the audience the hidden familial violence on which social harmony is based, and this film is no exception. When Vernon and Morris write of the more recent work of Almodóvar, they entitle their discussion "After the Fiesta" (11), in reference to a post-Movida Spain whose brightly lit avenues into the twenty-first century and the third millennium still house deep, murky side streets of conflict. In the resolution at the end of *Carne trémula*, Isabel is long gone, Clara is dead (as is her singular fascination with the art of the flamenco), David is banished from the space of domesticity into that domain relegated to the less-abled (the paraplegic wheelchair basketball league, albeit a profitable venture for leisure-wear manufacturers and sports fans alike). He is a part of the new in the most charitable way, but only in the terms spelled out by those who are in control. An onlooker at the feast of the millennium, David can only be a voice-over trying to be heard behind the fast-moving images of social and economic success. Cast against the backdrop of dramatic homage to Archibaldo de la Cruz and Luis Buñuel, *Carne trémula* houses morality in the eye of the beholder and not in the agents of the law. Has democratic Spain really been liberated from the past—what Buñuel envisioned in many films as so much dead meat, empty conventions, and ritualized discourse—or is it still haunted even as it emerges into the European Union? Does this "change," as Víctor calls it, signal the interruption of event into the leisure time of post-Franco freedom? Or, like Buñuel, does Almodóvar still intuit a dark side to upscale tedium?

So much has been written about the economic and political "pacts" during the nation's transition to democracy,[6] but we might see Almodóvar's films as having pacted with Spanish culture in their own way. The taming of the discourses of democracy has created the backdrop for a new round of consumer satiation and boredom played out in the time and space between the liberation of the marketplace and the celebration of unlimited personal expression. Paeans to the abolition of censorship and ideological commitment, the flourishing of theater and cinema, independent media productions and superproductions with international recognition, the erasure of the "difference" of the past in favor of the present-without-obstacle, must all be set against the narrative of eventual economic disenchantment of the 1990s. After the superproduction of the 1992 Olympics in Barcelona and the World Fair hosted by Sevilla the same year faded away, it meant less that "every citizen [had] access to culture" (Juliá 117) than that recession and government corruption were taking their toll on the nation's perception of its future. The general elections of 1996, the year during which Almodóvar began shooting *Carne trémula*, marked a second sense of transition in Spain and "the end of a long period of 'light and dark'" (Juliá 119). In the face of new crimes of greed such as illegal financing, tax fraud, embezzlement, bank scandals, and political corruption across seemingly all party lines and affiliations, facile notions of guilt and innocence seem increasingly like ghosts from the past. Whether set in a framework before or after the dictatorship, politics ends in *desencanto* ("disenchantment"). And we might well read this disenchantment as the social ill whose most visible symptom is boredom. Whether envisioning such moral categories as Francoist vestiges or as nostalgic remnants of a premodern past, they certainly inform this work and urge the spectator to imbed them in the current cultural moment. What kind of pact of mutual consent binds the bourgeois Archibaldo de la Cruz to revolutionary Mexico? What social conventions hold Elena, Víctor, and David in the web of collective social and economic relations of the 1990s? What benefits accrue to society from allowing Archi to continue his fantasies undetected and unimpeded? Are his obsessions and impulses just secrets we all share and agree never to discuss? When Víctor announces to his about-to-be-born son "¡No sabes cómo ha cambiado todo esto!" he is just hinting at the complexity we must decipher in Almodóvar's text. A public announcement that "things have changed" and that repression is over is not enough, for history can never be "over." In fact, that is one of the ideological truths on which current desires to consume are founded. History and event have passed from being part of a thick pall hanging over the present, tinging it with the vestiges of past grayness, to being the heavy albatross that can be cast off, something that hangs around the neck of the new Spain but which can be commodified and buried. Then, spending lavishly can keep it at bay (even if its ghost never quite disappears for good). As Conley concludes about the situation, "[u]nder the impact of global and flexible capitalism . . . the counterproductive potential of the Spanish past has to be eradicated" (xxiii). Given such a commercial domain for these cultural goods, the only icons left to preserve in the aesthetic realm are cinematic vestiges of the past, not literal references but the allegorical debris of the twentieth century. Hence Buñuel is simultaneously perversion (as part of the forbidden and/or forgotten past) and iconic image (in overt homage to chosen perverse figures of the past). By conjuring him up through Archibaldo, Almodóvar personifies a national absence whose very exile from the nation created, most paradoxically, "an immortal personification of Spanish cinema" (Conley xxiv).

THE DEMONIC SIDE
OF MODERNITY

Waiting for Satan at the Movies

Alex de la Iglesia's 1995 *El día de la bestia (The Day of the Beast)* and Alejandro Amenábar's 1996 *Tesis (Thesis)* have more in common than first meets the eye. We might begin with the obvious fact that each film narrative involves a suspenseful mystery of some sort to be pursued and solved, whether it be a missing classmate in the case of Amenábar's film or a search for the site on which the Antichrist will make his appearance in de la Iglesia's. But what could a self-proclaimed "satanic comedy" and a thriller set in the world of contemporary academia possibly share, and under what genre, if any, might we articulate a deeper discussion of their visions and effects?

I submit that the "rhetorics of horror," as Ken Gelder refers to the codes and devices articulated by a very broadly defined generic paradigm, "provide ways of defining . . . what is evil (and what is good) in societies, what is monstrous (and what is 'normal'), what should be seen (and what should remain hidden)" (1). The norm and any visions of deviance from it cover a range of possible dimensions, and the functions of "horror" in society, especially on a psychological level, may be varied and intertwined. Schneider establishes the conjunction of multiple subgenres under the overarching category of horror to indicate how broad this field is. He proposes that "[l]ike tragedy, horror promotes emotional catharsis in audiences; like fantasy, it offers viewers an escape from the tedium of everyday life; like comedy, it provides a relatively safe (because relatively disguised/distorted) forum for the expression of sociocultural fears" (168). The individual and collective healing process of catharsis parallels the masking of social anxieties under the guise of an experience of limits—wherein the horrible occurs or appears—from which we return, somehow nourished and refreshed by the emotional overload, to reassume our places in our cultures. It is the third category which provides the specific notion of the genre as an antidote to tedium and boredom that seems to offer the most to our argument here, grounding such films solidly within the territory of therapeutic shock which can be experienced merely as more paracinematic overload or, as Benjamin would have it, visualizing the potential for graphic over-the-top awakening of the benumbed spectator.

Gelder recognizes that there is a circular relationship between the "rhetorics of horror" he proposes onscreen and the societal context which has given rise to them and which defers to the visual images as vehicles to defuse real social horrors. Gelder reminds us that "[t]hese rhetorics may be alluded to by cinematic texts, but the very same sociopolitical system in which they are deployed worries about their real proliferation as well" (1). That is to say, societies produce both horror films and horrors of a more obvious material sort. Certain representations of evil, especially when conjured up in more modern contexts, don't so much tell literal tales as they do figurative ones; they engage the human body with spectacles of sensation and of affect until it is oversaturated, overwrought, and unable to escape. Evil's more traditional disguises might very well appear, but they are infused with something beyond the archaic and predictable forms of the evil or the demonic when they stand out against a contemporary backdrop to which the bodies at risk are inextricably bound. In order to see the horrors of today, directors may turn to modes of excess, to what Gelder appropriately terms "a lack of restraint" (2), whose abolition of clearcut boundaries, divisions, or obvious limits disorients the sleepwalking spectator and disturbs the expected frames of civilized, comprehensible images. Far from consoling the eyes of the observer and allowing for a continued walk through the thick fog of certainty, the graphic excesses of the horror genre create bridges between pre-Enlightenment society and modernity's discourses of reason. The laws of the familiar world seem to no longer explain what we see, and we are cast into the realm of darkness—dare I say the territory of the darkest angel—with few weapons of defense at our disposal.[1]

The dark anxieties that accompany the celebration of progress and the triumph of the modern—in particular at the turn of the third millennium—coexist like a photographic still and its negative, both of which form essential parts of the fabric of everyday life. Each has its place in what we might call "the phantasmagoria of progress" (Buck-Morss 106), a state of mind haunted by vestiges of what used to be or what might come into being. As we marvel at how a lens can stop somethig in mid-flight, or what a digital device might produce out of thin air (with help from our own fantasies and anxieties, of course), there is always the "other side." Alex de la Iglesia gives life to this vision in a television program entitled *La zona oscura (The Dark Zone)*, but these shadowy domains aren't always so easy to separate from what we solemnly refer to as the "real." What we see while awake and what comes to us in dreams are two sides of the same coin. Perhaps this should be an indication that the "real" encompasses more than we think or more than we are willing to admit into our scheme of things. That angst-ridden terrain on which visions of past and present clash, on which tradition and modernity come face-to-face, never ceases to fascinate the eye; where science, technology, and intellect reign, the ghosts of superstition, blind faith, temptation, and false innocence are never far away. As Professor Cavan, the host of a wildly popular esoteric late-night television program with a hint of self-help advice thrown in for good measure, proclaims to his numerous followers in *El día de la bestia*: "con mi ayuda podrás conseguir lo imposible" ("with my help you will attain the impossible"). There is nothing possible unless it is held up to the scrutiny of the impossible. Such are the promises of the media images that surround us; in the film, they not only sell books written by the professor, but also become the signposts of misreadings.

An audience's rapture with one side of this spectacle may seem to preclude the other, but the intensities and excesses of light are never located far from those spaces where illumination does not reach and which we must fill in with visions from our collective imaginary, with figures and hallucinations from our "internalization of monstrosity" (Monleon 22). In a traditional Gothic tale this definition would have pointed to cobwebbed corners and stairways, damp attics and cellars, castle towers and remote wings of mansions as the architectural embodiment of shadow and obscurity. The family's secrets, whether singular or collective, would inhabit the edges of these landscapes and the recesses of these buildings. At the beginning of the twenty-first century, however, our horrors inhabit a different venue, one more readily recognizable and therefore even more sinister to us. Our fears accompany us in the home, the school, the workplace, ourselves, and, most specifically, the crowds on the mean streets of our cities whose very existence calls to mind the utopian impulses of modernity's projects. The transparency of urban space long past, our cities (and perhaps we ourselves) have become

enigmas. The dark space of urban myth forms a counterpoint to the previous epic narratives of social and cultural construction, and between the
physical city and its imaginary counterpart there lies the in-betweenness
of excess. Despite living there, we may find our surroundings obscure
and opaque; human relations are reduced to time measurements and
detailed calculations in agendas, "personal digital assistants" (PDAs),
and even ticking fertility clocks. Just where we feel we should find
ouselves at home is the exact spot where we do not. In an effort to find
some way to talk about this punctuation of our living space by the inter-
ruptive phantoms of irrationality, that "double vision" of the city (78) to
which Donald refers, we might best summarize this sense of haunting in
terms of the Freudian uncanny. Freud used this term to represent how
modern, enlightened society is "always inhabited by its own otherness"
(Gelder 13), and how what is "old and long familiar" (Freud 195)
becomes frightening and uncertain to us in the wink of an eye. We are
both attracted and repelled by the traces of our "earlier" selves and more
"primitive" ways, mores considered long surpassed and vanquished by
the forces of modernity yet stubbornly and insistently lurking in the
shadows of our everyday life. When Schneider refers to the literal
embodiment of "surmounted beliefs" (170) and their power to horrify
the audience, it is this very frightful situation that he conjures up: what is
thought to be dead and gone comes back in unexpected places, at unexpected moments, and often in unexpected forms. Following Schneider's
division of the horror imaginary into "literal manifestations of paradigmatic uncanny images" and "metaphorical embodiments of paradigmatic
uncanny narratives" (174), it is the latter that seems most applicable to
understanding the works of Amenábar and de la Iglesia. The horror felt
by those witnessing such a resurrection is very real indeed, so real that
the body reacts in very physical ways to what is seen; but the tales they
tell lie far beyond the surface of the visible since they penetrate the
realms of the psychological imaginary.

Now we might surmise that there are a number of ways to portray
these conflicted relationships with our habitat onscreen, as many as there
are social horrors that are brought to light. These include familiar monsters set in defamiliarized settings—director Víctor Erice's 1973 film *El
espíritu de la colmena (The Spirit of the Beehive)* does just this with
images from James Whale's 1931 *Frankenstein*, for example, recontextu-
alized in Franco-era Spain. Others involve the breaking of a spell that
has kept us enthralled with an image but that suddenly reveals what
"ought to have remained secret and hidden but has come to light"
(Freud 200). The return to life of the dead—a concept long surpassed by
the advent of modern society—would seem challenged by the monstrous

figure come-to-life. Yet if we reread the film under Schneider's terms, it would most certainly exhibit the traces of a "metaphorical embodiment of uncanny narratives," narratives that pertain to Erice's time and place. What could be more horrifying in 1973 than the thought that an aging body might not die but might actually return? With Francisco Franco two years away from his ultimate demise, the return of the dead is an especially traumatic metaphor of the times. So Freud's Victorian mores regarding the human body aside, his term just might help us address what it is that has invaded our lives and our homes and has cast light on the traces of the *Unheimlich*—the unhomely, uncertain, unfriendly, other—within its walls and within ourselves. In the anticipatory moment of yet another leap into the "new," the visible confirmation of Western society's overinvestment in innovation, dynamism, and the ephemeral, we find ourselves burdened with—like it or not, since the baggage is stored in the images of our deepest fantasies—what Habermas calls "a longing for an undefiled, immaculate, and stable present" (5). While we compose paeans to newness, we have internalized a wish to languish in the comforts of today. As Benjamin sums up this bourgeois state of affairs, he concludes that we are "addicted to sleep" (Buck-Morss 105), because to awaken would stir up all of the ghosts which we refuse to see or which have been relegated to the realm of repression, night, and the darkness of the subconscious.[2] The exaltation of *la movida* left behind residues, not the least of which is *el desencanto* ("disenchantment"; the bursting of the bubble): astride two centuries and two millennia, we can only go forward with the cultural rubble of the past piled around our ankles. Amid so many possibilities, two of the most profound remnants of the twentieth century we have taken with us are the fetishizing of the visual (as discussed by Martin Jay in *Downcast Eyes*, on the "ocularcentricity" of Western culture) and the banalization of evil. While the latter echoes Hannah Arendt's study of Nazism and the Holocaust, we could extend the concept to include other wars as well (including recent episodes of ethnic cleansing in Eastern Europe), and so many more traumatic episodes of the past one hundred years which have been brought effortlessly and relentlessly into our homes by means of the media. Indeed, it is through the media that the primacy of vision and the banality of radical evil intersect.

The privileging of sight brings with it, of course, both tremendous enjoyment and extreme risk, both psychic and physical. So scopophilia and scopophobia—the lure and the repulsion of the visible—abide as one since vision "as social practice" (Jenks 2) represents the pleasure of access and the curse of a cult to the power of the "real" implied by that access. The fallacy of unmediated perception—what W. J. T. Mitchell refers to as "the innocent eye" (118) of both seeing and of analyzing or interpreting what is seen—is a subtext of both films under consideration here. In each, a purposeful confusion of object and representation is a symptom of social misreading by two self-declared "innocent" observers. In Amenábar's film, this is a first-year graduate student (played by Ana Torrent) with her eyes trained on an objective study of audiovisual violence for her "thesis;" in de la Iglesia's case, it is a Jesuit theologian (played by Alex Angulo), who when confronted with the omnipresence of the images of the mass media for the first time read them as literally as he has read the Revelations of St. John. Their single-minded fascination with "looking" (the first at murder and mayhem onscreen but not around her; the second at what he deems readable signs of the truth of his mission) creates a blind spot for each character, the "blindness at the center" that Jameson posits at the very core of cultural and economic colonization ("Class and Allegory" 292). As it infiltrates the seemingly impermeable doors and windows of domesticity and "the home," and, as each character confronts it, "urban space . . . is doubly textured. It is concrete, but just as brutally it is fantastic" (Donald 77). In the face of such a challenge to the clarity of a single line of sight, it will prove extremely dangerous to be naive. Our graduate student Angela finds a mystery inside the walls of the university, but her fears and fantasies follow her home at night and permeate her dreams. When the double visions coincide, she becomes the star of her own nightmare. And to the very end the priest Angel insists that his single-minded vision has brought a salvation of the social order by staving off an apocalyptic end of history. Yet we must recall, as Benjamin constantly reminds us, that the postponement of an encounter with our own demons is class related as befits those most comfortable with the way things are and those who have lost hope for the arrival of change. We hit the pause button on the VCR if what we are about to see might make us squeamish, and we stop even a metaphor of the Antichrist from bringing change to our way of life if that fear is even greater than seeing things continue just the way they are. With an eye on Benjamin's texts related to boredom as the postponement of great deeds and social possibilities, Buck-Morss judges that in this vision of events, things have ground to a standstill. She concludes: "If history, far from progressing with the pace of technology, is stuck like a broken record in the present structure of social relations, it is because the workers cannot afford to stop working, any more than the class that lives off this labor can afford to let history go forward" (105). For one class, boredom is the agony of everyday life; for the other, it is a fashionable alternative to societal change, a choice to be made and a will to be imposed. It is difficult to give up even boredom, as we are lulled by its daily panorama of new alternatives which we have, in reality, come to expect as part of the options of modernity. Like addicts who fear the symptoms of withdrawal from whatever drug keeps them from having to deal with the real, those who inhabit the modern world are haunted by the trauma—the horror—of awakening.

It is truly remarkable how Amenábar and de la Iglesia have assimilated and merged these visions of the horrifying and the banal into their films. Raised on the varied fare of international television and video, including all the hybrid forms and subgenres these formats foment, both employ the medium of the film itself to question the power of the cinema over spectators and its problematic relationship to the concept of "modernity" as a replacement for other (avowedly superceded) myths and cults. Through assorted tortuous adventures amid the landscapes of the "urban uncanny" and the "brutally fantastic" that we have mentioned from Donald's writings on the city (81), the directors disquietingly lead us to face a collection of our greatest fears in a habitat so frightening that we might be tempted to suppress the fact that they are indeed based on reality. Perhaps they are all too "real," and that is what unnerves the audience more; if we can classify disquieting images under the taxonomy of nightmare, then we could even relegate them to that sphere of anxiety tapped into by earlier by Spanish artist Francisco de Goya y Lucientes who, we reassure ourselves, was just a madman gone deaf during a time of complicated political intrigue across European cultural and geographical borders. But let us remember that the titles of so many of his sketches, lithographs, and black paintings reflect the same sense of horror we find in films almost two hundred years later. In one of the most recognizable of his works, a young man sits with his head resting on his forearms, having fallen asleep at midday over the intellectual pursuits on which he diligently had been working (as witnessed by the scattered papers on both table and floor). Above and around him cavort all sorts of monstrous creatures and a particularly malevolent-looking bat flutters treacherously close to his head. Goya entitles this metaphorical vision of slumber in terms of the spell that illogical dreams cast over us: *El sueño de la razón produce monstruos (The Dream of Reason Produces Monsters)*. There is no science in the world as this artist sees it; there is no logic in his aesthetic universe, but rather the liberation of our irrational, internalized monsters that take physical shape according to the greatest fears of our times. But even in films of the early twentieth century, Walter Benjamin observed a similar attack on the eye as an affirmation of the power of the cinematic image to release what we have done little to represent on a conscious level. If "the camera introduces us to unconscious optics as does psychoanalysis to unconscious impulses"

(Donald 84), it thereby demands that we leave behind the hypnotic stare of the sleepwalker and "look at" what we merely "see." I take the phrase "unconscious optics" in this case to mean the primarily ocular conventions of Western culture, as well as the blindness insinuated by the myth of unmediated perception, as the two come together in the conscious deciphering of what comes into our line of sight.

Usually used to orient the spectator within the films' narrative and to function as a metonymy for the rest of the text, the establishing shots that open *Tesis* and *El día de la bestia* function less to familiarize than to destabilize the audience, for they paradoxically negate our powers of vision and of hearing from the outset. Rather than recognition and shared community—the successful suturing of the viewer into the film; the "being there" of our direct access to the real—the directors have opted for censorship and exclusion as we enter their cinematic universes. The process of simultaneous inclusion and rejection thereby fetishizes, or re-fetishizes if we are to be exact, what is lacking (hearing and sight) and entices us with the illicitness and secrecy of their insinuation. We are there—at least the camera places us "there" in terms of a scene of action—but, ironically, we find we are excluded from full access to comprehension at the same time. And when we desperately try to regain our focus or to make audible what is not, prohibitions force us to turn to hypernarration to fill in for these absences. Words—dialogue, lyrics, confession—take the place of acts. We see no evil but at every turn hear innuendo about its presence amidst us; we overhear no revelations but watch as someone is motivated to act on them in scene after scene. Not so much representing "new decadent desires" (Lev 38), as some suggest have been awakened by the ubiquitous glitz of end-of-century consumption, these films instead appear to reaffirm a structural and visual dissonance between appearance and "fact" in the shadowy survival of twentieth-century anxieties and longings as the uncanny horrors of the twenty-first. Even when disguised in the form of sci-fi special effects or the much-touted use of cinema as the vehicle of images of the "New Spanish Woman,"[3] these two films remind us that by day we celebrate holidays, go to the office, and purchase goods, but by night we are still stalked by our own previous creations and impulses, no matter how hard we have individually or collectively worked to repress them. They may appear alien to us at first, but to our great discomfort—and perhaps that is the truly demonic or satanic part of the comedy—we find them still inhabiting the recesses of our imaginaries. What drives the two films is our own desperate need to see what is really going on, more than the solution of a mystery, as we mentioned in the beginning. As portrayed by de la Iglesia and Amenábar, cities are places in paracinematic works "where people kill time, they represent the space in which 'aberrant behavior begins'" (Hawkins 100). It is within their alleyways and dark passages that excesses thrive. But to label such spaces and visions aberrant (or not), we have to be made aware of what they look like and why they makes us feel edgy; the next step is to see whether there is such a clear separation between the spaces of "normal" city life and those of the deviant or eccentric. The conjuring up of Satan in a downtown apartment house, or the risk of disappearing into the underground world of pornography, sexual exploitation, and snuff are the narrative choices of Amenábar and de la Iglesia that are used to reveal the complex relationships between such worlds. Like Benjamin's "dream-worlds" (Gilloch 130) of Paris, Moscow, or Berlin, Madrid serves both directors as the setting for their visions of the exciting phantasmagoria of modernity, as well as for its extraordinary contradictions.

Contemporary Western culture, and Spain is no exception, is focused primarily on the world of youth—*la juventud*—as a source of both personal dreams and social disillusionment. Seemingly immune to the explicit images of sexuality and violence which have become commonplace since the touted post-Franco transition to democracy, contemporary generations of filmmakers find a rich source of material and great potential for commercial exploitation in youth's enthrallment with such images. In his self-proclaimed satanic parody, Basque director Alex de la Iglesia mixes together elements influenced by such recent popular American films as *Scream*, *The Omen*, and *The Exorcist* (the last of which is also enjoying renewed success in the United States with its rerelease in theaters and release on video in a director's cut that includes some previously edited and deleted scenes) and heavy metal recordings of the popular rock groups Def Con Dos (now disbanded) and Gran Wyoming to create a vision of the modern world in which the satanic is just another part of the everyday. In a city seemingly oblivious to real pain and suffering because it has preferred to train its eyes on the spectacle of purchasing power, de la Iglesia gives us the dark side of urban culture set amid crumbling and devastated streets filled with junkies, leftover punks, and the poor. This decay is not merely that of the narrow streets and cramped hostels tourists used to occupy but of its zombie-like, media-mad inhabitants as well. Lulled by the spectacles displayed on omnipresent screens—from homes to store displays to studios and offices—the masses do not seem to question how and why astrologist-television talk show host Professor Cavan (Armando De Razza) is the powerful overlord of his vast domain, nor when life became demonically attached to such technological weapons of culture from which so much pleasure is taken. Like Benjamin's shoppers and *flâneurs* who spent their

days on the streets of Paris and Berlin during earlier decades, the inhabitants of Madrid "are addicted to boredom" (Buck-Morss 105); they fill
all hours of the day and night with incessant media images which can be
consumed as if they were "real" objects in and of themselves. As witnessed by the huge audiences, enthusiastic applause, and the sheer quantity of spectators tuned in, technology is a refuge from the anxiety and
routine of life. The rapture of the public is evident in their eyes. Whether
news reports, talk shows, or exorcisms, these spectacles surround
madrileños, and there is no escape. Yet one aspect of media image consumption remains: how do we read their message? Is deciphering them
just another tedious burden, or is passivity the answer in the hopes that
the sensational and the abject will go away? The characters in both films
will find themselves thrust into the middle of this dilemma and have to
make choices.

Before the titles and credits appear, far from the center of action in
the big city, *El día de la bestia* opens with a long shot of a bleak, aging
church set amid the green hills of what we guess to be northern Spain. It
is a remote and seemingly peaceful counterpoint to the cauldron of violence of the Basque country that we associate with news reports. Bells
toll as if to call us to enter, producing a dissonance between sound and
image, since the dank, dark walls of the structure are not inviting to the
eye. Something disturbs the spectator about this venue; something does
not seem quite right. We long to peek inside but are fearful (if excited)
by what we might find. It is not until we enter the "holy space" that the
mystery may begin to present itself to us, however. Once the camera
places us inside the building, it focuses on a huge crucifix that dominates
the visual space in front of us and towers over the kneeling figure of a
solitary priest. The camera tracks down the center aisle. The priest is
soon joined by a second figure in black, and as we overhear the hushed
tones of their conversation we begin to realize that it is soon to become
the privileged exchange of a confession. We are immediately left with a
sense of curiosity regarding the situation and our relationship to it. Will
we be able to hear his words or not? Do we want to find out what he has
to confess? After the tantalizing lead-in of the words "no he pecado pero
voy a pecar" ("I haven't sinned but I am going to") and "es necesario el
mal" ("evil is a necessity"), the priest's words are drowned out by the
insistence of the bells. Gestures indicate that their exchange continues
but, in fear, the priest mutters that "nuestro enemigo es poderoso . . . es
posible que haya escuchado" ("our enemy is powerful . . . it's conceiv-
able he's overheard us"). Only a second or two elapses before the giant
cross falls heavily on the only witness—the second figure, gratefully, not
us—and the credits begin to roll. The scene changes abruptly. A sound-

track of very loud, heavy metal music accompanies the arrival onscreen of a bus that has just entered that emblematic site of hell on earth: Madrid. If looking to come face-to-face with Satan, I guess that would be where a Basque theologian might venture first. Given the tense and violent relationship between Basque separatists and the federal government in Madrid, the reading of the situation follows somewhat naturally. What the connection is between the previous exchange of words and the change of venue remains to be seen; both images and soundtrack demand attention, and it is difficult to figure out what to tackle first. As the priest exits the bus and enters the world of sinners, we are bombarded with images of the flip side of the cultural coin of the world he has left behind in the north. Smog, fumes, and dust fill the air; beggars dressed in ragged clothing (representing Mary, Joseph, and Jesus) plead for money from recent arrivals to the city, since this is Christmas Eve and a good season for charitable donations. In the rain, automobile accidents and victims line the streets; ambulances wail in the distance. Our senses are overwhelmed, and perhaps we are left to wonder where the priest will begin his quest for the devil with so many options from which to choose. Madrid appears just as New York, Washington, and Los Angeles have in apocalyptic films produced by Hollywood in the 1990s, from *Independence Day* to *Armageddon*. And after September 11, its eerie similarity to a new ground zero is uncanny.

Father Angel Berriartúa arrives at the *Puerta de Europa*, the door to the New Europe and gateway to the future as constructed and declared by the Socialist government while still in power, ready to take on Babylon. The portal to the future inhabits the same venue as the traces of the imperial past: Castilla (Castile). Little by little, in his casual conversations with passersby and store detectives, he reveals that he has spent the last twenty-five years as a *catedrático* secluded in the University of Deusto, studying the Apocalypse of St. John in order to decode its secrets. If we do some quick mathematics, twenty-five years before 1995—the date of the film—takes us back to 1970, a full five years before any of the transitions to democracy and squarely under the reign of Franco. Historical events have come and gone, but Angel has been deep at work trying to capture time once and for all. As we learn shortly thereafter, this text is not taken by him as allegorical, but as a cryptogram which, decoded with (of all things to be culled from Spanish cultural history) the traditional Jewish calendar and a lot of sophisticated mathematical calculations, prophesies the arrival of the Antichrist in Madrid on Christmas Eve 1995. This is the year before Spanish elections, mind you, and the apocalypse as a political image may not be all that far-fetched for many. The Socialists have been in power since 1982 but, with

the González government on shaky economic and moral terrain, maybe
it is really "the end." Solemnly vowing to sacrifice himself for the good
of modern society, Father Angel wanders under cover of darkness—a
constant in the city envisioned here—to commit as many sins as possible
and thereby conjure up the devil himself to reveal the whereabouts of
the birth of his son. The only way to stop history from going forward
toward its own end is to stave off the agent of that end. An "angel"—the
name of our priest—desperately seeks a "fallen angel"—the devil—to
stop the evil deed that might signal the end of modern history and bring
about a "new time." So much for modernity's overinvestment in the
new, since it sounds like the old, the routine of just waiting, looks pretty
good at this juncture. Since Benjamin assures us, however, that such
"[b]oredom is always the outer surface of unconscious happenings"
(Buck-Morss 407), a search for the mysterious site is the least of our
worries. What we must keep in mind is the trigger for the search, that
"uncanny" image or feeling that has been the impulse for Father Angel
to leave his Basque homeland and venture to Madrid. What the texts of
St. John have revealed to him, by means of some sophisticated and complex equations and a key kabbalistic guide, produces his need to keep
change from occurring and maintain the status quo.

It likely goes without saying that he cannot fulfill his mission in the
glaring light of day but only in that nocturnal world inhabited by the
phantoms that average shoppers on the Gran Vía can only guess at or
hear about on news reports and informational television programs.
Committing petty acts of thievery and evil such as stealing an unat-
tended suitcase, raiding the donations given the Holy Family by
passersby, and pilfering the wallet of a dying man, Angel wanders
around the old section of the center of Madrid in search of some sort of
sign that he is on the right track. Rather than be thwarted from accom-
plishing his goal, he finds what he considers a series of hints or omens
that he must follow. These range from nightclubs named Satanica to
window displays that promote Cavan's books, tapes, and zodiac readings; they also include a music store whose clerk (played by Santiago
Segura)—appropriately named José María—is a devoted fan of what the
priest reads literally as "Satan" and his music-driven worshipers. The
two make an extremely unlikely connection over the misinterpreted
conjunction of interests, and Angel establishes a base for his operations
with the help of his newfound friend and ally.

But the nocturnal dwellers of the city are like afterimages of the
day, photographic negatives, or ghosts in the machine of modernity.
The innocence of broad daylight is shadowed by the cynicism of the
darkness (not that of the devil but of the hours after nightfall). The

Figure 6.1. Father Angel Berriartúa (Alex Angulo)discovers satanic music.
Reprinted by permission of Lolafilms, S. A. Source: Filmoteca Española.

words of Angel's new landlady, the mistress of a *pensión* in ruins, makes the attitude of the city dwellers clear: "de noche putas, negros, drogadictos . . . qué asco" ("when night falls it's hookers, Blacks, drug addicts . . . how disgusting"). Her commentary on such a social mix is revealing: in her mind economic suffering, unemployed street youth, and racism combine to form the legions of modernity's nocturnal enemies. Almodóvar has shown us Barcelona-by-night in films such as *Todo sobre mi madre (All About My Mother)*, but his characters' feminine side almost always make them more difficult to judge and almost impossible to condemn. Their saving grace is their "real" innocence despite a life of poverty, crime, addiction, and the burning need for sex reassignment surgery. In *El día de la bestia*, the horrors of the city are that the only real innocent is Angel and he stubbornly refuses to see things any other way. The traditional embodiment of evil is literal, the devil incarnate, while what is truly horrible—women in prostitution, young addicts, immolated immigrants—is invisible to his eyes. So there are two other elements to this city of shadows: the first is Professor Cavan, purveyor of spectacular palmistry readings, staged exorcisms, and other assorted magic tricks for the sleepless multitudes dying to witness for themselves these over-the-top performances as "real TV" or reality shows (which have some element of staging to them). The second is a sinister group of hooded figures who roam the city after dark in vans and make it their professed moral duty to clean up the streets. In a disturbingly dark reflection of Angel's mission, *Limpia Madrid* (Clean Up Madrid) goes after homeless immigrants, beating or burning them to death while onlookers turn a blind eye. So violent as to seem unreal, the campaign seems to have enjoyed a lasting success, and law enforcement agencies have been reduced to reporting the outcome of their attacks as just so many statistics. Curiously, Angel finds mathematics a key to his first text (St. John) but neither hears nor sees it as a clue to the second (voice-over news reports of urban violence on the rise). Since the masses are lulled into stupor by the everyday sounds of the city, from ambulance sirens to gunshots twenty-four hours a day, what would it take to interrupt this routine? Has all sound become inarticulate, reduced to the levels of decibels and noise rather than divisible and identifiable? Has excess drowned out the human voice amid the cacophony of modernity, and can this voice be recovered?

As the priest continues his sinning, committing acts of petty theft and meanspirited actions towards invalids, the poor, and the elderly, Cavan's voice drones on in the background as a constant counterpoint to the world outside the television studio. Blatantly and unabashedly unaware of the difference between performance and "reality," Angel confesses his innocence to the man he hopes will be his direct conduit to the devil. Upon seeing Cavan's program for the first time on a TV in a bar he enters in the company of his new companion José María (the record store clerk), Angel takes a step back in amazement. He has never owned a television set; in his eyes Cavan, for all intents and purposes, is truly a connection to the underworld and not a media personality. His literal reading of a written text (the prophecies of St. John) and subsequently of a staged program by a parapsychologist, make him blind to the violence and evil surrounding him in the streets and alleys of this modern city. He might have left Deusto behind, but the veil over his understanding is not lifted by the sights all around him. The unlikely trio of Cavan, Angel, and José María—a diehard heavy metal devotee despite what appears to be advancing middle age, and from the working-class neighborhood of Carabanchel, he sees fit to tell this newcomer—face down the forces of the underworld in the shadow of the Kio Towers, those architectural symbols of Spain's definitive entry into twenty-first century Europe and monuments to progress and modernity. The director could not have chosen a more symbolic and evocative setting for the encounter between the forces of good and evil, yet it is incumbent upon the audience to read beyond and not relegate Angel and his cohorts to the terrain of the literal. A demonic figure should be a goat, just as it appears in Goya's dark series *Los caprichos*, and so it is in this film. But it would detract from the complexity of meanings to read Goya's *macho cabrío* ("he-goat"; the devil manifested in animal form) on the surface as a mere literalization of the devil, as would also be the case in de la Iglesia's film. Each time it appears, the image overwhelms the spectator with the effects of making "evil" take on a zoomorphic shape; but if we were to revel in the details of Goya's etchings or in the special effects of de la Iglesia's film, we would truly be trapped by the realm of the purely visible and lose the phantasmagoric dimension of horror they propose. The chances of a goat coming into our elegant apartment house on the chic calle Serrano, or of catching a glimpse of a horned creature as we cross the downtown streets, are remote indeed. Yet the ghostly apparition of demonic forces in the middle of the constructs of high culture haunts the frames of this film from beginning to end. Light, beauty, and progress have their counterpoints in the perverse attraction of darkness and evil, of vestigial forces that we are unaware still lurk inside our collective imaginary and within the walls of our modern edifices. Entering the spaces of modernity is costly, and it does not come with a clean break from all that we were before. So the apparition of the goat reminds us, as do the blood of the virgin and the improvised, white-bread "host" in the drinking-glass chalice that Angel uses to invoke demons. One just needs the right time and place to mix the ingredients, and the past miraculously, or uncannily, comes to life in front of our very eyes. Is this a comedy, then, or a satanic comedy whose "estranged" narrative is a metaphor for the greatest fears of the new millennium that we have carried over with us from the previous one and don't seem to recognize?

While he seeks to contact the reigning power of "el mundo de las tinieblas" ("the empire of darkness"), Angel has lost sight of the dark, fascist horrors under his very nose. Television fare may pander to the hopes and fears of a viewing audience, but it is outside their living rooms that the real battle for modernity is taking place. The spectacle of ritualized horror, not too distant in the European past to be repressed but close enough to the cultural surface to return as a narrative of the "uncanny" we have wrought upon ourselves, is drowned out by the insistent images of the media performing a nightly sleight of hand. Reports of accidents, homicides, and carnage on the news become, as Baudrillard has shown, just so many indistinguishable simulacra that have taken the place of the "real." We no longer need to look out the windows because we have a window on reality in each and every living room: the television screen and its digested form of the "real." If a news anchor doesn't report something, it does not happen (or it is as if it had not). Baudrillard writes,

> Such is simulation, insofar as it is opposed to representation. Representation stems from the principle of the equivalence of the sign and the real. . . . Simulation, on the contrary, stems from the utopia of the principle of equivalence, *from the radical negation of the sign as value*, from the sign as the reversion and death sentence of every reference. (6)

By inference, even the concept of the "real" becomes an issue of unreality since it matters not what once might have held true and is now lost, but that we now inhabit the absence, the lack of need for the real since simulation refers to and replaces itself, closing off all necessary contingency. When James Donald submits to us the idea that "the city is not a place" (92), he prefigures this type of urban setting vividly imagined by director de la Iglesia. In his view it is instead "a mode of seeing" (92) and, as such, the space where celestial angels and fallen ones collide, where the dreams of modernity confront nightmares from the past, all within the space of electronic waves that capture the images already interpreted by technological means, or produced by those same means from scratch in the twenty-first century digital age.

It is significant that *El día de la bestia* ends with a shot of two scruffy beggars on a park bench in Madrid's El Retiro park. As children play and couples stroll, the camera tracks in on a close shot of these figures sitting alone, oblivious to almost all around them. In closeup, we come to realize they are Angel and Cavan, recognizable even if somewhat battered. The one thing they cannot take their eyes off is a television screen. They are transfixed by the image of a man on the screen of a small TV placed, facing the camera, on the counter of a kiosk for the entertainment of customers who come by for refreshments. They gaze intently at the face of Cavan's replacement. Obviously, *La zona oscura*, as we are reminded the show is called, must go on. After a momentary tribute by the new emcee to the disappeared previous host Cavan, everything proceeds as usual, to the excitement of the audience. It is not the individual they have come to endorse but the function he provides: he entertains, he brings the outside into the home, he is the true intermediary—not so much between man and Satan but between the "real" and the spectator. The world has not come to an end, and our two protagonists have survived, if a bit worse for wear. They have shared an experience of the limits and now are inseparable companions. Religion and media spectacle have entered into a pact: unable to communicate their heroic feat to anyone, except of course us, they now inhabit the dark side of the city they came to save. Their story—the one we ourselves have been witness to onscreen—joins the other dark urban legends that haunt the modern metropolis. As they stroll off into the distance and the closing credits roll, Cavan leans heavily on Angel's shoulder. This seer of the future and promoter of exciting encounters with the devil has been left half-blinded by his own encounter not with Satan but with the legions of Limpia Madrid and their liberal use of gasoline to remove all traces of "difference" from the city. Let us not lose sight of the fact that Cavan is Italian, a foreigner, who is the media mogul. For some forces in society, he is an outsider, an interloper, a disrupter of the purity of their vision of Spain's future that carries on the prejudices of the past. With our own eyes we saw José María, enthralled by Satanica and the seemingly innocent pastimes of heavy metal fans, sacrificed to the goat/devil who appeared on a crossbeam of the building construction site, lured by the prospect of really meeting up with this enticing figure from another world. But Angel, armed with sophisticated weapons he has taken from the street criminals and an obsession with keeping history at bay, guns down the vigilantes who come to immolate Cavan under the shadow of the arches. Rather than sight restored by their survival, we find two figures reassured in their blindness who support one another. They think they have saved the world.

In *Tesis*, Amenábar's vision of darkness is set in the same metropolitan space of Madrid, but this time around it is enclosed within the sacred halls of academia in which at least some of us find, or think we find, a refuge from the "real." We too will be shown as naive in our vision, of course, as the "phantasmagoria of progress" witnessed in the overabundance of material goods and pleasures in modern consumer society meets face-to-face with our "internalization of monstrosity," as Monleon has called it (20). At what point will the infinite horizons of the marketplace become an overwhelming sight? When does a prosperous life of plenty turn into a harrowing nightmare of excess? We hear raucous voices and watch as hordes of students congregate at the gates of a university's School of Mass Communications; the masses are doubly present, in both the quantities of enrollees and classes, and in their attendant interest in the media that addresses them daily as consumers. Enticed by the larger-than-life images of splendor and power emanating from television sets and film screens, along with the accompanying fantasies of fandom, money, and fame, these students make their way through the maze of university requirements to exit the other side into Baudrillard's world of simulacra. And, fulfilling its promises of technological preparation for the new generations, the halls of academia reflect society's interest in all the hardware and software necessary to compete on a world-wide scale and in preparing the citizens of the twenty-first century. As the inheritors of the world on the move first portrayed in the early, *movida*-era films of Pedro Almodóvar, Angela and her classmates inhabit a contemporary city, "attractively 'modernized' with sleek university buildings, cosmopolitan professors, and carefree students," but it is also a world which simultaneously "harbors a darkness" (Lev 35). Such obscurity dwells not only among the architectural constructs such as Gothic mansions and labyrinthine tunnels in the university's basement, but amid the deepest labyrinths of the human psyche as well. In this urban capital, dreams of unlimited pleasure coexist with the nightmares envisioned almost two decades earlier by Goya. Although the twist on the situation is that evil inhabits the body of youth and physical beauty (Bosco, played by Eduardo Noriega) and moral goodness is disguised in the countenance of the long-haired social outcast Chema (Fele Martínez), Amenábar's representation of the two sides of modernity is still not far from Goya's empires of day and night or light and darkness.

What no one among them appears to think about, however, is the more sinister side of this promissory world. Occupied with their studies, and with the usual social dimensions of higher education, students chat in halls, exchange routine gossip, and keep agendas of their activities. They converge over the sights and sounds of the classroom and the café, the family dinner table and the movie theater; they seek out companions and lovers. But not far from the klieg lights, soundstages, and cameras of commercial filming lie those underground places where snuff films are made (or staged, depending on one's point of view). Alongside the transparent life of the cities of glass there are defamiliarized spaces, ones in which such grainy products avidly exploit an audience's fascination with watching life ebb away from a human body and taking mutilation and violence further than the cleaned-up, recognizable over-the-counter productions available at Blockbuster or its equivalents. The stuff of urban legend—in the United States, reports of snuff films began to surface in the mid-1970s and continue to proliferate to this day—the enticement of having access to the "real" torture of helpless women on screen insinuates a whole new dimension into Gelder's "rhetorics of horror." While ghastly figures do not literally walk the streets of Madrid, what different kinds of monsters might hide in the shadows of these underground productions, and what monstrous creatures live among us and purchase them? The unrecognizable profile of those belonging to such an underground economy of fantasy makes them even more horrifying. And the mere fact that there is money involved in these works and in the myths surrounding them as well (for there is always profit to be made in the

*Figure 6.2. Classmates Angela (Ana Torrent) and Chema (Fele Martínez) share
the dark side of videos. Reprinted by permission of Las Producciones del
Escorpión, S. L. Source: Filmoteca Española.*

dark corners of the liminal and the private, in the secret fantasies of those
who make the underground films and those they know will purchase
them), adds to their forbidden aura of enticement. In the incessant chip-
ping away at the limits of reason by the presence of these artifacts we are
reminded—in the tongue-in-cheek phrase that French anthropologist
Bruno Latour has used for the title of his book—that we "never *have*
been modern." What is modernity anyway? The concept and term continue to be hotly debated. Perhaps this is the greatest "surmounted" fear
come to light: that modernity is a masquerade, and that we are but a
compilation of our previous cultural lives and selves which we cannot
shake and which can be conjured up by titillating insinuations of the
horrors we carry within. If indeed snuff's "reputation precede[s] it"
(Hawkins 137), and the director's manipulation of documentary signals
lures the spectator into watching a "real" murder being committed, we
find ourselves part of an uncanny triangle. From director to victim/par-
ticipant to viewer, the complicity is truly horrifying, even if the film is
revealed as a spectacular hoax, for as Linda Williams so clearly points
out, "the idea of snuff continue[s] to haunt the imagination" (192).

Never mind whether it is staged or real, implicit in the fact that there is a market for this genre of cinema is the insinuated enjoyment (by at least some) of watching filmed and recorded acts of violence against women. And it becomes even more terrifying to consider that this is part of a regular routine of consumption.

As a graduate student dutifully researching her master's thesis, Angela (the character played by Ana Torrent, memorable for her roles as a mystified young child in the early films of Spanish directors Carlos Saura and Victor Erice) is drawn deeper and deeper into a mystery she stumbles upon while in the process of doing her schoolwork. Angela gets caught up in the public's fascination with what we might call the uncanny on film: human autopsies, ritualized killings of young girls, accidental and staged acts of violence, and the twilight world of exploitation films which flourish across the European continent (and, of course, the Americas as well). These films are merely a rumor at the beginning of *Tesis*, but by the end of the movie they are more than that. Her supposedly objective interest in such texts and the perpetuation of their enthrallment of the audience feed some secret fascination she seems to have with the relationship between visual images and the spectator. Perhaps owing to their ubiquitous presence in modern life, or perhaps for other, more sinister reasons not immediately revealed, Angela spends quite a large amount of time looking for information about forbidden productions and secret stashes of films. This is not merely intellectual work but something more, or something "else," that drives her.

One could not imagine, perhaps, a more modern project for a graduate degree in the world of today's academic subjects: the sophisticated and complex interaction between image and eye, between lens and audience, between the representations of art and the objects of real life. Joining the films of Brian De Palma, David Cronenberg's *Crash*, and the recent film *8MM* starring Nicholas Cage, Amenábar's film opens the gate to this dark side of the media and its potential to enthrall us, "exciting fear" as Freud sees it (193), fear both of what we already suspect might arouse our repulsion and horror (from having experienced it before and now reliving the experience, as with a compulsion) and perhaps, in a different sense, of our fascination with that very horror and its possible repetition. He demands that, through Angela, we consider why we are hypnotized and intrigued by the explosive gore and extreme violence of reality films and television shows, of paracinema and its possible role as a rouser-of-dreamers rather than just a part of routine alongside other representations of the secret acts of violence committed by human beings on one another. But then the director edits; he steps in and, paradoxically, keeps us from seeing just what we thought we were there to see. We are put in the place of Angela, literally looking through her eyes most of the time, as if she could filter for us what we dare not look at with our own. If Alex de la Iglesia's film ends with a thwarted demonic apocalypse conjured up from the depths of the inferno and played out on the brutal stage of the modern city, then Alejandro Amenábar finds the devil alive and well within us, individually and collectively, capable of being invoked each and every time we pop a videocassette into the VCR. We no longer have to worry about horror finding us alone in a dark alley at midnight; we bring it into our daily routines and use its images as a break from the boredom of a loss of feeling and emotion. We have actually found entertainment in the demonic. Since wars, famines, diseases and plagues have become the standard fare we watch as we prepare our meals or wash our clothing or dress for work, what are the horrors that might make us stop in our tracks and take notice? Do any remain, or has simulation reassured us that everything is an act, that some artist or artisan has had a hand in whatever we cast our eyes upon? Baudrillard clarifies that "[t]o dissimulate is to pretend not to have what one has. To simulate is to feign to have what one doesn't have" (3). Has our own tedious consumption of the image made us *hope* that something is what it isn't ("real" as opposed to staged), desperately clutching at the myths and legends of snuff to produce some semblance of excitement in an otherwise dreary existence? No longer chased by the phantoms of want and scarcity, the middle classes expect the new as part and parcel of the everyday. So is snuff just another dull, drab work of hype because something else will replace it before our eyes soon enough? The options and alternatives are positively horrific, "turn[ing] away from 'infinite progress,' 'moral improvement,' and human freedom [as goals of Western culture] often to foreground their opposites: enslavement, degradation, and a level of regression that can seem to take us out of modernity altogether and into something much more 'primal'" (Gelder 3). The coexistence of reason and unreason in the same geographies produces films such as *Tesis*, which address the shock of the two realms seeping into one another despite civilization's greatest efforts to keep the demons in their place (the past and the unconscious).

Tesis literally puts us in the dark from scene one. Nothing appears onscreen but pitch blackness. A voice-over calmly announces that passengers will have to exit the subway cars because there has been an emergency of some sort and the train cannot pull completely into the station. The last few yards have to be traversed on foot. Nothing is spelled out yet: no details, no descriptions of this interruption in daily routine. In the space between the stopped cars and an on-time arrival, and in the time gap between being there and stopping short, we are left in the brief moment of the uncanny. What has happened? How do we fill in the missing pieces? What does our imaginary do with the temporal and spatial darkness in this instance? Is commuter time just on hold, or is this a pause in modernity that allows for something else to seep in, something infinitely more insidious than just a brake fire or a machine malfunction?

Images begin to appear onscreen of commuters matter-of-factly obeying orders from a disembodied voice as we simultaneously hear that a man has jumped to his death on the tracks. "Les aconsejo que no miren a la vía" ("I advise you not to look at the tracks"), we are warned, because it is too much to see. The body has been cut in half, your day will be ruined. Amid the crowds milling on the platform, Angela emerges, literally standing out from the multitude. Her expressive, dark eyes—ones we recall with insistence from the faces of the abandoned postwar children of *Cría (Raise Ravens)* and *El espíritu de la colmena*— are open wide as she steps out of the throng and edges closer to the scene of the crime. Like a sleepwalker—Walter Benjamin's image of the awakening power of the cinema immediately comes to mind, literalized in her somnambulistic movement and vacant stare—Angela seems transfixed by the possibility of actually witnessing what we soon learn she is writing about for an academic degree—not media representations of violence this time, though, but the "real thing." Voices of officials repeating "no sean morbosos" (don't be morbid, but also a hint at morbid pleasures) form a counterpoint to her eager face and insistent gait, shot in extreme slow motion. The space closes as she inches her way toward the edge of the platform, but time stands still as it is slowed down by the camera. The angle of vision changes, then, and we no longer look *at* her but *with* her, her gaze drawn downward into the dark, promising abyss of the tracks. As it jostles its way among the crowds of commuters, the camera follows her progress and our anticipation grows. With her, we edge closer and closer. Just as the music intensifies and our own deep breathing makes us think we will be given access to this scene—and before we have a chance to ask ourselves whether we really want to see it after all— she is pulled back from the edge and there is a jump cut to the recognizable buildings of the university. From death to life is just a quick cut of the camera. We are saved from our own burning wish to look, and Angela returns to the safe halls of academic endeavors. While the camera seems to pull us back from the precipice of our own temptations, this reprieve will not last long.

Meeting with her advisor Professor Figueroa, Angela declares over and over that the topic she is studying, "images of audiovisual violence," is not really of interest to her personally, but is merely material for her thesis. If Father Angel had a naive vision of the problematic connection between reality and representation, Angela seems no more aware than he that a claim of objectivity does not seem to function here and that perhaps it should not do so. They are like two different universes. She is not in Deusto, nor has she led a cloistered life, but the uncertain, the unfriendly, the "other" that is evoked by images of suicide, of mutilation, and of torture—will they be "muy fuerte, muy fuerte" ("too strong, too much"), as her classmate and admirer Chema will warn her repeatedly? Or is it all hype and they will look no different than the evening news footage of Bosnia or Rwanda or any other modern-day killing field? When the mediating eye of the movie or television camera is absent, violence is too much, too real; it cannot be seen. But with the presence of the lens we return to the comfortable, recognizable terrain of the simulacrum and of the discriminating filter of academia. We need something as a buffer between the evils around us and our perception of them; we are lured to horror films as metaphors for our excesses and for the horrors we live amid.

So a spectator might well ask: Since we all know we are looking through the lens of a camera as we watch this film, what might we expect to see down the line? Are the artificial divisions constructed between "art" and "life" so clearly drawn as to help us distinguish which is which and to thus feel safe? Can we distinguish what is real and what is not as easily as we might wish to? Can one become the other at a moment's notice, perhaps even before our very eyes and throw us off track? Could the news footage of a suicide on the rails turn into tomorrow's backroom video rental? For whom is this interest in morbidity, in the twilight between life and death, the vision of art and for whom is this pornography?[4] The temptation of what throughout the film is referred to variously as "*el cine de verdad*" ("real cinema") and "*basura*" ("garbage"; "trash") is a lingering promise of which we just can't let go. Nor can Angela: she needs to finish her thesis and graduate, but she is also so obviously enticed by the secret videos rumored to be in the school's film archives that she has Figueroa risk his reputation and his life to bring them to her. Of course, he must die in the attempt, both to strengthen the tension of the film's mystery narrative and to show that pleasure and risk are like evil twins. After the professor tells her he will be called "*un sádico*" ("a sadist") if he requests the prohibited videos, and pleads with her to use only material accessible to the general public, the audience becomes aware that there will be no immunity, either for the academic or for the spectator. Once you are enticed to look, there is no turning back; there is no "immaculate perception" (Jenks 5) but rather a constant transformation of the subject by what is seen and an

Figure 6.3. Director Bosco (Eduardo Noriega) sets up the scene of the crime. Reprinted by permission of Las Producciones del Escorpión, S. L. Source: Filmoteca Española.

undeniable revocation of the concept of innocence. And, it seems, there will be no witnesses to recount what happened.

But the unspeakable (snuff) becomes the invisible in *Tesis*, since the only glimpse we catch of the images on Angela's television screen are in pause mode; the rest of the time we watch *her* watching something we can only imagine and that, in the end, the voice-over narrator warns us about. That is, she does play the videotape, but long after her initial refusal to look. Angela censors the film as fare inappropriate for her younger sibling, but fear overtakes her in her own research as well. She returns several times, remote control in hand, unwilling to let the film go unseen yet dreading the final visual confrontation with the actual images. We are asked to take for granted their excesses, for as viewers we only get to see Angela vomiting after finally acquiescing to Chema and accompanying him back to his flat to screen the footage. Maybe her thesis will be "too much" for her to pursue. What is the strange, uncanny pact established between director and viewer, and between Amenábar and ourselves, that makes us—along with Angela, our surrogate eyes and ears—watch a forehead being sliced open or a woman's torso split in two? What moves Angela from being reticent and *"moji-gata"* ("wimpy") to defying Chema's warning "no mires, no mires" ("don't look, don't look") when she can no longer resist the temptation to look? The gamut of genres he recites to her tells us that this screening request is no simple matter: there is "porno, gore, Oriental," lynchings, fresh blood, and all kinds of "action" films—and who knows what other delights—he has collected inside his locked cabinet. A devotee of exploitation and splatter films, Chema not only views them but forms a collection, catalogues them, and even has a private rating system of sorts for them. And in a twist of the mystery plot, he confesses to Angela that he has invited her to his dark and macabre apartment, inherited from a dead grandmother, because he thinks she is pretty. As far as the solving of the mysterious, we cannot leave our suspicions of Chema far behind. But what would make him any more—or less—monstrous than those who actually produce the films? Is the consumer somehow just another innocent, a victim caught up in the thrilling possibilities of the market-place and lured out of complacency into purchasing some real excite-ment? If mundane life no longer is the source of such stimulation, then extreme real-life videos and films might offer an alternative. But do they come from parts of society we just don't see, or are they complementary aspects of the "real" like the exotic spicy ingredients added to a dull recipe to bring it to life?

Alone at home, Angela can't bring herself to watch the screen. She dims the image on the TV screen to black as she puts on headphones and continues to listen to the sound of punches and slaps and a woman's screams and protests. What draws Chema to create a monu-ment to these films by collecting them is his insistence, in an incredu-lous tone, "pero esto es real" ("but this is real"). Her screams are not realistic, but real, and this is what keeps him watching. The twist is thrown into the plot when he murmurs to her, quite calmly and emphatically, "esa tía la conozco" ("hey, I know this chick"). How real is real, and just when or how does the representation and editing of real scenes become unedited "reality"? The space between fantasy and the real has been bridged by the writhing, tortured body of a young woman, a fellow graduate student of communications. The worst fate that can befall such a video reality show is to be called "apocryphal" (Lev 34), the false counterpart of pornography and the even darker side of what is already sometimes quite sinister but still falls into the realm of entertainment. Chema insists that as art all of his videos are "educa-tional," but perhaps they will teach us more about ourselves than any-thing else, making the uncanny, "old and long familiar," resurface in a moment of conscious, critical vision. Once we have seen it all in the

Figure 6.4. Angela (Ana Torrent) becomes the captive in an underground video shoot. Reprinted by permission of Las Producciones del Escorpión. S. L. Source: Filmoteca Española.

media, what could be so shocking, so intense, so uncanny, as to rouse us from our lethargy of looking but not seeing?

What Freud refers to as a "quality of feeling" (194) would infer the apparition of some phantom capable of such horror that it stirred up our most repressed qualms and fears and liberated them through some object or image to which we have become accustomed. Alex de la Iglesia's special effects are one thing: horned goats, bloodletting, and dense red smoke are not new to films when the devil makes an appearance. In fact, they are predictable fare. But Amenábar's "effects" are more subtly insinuated by the suggestion of "intellectual uncertainty" (Freud 206) as to our reaction to the existence of snuff. (I suppose the existence of the goat in a fancy Madrid apartment might, for some, be just as uncanny— but for most it also acquires the elements of comedy and excess, given the context in which it is conjured up and the exaggerated demeanor of the characters doing the conjuring.) We are not merely frightened by the horrors we imagine—whether they be perpetrated by the Antichrist, a fascist vigilante group, or a filmmaker-torturer-for-profit—but by the fact that we are forced to consider these things as "secretly familiar" (Freud 222) to us. We just thought, or convinced ourselves, that they were long gone after the advent of modern times. Racism, xenophobia, religious cults, and human sacrifice call forth all that we say we have left behind. Are we indeed so uncannily helpless as to be drawn, as if under a spell, to watch and even enjoy unspeakably inhuman acts represented onscreen? Or is feigned helplessness merely a spectacular *act* of modernity that allows us to recover our instinctual enthrallment with blood and lust for a moment, at home, in the privacy of our own living rooms? The pretense of professional research has a familiar ring; it provides camouflage for something more basic that exerts a fatal attraction on us. We *do* want to look, but we don't want to admit that we do. We have become immune to so much, maybe we just want to see if something, anything, can have an effect on us. Angela has a compulsion to return to the snuff videos, drawn in by Chema and his fascination with their spectacular crimes, but also by her own undeniable curiosity. Through her, we are placed squarely within a more startling realm, for we *want* to follow her. The evocation of that hidden desire has been conjured up by the temptations of Angela and by our vicarious explorations of those instincts through her. Our eyes don't close or look away, despite the warning at the end of the film that all of this might be too much for the unwary viewer and that the images the police have confiscated and are about to appear onscreen are *"fuertes"* ("strong", "shocking", "excessive"). But given what we have already seen, this comes either too late for some or it is fairly artificial, coming from a prime source of titillation and seduction. After all, we have placed such stock in our power of sight that we are drawn irresistibly to see what might be in these images and find it almost impossible to look away. The immediate comprehension, control, and gratification promised by the media exert their influence over us and we are bound to look.

De la Iglesia does not condemn his characters' search for a future salvation of humankind in a deciphering of mystical writings, nor does he fault the entertainment value of music or television programming. He even gives us privileged access behind the scenes of its production. The problem arises when the value of any of these enterprises is raised to a cult status: theological, satanic, New Age, technological or otherwise, a cult is still a cult. In a nation whose transition out of an era in which a personality cult was installed and enforced so deeply and uncannily for so very long, as it is only all too easy to recall, each director uses the very medium we seem to worship and take for granted as the sign of the modern to point up the pitfalls of its elevation to an absolute. As Marshall McLuhan wrote almost half a century ago, the medium IS the message: our twenty-first century "rhetorics of horror" inhabit what we also consider our most privileged site of pleasure.

7

A FEW LAST WORDS

Waiting in the Anteroom of the
Twenty-First Century

It has been a quarter of a century since Laura Mulvey first posited an analysis of the technological strategies and narrative structures that might account for the spectator's pleasurable experience of viewing films in her widely cited 1975 article "Visual Pleasure and Narrative Cinema." Since then, the cinematic experience has undergone increasing critical scrutiny as interest in the phenomenon of visual consumption has grown. Not merely the pleasure of watching but also the trauma of looking have both become objects of investigation, for it is in the realm of the disruptive rather than the distracted that we might find the riches of an encounter with what Benjamin sees as the launching of an object or image from a mute standstill apart from historicity into a trajectory filled an electrical charge that can spark recognition. He writes optimistically of this active dialectical interpretation: "If the pre-history of an object reveals its possibility (including its utopian potential), its after-history is that which, as an object of natural history, it has in fact become" (Buck-Morss 219). Pre-history and after-history are linked across the problematized spaces of representation and it is in these that the limbo of the present acquires visible form. Violently forced out of an ideologically naturalized continuum—of events, of products, of the artifacts and remnants of so-called progress—the previously fossilized image can be released to shatter any and all perceptions of routine recognizability. No longer a remnant of the past encased in the rock of reified tradition or myth, the image/object may be freed into the realm of contradiction through what Hawkins calls the "psychotronic style" of a cinema that rests on the "scalpel's edge" (83) of a false equilibrium it proposes to upset at every turn. While many recent United States productions have chosen to develop the literal aspect of the razor's edge through slasher films and the like, with the exception of Jess Franco, Mexican and Spanish directors in general have interpreted this more allegorically. There are no blades but demons, dogs, bondage, flames, drugs, and bullets which hold the human body on the edge.

The engagement of such texts of paracinema with the body of the spectator—whether it be in the shape of porn, gore, splatter, schlock, horror, exploitation or other cinematic genres of excess such as melodrama and parody—cuts across the space between screen and eye, as well as across leisure time, to produce an arousal from the terrains of lethargy and boredom. These so-called body genres we have been examining evoke a different kind of pleasure in the audience, a response less theorized, more spasmodic and potentially more explosive in a social sense than what is considered standard high-art cinema. In the transnational smorgasbord of consumption at the end of the twentieth century, the cinema of excess fills a big platter at the center of our feast-for-the-eyes and it is difficult to pass through the modern arcades of the mass media—from commercial television to the digital marketplace—without indulging. Whether in the living room, the office, or the theater, films and video accompany the ritual acts of eating (whether TV dinner or snacks, it makes little difference to the one who indulges), but they also offer a fare of their own. Caches of fantasies, the images made visible for those inhabitants of the modern metropolis who take refuge from those very cities within the four walls of domestic serenity represent a (false) haven from the brutality of history couched in the drab tones of monotony and predictability. Benjamin's description of the interior spaces of boredom is vivid in its suggestiveness for breaking through this false surface to reach the sublimated desires seething below: "Boredom is a warm gray fabric lined on the inside with the most lustrous and colorful of silks. In this fabric we wrap ourselves when we dream" (1999 105). But how might this be achieved? Craving stimulation but simultaneously no longer responding to it requires that such visual fare reach out further, more excessively, to excite the spectator into increasingly spectacular arousal from a lethargy of despair or inertia. From a phantasmagoria of architectural forms and consumer products whose immoderation incited Benjamin to both ecstasy and critique, utopian wish-images have moved into the realm of representation frozen onscreen in condensed icons of desire and frustration. To stimulate a real hunger for these utopian social impulses, not merely a Pavlovian response to a recognizable visual stimulus, paracinema attacks the ceremony of plenitude with an eye toward the repulsiveness of excess.

The introduction of the metaphor of ingestion—feast, fast, or any other references to the extremes of absorption of food by the human body—is not gratuitous here and it brings us back full circle to the fact that goods and images are, after all, consumed. While Jameson urges us to recall that we are in fact "a public with an appetite for the documentary fact" ("Class and Allegory" 293), we might also extend this metaphor of absorption to a thirst for blood, a hunger for excitement, or even the devouring of images with our eyes. What holds most currency in the market of exchange is the question of quantity or variety, and this certainly is the case when we speak of the cinema. We have become ravenous for something to stave off a hunger that gnaws at us unless we ingest more and more. Gluttony and compulsion would seem to name two sides of the same activity of the modern consumer, who belongs to a dreaming global collective whose greatest desire is to escape the ultimate terror of society: boredom. What better than to seek excitement in either overwhelming the body with sumptuous food or overtaxing the eye with intoxicating images? This preponderance of saturation is the concrete representation, Jameson's narrative "figuration" ("Class and Allegory" 300), of what we cannot show with any other conventions. In the process of coming to terms with our fears and anguish over the global project of modernity, we have projected our horrors onto the screen in these concrete images.

With a view to this conjunction of fleeting types of corporal saturation, Benjamin

> does not look at books from the perspective of the humanities, but studies them as elements of "food chemistry." Reading is a meal. . . . The "pleasure of consumption" throws passionate reading into the sharpest conceivable contrast to what criticism routinely assumes is the reader's pleasure: substitution. The pleasure felt in gazing at [the exquisite dish on the dining table] is only heightened by the pleasure of destruction that lies ahead. . . . [T]he critic's destructive nature is firmly founded on the act of reading itself. The voracious reader reads by consuming—driven by an appetite for destruction . . . and the ecstasy of consuming the world's substance. (Bolz and Van Reijen 10)

Nourishment is only part of the experience; the use-value and depletion of the dish taken apart into morsels are the processes of destruction that create new meanings through the serving up and tearing apart of the old (pre-texts). Neither one stands on its own but instead forms an ingredient in the admixture of cultural options that combine and recombine in transient, sometimes ghostlike, images. To break into the stoicism of the bored observer of these contours of the modern, to stir up the forgetfulness of one unmoved by his or her surroundings, involves severing the comfortable gaze, bringing the whirlwind of the marketplace to a standstill. Paracinema is just one manner of interrupting the presumedly unequivocal course of world events, from (the myth of) a fulfilling everyday work routine in *Danzón* to the pursuit of future success through advanced education in *Tesis*. The feeling of inertia created by boredom, viewed by directors from María Novaro to Alejandro Amenábar and Alex de la Iglesia as the site on which to focus in order to shock the spectator out of habitual lethargy and social blindness, is exaggerated in the films we have looked at so as to bring time to a standstill. Julia leaves time behind in the capital for the hazy timelessness of Veracruz; Father Angel seeks to bring history to a halt by conjuring up the devil himself; Archibaldo de la Cruz burns all traces of his crimes but repeats them as a cyclical ritual, untouched by the ravages of historical changes taking place around him; and all three narratives of *Amores perros* portray characters whose ambition is to erase the traces of "event" (from accident scars to personal relationships gone sour, and from risky political commitment to the enforcement of family values).

The acquired immunity of the middle classes to the effects of a daily saturation of the eye by commodities, material comforts, and technological innovations can only be critically assailed by such a rupture in the field of vision as one encounters in the juxtaposition of images and objects which provoke and disconcert the spectator. Benjamin intended cinematic montage to have such a potential "to startle, to make manifest that which lies hidden and forgotten" (Gilloch 115), and paracinema seems to be the inheritor of this type of disruptive aesthetic first promoted by Eisenstein. But while Benjamin saw the boulevards of nineteenth-century Paris as material proof of modernity's presence—in the overflowing crowds lulled by street after street of glittering casinos, cafés, and shop windows replete with merchandise ready for the taking—what of the retreat from the streets of 1990s Madrid or Mexico City into the privatized realms of consumption as evidence of belonging to twenty-first century globalization? How might historical objects be pried from their sedimentary social contexts when the collective life of boredom has withdrawn from the collective public sphere into the singularly domestic? Can we just stop and edit out—fast forward, rewind, or retape—what we don't wish to see, as we do with our VCRs? The editing function of our own machines would seem to hint at our mastery over what might disrupt or provoke, allowing for the continuance of the soothing dream state in the privacy of our own homes.

Since Spacks defines one aspect of boredom as "the incapacity to engage fully: with people, with action (one may act, but without complete emotional participation), with one's own ideas" (165), then perhaps we have come a long way toward identifying a peculiar double set of phenomena. On the one hand, traditional discourses of nationalism are being replaced with those of sweeping global markets and transnational interests, which are plied onscreen to a virtual audience of millions. But on the other hand, consumers are retreating into the sanctity of the home and into an increased concentration on the individual who reaps the rewards of modernity's banquet without an eye to the broader implications of these radical changes. The incomplete emotional participation and the lack of being roused out of the sleepwalker's rounds of the marketplace connect the two aspects of the quotidian: if one feels part of the global project owing to one's ability to acquire the products available as a result of the demolition of geographical barriers and economic obstacles, these are acts—paradoxically—done *at home* and not as part of the interests of a class or group. The QVC Network, MSNBC's virtual shopping mall, the Internet, and satellite or cable television all contribute to the privatizing of consumption. But once the consumer has made a purchase, or several, or many, this becomes a naturalized routine and just another repetitive aspect of daily life. It is no longer a special, satisfying process but a highly unsatisfying one, for it perpetuates its own cause and leads nowhere in the long run. The very miseries of boredom are its appearance as the symptom of an absence: it conjures up desire(s) while blocking their potential for pleasures, that destructive potential of ingestion that Benjamin so rigorously defended. The more one has access to, the less satisfaction there is, for it brings little nourishment despite filling the body. While generating desires and goods, the modern marketplace also generates the capital that accumulates, but brings fewer emotional rewards. One may contemplate riches or feasts but they may be accompanied by emotional and psychological starvation. As Spacks concludes of this desperate but tedious situation, "the victim of boredom finds all outlets mysteriously blocked" (165), especially the outlets of personal pleasure. Daily life is lit by the dull light of material plenty amid the constant haze of emotional dearth (and, after September 11, by newly interiorized fears). It appears certain that after the Trade Center disaster the angst-ridden aspect of boredom has been greatly enhanced. As we await the return of "normal" life, we are awash in the indulgences that are intended to counteract anguish: food, family, and more time to kill since we have reduced the radius of travel.

The growth of the modern film industry in Europe and Latin America, spurred by Hollywood's investment in and domination of the marketplace, continues to be haunted by traces of that monopoly over images and genres. Its replacement by television and video in our end-of-century, technology-driven global society has merely displaced the arena of consumption from the collective audience to the individual spectator, populating the visual field with increased distractions that have been naturalized into everyday life by technological means and through the process of repetition. From the ubiquitous appearance of commercial products as part of the background noise of the "modern" to the promotion of alien genres (talk shows and sitcoms) as a necessity for belonging to the global world as an equal partner, films on large and small screens alike form an information chain across space and time. Embedded in the links of this chain is a new set of images, conventions, and codes that lack the stimulus Benjamin required as a catalyst for disruption. While they appear to fill what might otherwise be perceived as empty time with their sheer overbearing presence, the images from film and video are often merely consumed as one delectable course in the great and endless banquet of modernity. They nurture the social body and keep its economic system alive, yet they just whet the appetite for more. They never actually go beyond the temptingly appetizing appearance of the dishes served up. However, the tiny spark that conceivably might ignite a change in the spectator's vision of what Benjamin called "the strongest narcotic of the century" (Buck-Morss 218) is the provocation of excess and saturation. The cultural dinner table must become a battlefield, not a lounge.

From the Mexico City suburb of Coyoacán to Madrid's blue-collar neighborhood of Carabanchel, whether from the side of illumination or from a somewhat darker angle, the "surprise" of cultural products of which Jameson simultaneously warns and regales us hints at the powers of excess over the vapidness of such culinary distraction. In an allegory of the ubiquitousness and thoroughly overwhelming presence of commodities for our consumption (if not true delectation), the cinema of excess forces us to ingest even when we feel satiated and langorous. Films such as *Carne trémula* or *Danzón* on the one hand, and *Amores perros* or *Tesis* on the other, force-feed us after we have pushed our chairs back from the table of plenty. As we are tempted to drift into the timeless time of post-prandial sweets, leisure relaxation, or pleasant liqueurs, Almodóvar, González Iñárritu and Amenábar make us watch our own feeding frenzy in the guise of entertainment. Of course, we don't actually imbibe blood, but we do reach excesses and immoderations similar to those we see allegorized onscreen, whether we immediately recognize ourselves as participants or not. It is not a pretty sight, but images of beauty, or even grotesque beauty, no longer wake us from our glutted slumber. Something more jarring and insistent is needed if we are to feel what we have so far managed to ignore. Quadriplegics, stalkers of women, tremendous multiple car crashes, and psychological mutilation, however, might disturb us into pondering our illusions of civility as we fill our mouths with popcorn and our days with the boring but triumphant rhetoric of routine. The satiation of the digestive system is rivaled only by the oversaturation of the nervous system by these films through the use of excesses of color (red and more red), sound (thumping music, heavy metal or otherwise), sheer noise (of urban violence and street crime), and raw emotion (of kidnappings, disappearances, torture, and bondage). If we have become immunized to such overload within our own cultures, perhaps a distancing effect can be created with films set in Mexico or Spain. If *Scream* fails to arouse an audience, perhaps *Amores perros* will, since its director may be influenced by American movies but his image of the city is alien enough to provoke a new look at what happens along its streets.

The proof of the effects of affect is the fact that *Amores perros* carries a disclaimer at the beginning of the film, ostensibly for squeamish audiences everywhere. As the credits roll we read the statement that no dogs have been harmed in the process of filming this story so one shouldn't believe one's eyes. If dogfights or life-threatening injuries look all too "real," we should keep in mind the disclaimer at all costs: our eyes are playing tricks on us. While we have become accustomed to special effects and artificial blood, we know the "real thing" when we see it. Or do we? The words obviously are meant to reassure the audience, but they actually have the opposite effect. We might be made to look even more carefully at what we have been told isn't the case: we want to know if what they say is not real looks real after all. And when it does, what might one do? The crisis of the eye continues.

Critics in the United States conclude that the aggressive nature of the film is owing to the fact that it was shot in "Mexico City, where the violence, unlike the violence of *Pulp Fiction*, is altogether real" (Hirschberg 32). The scenes are not part of our daily life for we, after all, are modern. We have to be displaced from home, driven madly through the capital of somewhere else, to see that "our" brand of violence is different from the "real thing." We use a Hollywood set; and Quentin Tarantino or David Cronenberg, for all the critical reaction against their fictions, are just a couple of American directors shooting on back lots. It takes the Mexican director González Iñárritu to give the "real" the tinge of difference, "a most un-American touch" (Hirschberg 32): dogfights and collective celebrations of blood sport. Hirschberg calls the result "visceral" (32) and she is right, since paracinema aims for the gut. But are there not equivalents in other cultures? Maybe congested urban freeways are our arenas for spilling blood and taking out the frustrations of endless commuter tedium. Maybe the Spanish *Semana Santa* (Holy Week) free-for-alls on the highways from Madrid to the coastal resorts are the new and unrecognized stages for our rituals of violence, some of which are speeded up to the chaotic rhythms of automotive traffic while others are slowed to the boring cadence of the *danzón*. Bakhtin's chronotope has perhaps been expanded to unrecognized—perhaps even "unfigurable" at the beginning—proportions and unsuspected convolutions. What melodrama slows down to a teary drone brutally ruptures the continuum of object and event as much as the scenes splatter films show at a breakneck pace cast spectators headlong into disaster before they know what has happened. These films fill our eyes and ears to the point of explosion. There is no moderation but insistent repetition. None could leave the spectator unmoved as we open our eyes to the spectacle of the human body trapped in the moment of "orgasm in porn, of terror and violence in horror, of weeping in melodrama" (Hawkins 5). All three instants freeze rational analysis and cast us headlong into territory we thought we had long ago tamed. Even a lack of affect can be exploited for such ends, much as Amenábar does in *Abre los ojos* (*Open Your Eyes*) the narrative of which is also constructed around a car accident but whose characters seem to sleepwalk through Madrid. We have become numb to the by-now boring side of ecstasy and pleasure; the time has come to sidle up to fear, terror, grief, and anguish in quantities overwhelming to the senses. After all, as we have come to identify, what we seek as enjoyment can be elicited as much by destruction as by the evocation of a passive pleasure we have come to expect. It may take a process of self-discovery to recognize our dreams once they have been exteriorized, but when the gloomy wrapping has been removed, the hidden hues of our secret expectations can come forth.

What Benjamin evokes as the warm, fuzzy gray fabric that covers the concealed folds of fantasy is perhaps our best social performance. The drab hues of everyday life, punctuated as they are by expected and ceremonialized moments of pleasure (the equation of acquisition + consumption + expenditure), hide the scarlet tones of the sublimated violence that holds a mellow surface glow of boredom in place. The cinematic trick is to evoke the extremes of blood-red or jaundiced yellow or ghostly white just as we are bedding down under the gray flannel blanket of our dreams. Ted Turner's colorized masterpieces of yesteryear are the models we anticipate, but even their garish tones seem to fit into a harmonious whole and a cultural lineage of images. Amenábar, Almodóvar, Buñuel, Hermosillo, Novaro, and de la Iglesia all turn the docility of daily life inside out with a bombardment of prime colors and primal noise. Colors and sounds act as symptoms of an absence uncannily evoked through traumatic vision and shock value, what Susan Hayward calls "style [used] as meaning" (107). As we have seen in cinematic melodrama, this is the chiaroscuro of a triangular relationship, which conceals as much as it reveals; as we have looked at in horror films, this is the devil among us or the fires of hell that burn within us. The first is pure darkness, the second intense light. Archibaldo de la Cruz's fantasy of burning a mannequin double of Lavinia, Father Angel's quest for the material evocation of the devil, or university student Angela's conjuring up of evil in its modern disguise all belong to the uncanny evocation of the dangers wrought by an inability to see. In melodrama what eludes our gaze inhabits the corners; in the cinema of excess it dwells in the midst of flames. We conceivably can recover such an ability by evoking to excess, by taking pleasure from the fact that "so many people find [such visions of modern horror] disturbing, distasteful, or even downright unacceptable" (Gelder 5). Rather than minimize the effect of the cinematic styles of excess, these films' message is that we need to be incited to such extremes or risk them once again becoming humdrum and predictable.

Only in the hidden recesses of the home and in the anxiety-provoking rituals of paracinema might we find the intensities and excesses we have overlooked in order to live amid a boredom of our own devising. In evincing desires, or rather dangerous desires, we have normalized boredom into a quality of reassurance; everything has its place, even horror, at least until it moves elsewhere and gives us that Jamesonian cultural surprise. The "suspended attention" (Spacks 261) inherited by the modern state of middle-class boredom still allows, however, for a hopeful vision of such tedium, with the activated gaze coming alive when faced head-on with visions of uncannily traumatic images. Given the more difficult discussion of an aesthetics of paracinema, the conventions of genres such as snuff films, horror, Euro-trash, and sci-fi terror hit the viewer with "all manner of cultural detritus" (Sconce 372) much more akin to the heterogeneous pile of twentieth-century rubbish at the feet of Benjamin's Angel of History than to the museum exhibits used to house official collections of the historical continuum of nations. Just as Gelder reminds us that horror texts—which we have taken here in the broadest sense of the term—represent the entanglement of the primal and the modern (3), similar to Benjamin's pre-texts and after-texts, so we might conclude that paracinema incarnates "the frenzied subject of excess" (Gelder 3) with all of its contemporary contradictions presented simultaneously. Such are the images that pull us out of the sanctuary of the familiar into the battleground of conflicting sensations and the sensational in daily life.

The recovery of controversy, the focusing on surplus and overflow—being inundated by too much as well as feeling adrift amid too little—is both a paracinematic device and a spinning constellation of textual fragments. Let us remember that the "pleasure of destruction" is a two-way street: one may take nourishment from the dismantling of what are deemed to be perfect edifices which we ourselves may have constructed or delicious feasts we have concocted for our own enjoyment. In and of themselves, these constructions are only monuments to routine or accumulations of objects on display (in most cases to prove one has the means to acquire the ingredients necessary for their production). Dissonance and indigestion are the more valuable stock-in-trade of these types of films if we look at them outside the realm of cult value. When we focus on animal blood, human sacrifice, snuff violence, the erotics of torture, the stark artifices of scarlet makeup and clothing at center screen, and never let the images disappear from view no matter how hard we blink our eyes or try to look away, maintaining a dream state becomes increasingly difficult. That we are all just meat dressed in the alluring trappings of modernity is made most evident in the fetishized legs, paralyzed limbs, and bloodied torsos of accident victims; in the burned fragments of fashion models and bullet-ridden brides-to-be; in the drugged virgins, objects of sexual obsession, and bound students of all seven films we have looked at. After sitting through more than one double feature or several evenings with the VCR at our side, we are left with a query whose answer is yet to be written: Is the cinema of excess part of technology's capacity to adapt to changing times or might in it lie the possibility of emancipation from our dream state?

These films should haunt Western society for some time to come since they bring the unexpected into view without creating an aura of fascination and wonder to surround the brutality of the images. Whether they take the shape of the demonic, the cruelly inhumane, or the irrationally savage, the spectator is left to scavenge among the ruins of modernity's project to see if there is anything salvageable. This takes effort, of course; it cannot be done from the depths of an easy chair or from the back row of the movie theater. Let us for now entertain the utopian notion that these startling images might not join the legions of cultural assumptions that assimilate even the most shocking into neat categories of the mundane and marketable. It is fairly unlikely that the auteurship of paracinema will become the subject of debate or analysis, although what is once cutting edge can turn into mainstream with the blink of an eye. Just as we recall that Spain "didn't have the same literary tradition of horror that England, Germany, the United States, and even France had, and so it drew on different sources. Directors borrowed stories from other traditions and 'nationalized' them with Spanish iconography" (Hawkins 93), so the cinemas of excess run the risk of not just "nationalizing" but "naturalizing" as part of everyday life. In the global marketplace of visual images, so much becomes second nature almost overnight; even the threat of nuclear war has changed, in an instant it seems, from unthinkable nightmare to frequent public conjecture (on May 26, 2002, the *New York Times* carried a long article in its Sunday magazine devoted to the details of possible nuclear scenarios after 9-11 and how to prepare for them).[1] For now, the resonances of paracinema and melodrama, their psychological carnage and physical violence, force us to engage with our own discontents in a way other than curling up and taking a nap in front of the television. With the turn of the century and our entry into a new millennium, maybe we must be forced "to let history go forward" (Buck-Morss 105).[2] Even if we don't know what we are waiting for, we must break our addiction to sleep and let the dogs out, for the frightening visions of sleep cannot hold a candle to the potential horrors of our waking hours.

$$\boxed{\text{Notes}}$$

CHAPTER 1. AT THE MILLENNIUM

1. Fredric Jameson writes of the shift from a consideration of class issues to a fundamental interest in citizens of international marketplaces in the "identical consumers interchangeable with everybody else" as we witness the "transformation of both bourgeois and worker into that new grey organization person known as the consumer" ("Class and Allegory" 288–89). Using the same economic filter for his vision of late-twentieth-century American culture, he finds that the only way to cut through the haze of boredom is "the experience of inflation itself, which is the privileged phenomenon through which a middle-class audience suddenly comes to an unpleasant consciousness of its own historicity" ("Class and Allegory" 296). I propose that the shock value of economic inflation corresponds on screen to the excesses of melodrama and "paracinema," the term used by Geoffrey Sconce and others to address the current spate of films whose violence goes way beyond all notion of ordinary border or boundary into the terrain of an explosion and exploitation of all senses being called on to respond to social platitudes. Inflation, of course, is the presence of an overwhelming amount of money whose material value is decreased and whose exchange value is less than what is represented on its visible surface. Inflated rhetoric or cinematic excess would function in similar fashion: sheer material accumulation whose individual components, when taken in isolation, mean less than what they did previously in conjunction. It is the bombardment of the excessive that brings our senses—especially the visual—to saturation, much as the market is saturated by (devalued) currency. An inflationary economy is the result of both too much and too little: the overpresence of banknotes and the diminution of their purchasing power.

2. Bakhtin's insistence on the irreducible connectivity of the dimensions of time and space into what he terms the "chronotope" ("time space") addresses "[t]he

process of assimilating real historical time and space in literature" (84). While he chooses to limit his discussion to the literary field alone, leaving aside for the time being all other areas of culture, it seems logical to posit its possible extension to film and other more recent artifacts of contemporary social and cultural history. What the novel was to the early twentieth century, the cinema is to its closing decades.

3. Benjamin's faith in the potential power of the camera lens to help the spectator focus on the unseen or encounter the unexpected within the doldrums of everyday life is echoed in Bentham's architectural structure based on insinuated observation and threatened punishment for the commission of social "evils." While Benjamin posits the intervention of the camera's gaze as a presence, however, Bentham relies on the "dark spot" (15) at the center of the absent observer's allseeing power. That is to say, Bentham proposes the illusion of surveillance by a "wakeful, watchful eye" (16). In the same way, Goytisolo finds vestiges of the assimilated control of the panopticon in the systematic "autocensura" (15) or selfcensorship implanted in the psyche of generations of Spaniards under Franco's rule. Goytisolo continues: "Lucha no exterior sino interna contra el modelo de censura intrasíquica, de censura incluida en el 'mecanismo del alma,' según la conocida expresión de Freud . . . , [somos] víctimas [tal vez] ya para siempre de un esterilizador Super-Ego, proyección interiorizada de su ilimitado poder" ("Not an external but an internal battle against the intra-psychic model of censorship included in Freud's well-known 'mechanism of the soul' . . . , [we are] victims [perhaps] now and forever of a sterilizing Super-Ego, the interiorized projection of his limitless power"; 16). So it ends up that, for Goytisolo, the inspector has taken up residence within and not outside the boundaries of the individual, making the omnipresence (and, one concludes, omniscience) of the gaze even more pernicious. Immense potential energy restrained from creative expression was doomed to remain in the realm of impossibility and only found outlets in that corelative of boredom, psychosis or, as Goytisolo writes, "neurosis, malevolencia, alcoholismo, agresividad, impulsos suicidas, pequeños infiernos privados" ("neurosis, spite and revenge, alcoholism, aggression, suicidal impulses, little private hells"; 16). I would conjecture that the first and the last of these symptoms—neurosis and the sheer hell of living—collapse into the routine of boredom after many decades of psychic control.

4. In a recent article, Mexican film critic Gustavo García complains that each time Mexican cinema appears to be on the verge of a renaissance things cool off. With the critical and commercial success of recent films such as *Amores perros* and the release of twenty-seven full-length feature films (double the number of the previous year) in 2000, there was much cause for optimism. But within the first few weeks of their appearance in theaters, attendance dropped off precipitously. García writes: "Otra vez, empezar desde cero. . . . sea la que sea la película, el público simplemente no ha ido a verlas . . ." ("Once again we have to start from scratch . . . whatever the movies, the audiences just haven't shown up to see them"; 2001 1). What he calls a sense of collective indifference (2) has been

one of the greatest factors contributing to the difficulties encountered by Mexican directors and producers and to the possible demise of the national industry. The general social apathy, plus a lack of interest in either large or small domestic productions, reflect the trend toward lolling inside the walls of a supposed domestic tranquility while the economic and political wars go on outside. It is important to note that two years after this judgment, however, García Tsao and other films critics find many more reasons for optimism (2002 44).

5. The reference here is to Spanish writer and journalist Carmen Rico Godoy's wildly popular tongue-in-cheek novel *Cómo ser una mujer y no morir en el intento (How to Be a Woman and Not Die in the Process)*.

CHAPTER 2. JAIME HUMBERTO HERMOSILLO'S *LA TAREA*

1. With great acuity, Rich suggests that audiences setting out to "discover" Latin American cinema for the first time reflect both Western society's fascination with the veracity of the visual and the "outsider" vision of Latin America as a geographical place steeped in a "realism" whose intrinsic "magic" explains away any rough edges, violent events, or historical processes (1997 273). The enormous variety of films produced in the last two decades of the twentieth century presents a much more diverse collection of texts and strategies than appear at first glance. Martin agrees, writing of the recent works of Latin American cinema as a "loosely constituted, dynamic, and unfinished movement of 'films of a new kind' . . . [it is not an] autonomous, unified, and monolithic project . . . [but a series of cinematic texts with] representational strategies . . . as diverse as the population groups and hybrid cultures of Latin America" (16). An emphasis on the expression and affirmation of national identities—in whatever images might be envisioned by the particular director—in the face of ever-changing social and economic conditions certainly runs through the body of cinematic works produced during the entire critical period between the 1950s and the early 1990s.

2. The media conglomerate Televisa has tapped into this lucrative consumer market by producing television series such as *Sopa de videos* (*Video Soup*, a play on the phrase *Sopa de fideos* ["noodle soup"]), a show similar to the long-running United States program *Candid Camera* and by sponsoring a series of film comedies with titles like *Risa en vacaciones (Vacation Laughs)* which number over a dozen and are still going strong. Both are more risqué and offensive in their pranks and situations than either of the United States-based models.

3. Linda Williams examines recent considerations of "a spectrum of pornographies (and sexualities)" rather than drawing a distinction between hard/soft porn in which "men's sexuality [is seen as] pornographic and women's as erotic" (6). Yet she herself makes the two appear synonymous by referring to them interchangeably as "soft-core *or* 'erotic' pornography" (6; my emphasis). In the current market, the more explicitly represented sexual acts of a particular

film cannot be adjudicated as a "women's story" or a narrative for men but possibly as either or both. Video pornography (or erotica, depending on how one decides to use these classifications) "aimed formerly only at men now [reaches] a 'couples' and even a new women's market" (6), Williams concludes. I find *La tarea* a good example of this trend in Mexico, at least among the middle classes whose viewing habits offer an intriguing glimpse into the repercussions of social values and mores behind closed doors.

Hermosillo's film also represents contemporary "Mexican culture" in the international video marketplace. In that case, audiences abroad may not find traditional gender stereotypes playing out as expected when the film is placed in the context of previously released melodramas. However, it is also possible to conclude that María/Virginia is just the new incarnation of the *dominadora*, the dominating woman who has found a different way of vying for power within the walls of the family compound. And she has added humor to the standard narrative of seduction and its consequences, thereby defusing an overt challenge to masculine power while still leaving the door open to possibilities.

4. Although in her study of Western culture Marjorie Garber explores the concept of "transvestism" in a variety of guises and cultures, I am interested particularly in the term "legibility," which she uses in the broader sense of identities being rendered visible and/or decipherable in changing contexts. This parallels the changing of clothing and other articles of gender-tagged identification which are taken as signs about their wearer's identity. How the erotic and pornographic are "marked" or take on aspects of one another's visible signs of identity, and how they are read by contemporary Mexican society, are the broad areas under examination here.

5. Torrents calls this film a "sophisticated" variety of comedy (227), García Tsao refers to it as an "erotic comedy" (1995, 223), and Maciel prefers to say it is an "artistic" comedy (42). All three seem to agree on an element of humor found at the heart of Hermosillo's text. As other recent directors have found, it is much easier to couch a message in a lighter package than to beat an audience over the head with it. One might wonder whether the social message, the "tragedy" of José/Marcelo and his imbrication in Virginia's plot to make the film and keep us in suspense, is easier for the spectator to swallow when combined with a dose of the comic to take the edge off.

CHAPTER 3. HOW I SPENT MY SUMMER VACATION

1. It is the transvestite Susy who teaches Julia how to dress and apply makeup in accordance with a color scheme appropriate to her personality. Julia, it seems, has succumbed to the drab colorlessness of everyday life. According to Susy, she needs to clothe herself in scarlet tones and bright lipstick to be seen and therefore precipitate events on the port. She is an invisible woman if unpainted and uncostumed; but she is not comfortable with the changes wrought by cosmetics

and artifice. A "natural" woman, unlike Susy and Karla one supposes, Julia quickly rejects this idea of personal spectacle as she looks for Carmelo amid the ships docked for the night. She rubs away all traces of lipstick and removes the red flower from behind her ear since they might cause her to stand out from the routine image of a middle-aged woman. Julia aspires to plainness, and luxuriates in that image.

2. This souvenir is listed in the filmscript but omitted from the final version of the movie.

3. Mexican critic Miguel de la Vega sums up what the new global film-going public looks for in a production and what a director must present to insure financial success :" . . . par de besos, par de nalgas, un poquito de homosexuali-dad . . . eso les encanta" ("a couple of kisses, a couple of bare buttocks, a little homosexuality . . . that's want they want"; 51). Although his comments are aimed at the films of Jaime Humberto Hermosillo, they describe what one sees in *Danzón* and, for that matter, *La tarea* or *Like Water for Chocolate*, or a number of other feature-length films recently produced in Mexico.

CHAPTER 4. *AMORES PERROS*

1. As mentioned previously, García Tsao, an optimist at heart, credits this rebirth to "the same middle class that had turned its back on domestically made films for decades . . . a new kind of audience, basically young, that goes to shop-ping-mall multi-cinemas attracted by films that portray their own culture." Rather than a utopian vision of complete "resurrection," however, García Tsao calls the current trend a "recovery" (2002 44) of the Mexican film industry.

2. Hirschberg tells her American audience that "[u]nlike most foreign films, the movie starts big, in an American sense" (32). Perhaps this is to reassure those who still regard foreign productions to be of the black-and-white variety or who continue to judge subtitles as somehow inferior to the earsplitting decibels of films like *Armageddon* or *Independence Day*. *Amores perros* rewards such an audience on two levels, then, for it overwhelms both the eyes and the ears. A mere two years later, González Iñárritu's film was surpassed by the publicity and hype surrounding *El crimen del padre Amaro (The Crime of Father Amaro*; 2002). Directed by Carlos Carrera and with a screenplay by Vicente Leñero, this film opened in an unprecedented four hundred movie theaters across Mexico on August 16, 2002, beating *Amores perros* by almost one hundred percent. An adaptation of an 1876 novel by Brazilian writer Eça de Queiroz, this block-buster—and scandal in the eyes of the Catholic Church—stars the now-teen-heartthrob Gael García Bernal in the title role.

3. Rainer calls this film "an homage to the Buñuel who made *Los olvidados*" (108) and there is great credence to such a comparison of street violence and its

less-than-subtle infiltration of the national psyche. Yet I would suggest that there are additional crossovers between the visions of the two directors regarding issues of gender and violence, and regarding the entire structure of political, social, and moral values on which the edifice of the nation is constructed. This comparison could then be extended to include the characters and situations presented in such Buñuel films as *Viridiana*, *The Discreet Charm of the Bourgeoisie*, and *Archibaldo de la Cruz*, among others. Of all the critics to review the film, only B. Ruby Rich mentions the real bridge between the two generations of filmmakers represented by the earlier Buñuel and the Generation X González Iñárritu, however: Arturo Ripstein (2001 35). While not developing the potential parallels between similar visions of the underclasses in the godfather of modern Mexican cinema (the Ripstein of *Profundo carmesí* [*Deep Crimson*]) and in the works of the new generation, Rich signals the important confluence of violence, degradation, and poverty (of pocketbook and of spirit) at the heart of both directors' films.

4. In 2000 the British writer and social activist John Berger published *King, a Street Story*, the chronicle of a twenty-four-hour period in the life of a homeless dog narrated by himself. Living amid the outcast remnants of twentieth-century consumerism, King uses all his wits to survive (barely) and, through him, Berger reminds the reader that among what human beings have abandoned is their compassion. This short fiction comes extremely close to the sentiment evoked by González Iñárritu in *Amores perros* where love, devotion, and obedience all belong to the animal kingdom most certainly, but not to the domain of humans who exhibit the emotional characteristics associated more with survival and instinct than with reason and thought. Perhaps one is led to conclude in both cases that any and all acts of violence evident in the social world are to be blamed on human beings and their lack of morality rather than on some inherent characteristic of all animals regardless of species.

5. The rock bands represented on the soundtrack of *Amores perros* have released a CD that includes numerous tracks beyond the film score. Opening in the Hard Rock Cafe to packed crowds in the upscale suburbs of Las Lomas and Coyoacán, Espuela de Oro, Meme del Real, Nrü, Zurdok, and others represented on videoclips in the background covered the numbers solicited by the director for his film. Each had to include the words "Amores perros" in the title as a prerequisite. Seen as yet another chance to promote the film-event-of-the-summer, the reviewer Patricia Peñaloza finds this "película-evento-producto" ("film/event/merchandise"; 1) of uneven quality at best, and socially revealing as well for its choice of venue: "el hábitat de Valeria" ("the habitat of Valeria"), the model of feminine perfection in the film. For this reason, she calls the gig "noche de perros fresas . . . y [de] pirruris" ("a night for yuppie dogs . . . and for spoiled rich kids"; 1).

6. The narrative voice in the first person tells the reader on the very first page of *La región más transparente*:

> Mi nombre es Ixca Cienfuegos. Nací y vivo en México, D. F. Esto no es grave. En México no hay tragedia: todo se vuelve afrenta. Afrenta, esta

sangre que me punza como filo de maguey. Afrenta, mi parálisis desenfre-
nada que todas las auroras tiñe de coágulos. Y mi eterno salto mortal hacia
mañana. (My name is Ixca Cienfuegos. Born and bred in Mexico City.
That's not so serious. In Mexico, there are no tragedies; everything is an
offense. An offense, the blood that slashes me like a sharp spike of cactus.
An offense, my uncontrollable paralysis that bathes each dawn with clots.
And my eternal death spiral toward tomorrow).

I offer my own translation of the lines rather than the standard English version
since I find the emphasis on paralysis (boredom, impotence, eventless time) so
much more obvious than the previous translation has made it appear.

CHAPTER 5. STILL JUST A DRESS REHEARSAL?

1. Baudrillard writes: "Rather than creating communication, [the sign] exhausts
itself in the act of staging communication . . . [a] kind of phantom content . . . ,
[an] awakening dream of communication" (80). The commodity is a lure for the
consumer, taunting him or her to come closer but turning out to be an "unlocat-
able reality" (81) for its very recycling. It came from somewhere else, but that
place is no longer traceable. He concludes that "[h]istory is our last referential,
that is to say our myth" (43). The greatest traumatic event, then, is the loss of
historical referent. From that point on, all is time without event.

2. In his review of the film Charles Taylor calls the texts of Rendell and
Almodóvar a "strange fit" of emotional disparities owing to the Spanish director's penchant for excess and the crime writer's cool tone of morbidity. Taylor
concludes: "He has always loved characters who are too emotional, too dramatic, too passionate, too everything" (1). This over-the-top excess is, of course,
the staple of melodrama.

3. Berardinelli finds this film a thriller but of the psychological variety rather
than a crime story per se. He writes: "The ending is surprising, not because it
doesn't fit, but because, knowing what we do about the involved parties, it's the
perfect way to offer closure to the tale" (1). The perceived shift in codes might
well be viewed as Almodóvar's response to the transformation of cold-blooded
British mystery into fiery (a la Buñuel's character Archibaldo) Spanish melodrama.

4. Reviewers are in agreement regarding the role of the passions in the lives of
these characters, as well as in the development of most of Almodóvar's films.
Hury asks: "Are we fated to live out our passions or do our passions determine
our fate? And how much choice can we exercise in embracing either view?" (1)
Whether one is overdetermined by an obsession with passion, or passionate
because one is by nature melodramatic, Carne trémula goes beyond the statistics
of crime with which the turn of the century seems to be obsessed to reach the

inner workings of those we might call criminals or who might commit acts judged thus.

5. Perhaps this film reinscribes on the screen what Vernon and Morris deem as an element lacking in the portrayal of Spanish society in Almodóvar's film *Atame*, in which they note the re-closeting of the erotic: ". . . if the film continues to affirm eros's transformative power over the pair of unlikely lovers, it nevertheless suggests that their love can develop only in isolation from a larger society no longer open to the collective ravages of desire" (12). While the realm of domestic melodrama might appear to be a private affair, it cannot be considered in any sense isolated or separate from the social norms of the day. In fact, as Brooks and others have suggested, the triangular structure of the melodrama allows us to view just those secret and secretive aspects of social life the greater collective body most wishes to suppress from public display. This genre is the escape valve for social control, used so expertly during the time of Franco to keep the fabric of civil life from unraveling and to legitimize the form it took. The "fatherland" was held together by an appeal to the domestic kingdom of the mother, and her sacrifices for the greater good were part and parcel of the institutionalized vision of the family. Familial love—that great passion at the center of melodrama—hurt, but the more pain it induced the more proof of one's loyalty. Conley mentions Almodóvar as a director "who projects scenarios of perversion . . . to reshape political allegories of repression into films that seek a mark that will buy into 'modern female subjectivity' insofar as the director equates the family romance with the overbearing 'maternal' aura of Francoist icons" (xvii). An allegory needs the reference to a context for it to play out, giving melodrama's codes a direct link with the social.

6. The political and economic crises of the late 1970s resulted in the Pactos de Moncloa, establishing an economic policy of national regeneration alongside wage controls, and setting the stage for the adoption of a constitution. Of course, of all those involved in the elaboration of such agreements, not all consider that they benefit equally from the final arrangements. Juliá notes that the Basque Nationalists' refusal to participate in the talks of this pact set up one of many schisms in the deal (110–11).

CHAPTER 6. THE DEMONIC SIDE OF MODERNITY

1. Figures of dangerous obscurity and infernal evil have reappeared over the centuries, some in more recognizable disguise and others conjuring up a more mundane reapparition of the devil, Satan, and his henchmen. From multitudes of little men with horns and pitchforks in the most traditional form to red-eyed goats and other wicked creatures of the night, the variations on a single theme abound. Yet Murnau's 1922 film *Nosferatu* might begin to give us an idea of how horrors of a different and more everyday sort begin to be embedded in the historically aligned figure of evil. What Schreck calls "the first genuine vampire

film" (35), Murnau's text belongs to both the netherworld and to the time of a Christian European fear of something "other" infiltrating its borders. Equally occult legend and allegory of (Jewish? Black Death?) invasion or contamination, the image of Nosferatu blends the idea of a life on the surface of society with the need to decode a secret level of existence and meaning in a series of mysterious messages and symbols. We might conclude the same of de la Iglesia's and Amenábar's films in that each forces the spectator to become an adept at reading and deciphering signs in order to understand things beyond the level of the literal. For de la Iglesia's characters Angel and José María, the hermetic kabbalah has become Revelations and heavy metal respectively. In the first case, we still have a horned figure to hold onto, while in the second we have to learn to decode evil in new guises. Schreck titles his chapter on Murnau and his successors "When Satan Was Silent," and this suggestion of a hidden spirit of the demonic could be useful for contemporary Spain. Given modernity's silencing of the most visible forms of past evils—dictatorship, civil war, and the like—the first impression is that of a new beginning and the abolition of "la leyenda negra" ("the Black Legend" of Spain's past, filled with conquests, death, colonization, and the Inquisition). Yet the falsity of such claims, their true nature as a spectacular cultural and political advertising campaign, is made evident by both filmmakers and evil takes its place at the end of the century as a motivation for artistic creation. Schreck vividly points out that Faust is not the only legendary incarnation of a satanic image in such texts, but that "[a]ccording to tradition, the Devil has always been a celebrated patron of the arts" (24).

2. Lacking what he calls the "textual imprint" (85) of a cultural or historical phenomenon, González Requena situates this absence in the field of the unrepresentable—for Jameson, the "unfigurable"—and the deepest recesses of the human psyche, precluding representation but inciting psychosis. This is what he terms "the performance of a radical absence. . . . It is something . . . that does not attain a positive form: the presence of a black hole or a radical void that, nevertheless, in its negativity, is traced through determined effects" (87). So we are left with an exclusion, except for the telltale symptoms that periodically float to the surface of the conscious mind.

3. The rise of women in the role of film directors and screen stars has been hailed by many in Spain and the rest of Europe as the advent of a turnabout in the representation of female characters and of gender identity in general. Much hope was invested in their arrival on the public scene "to deconstruct traditional unidimensional notions of femininity in Spanish cinema" (Jordan and Morgan-Tamosunas 127). The sense of ambiguity in characters presented in films by Pedro Almodóvar and Bigas Luna, for instance, has contributed to an affirmation of the "new" woman who is cast at the center of the narrative story being told. But it also creates the vision of the "new" man, as embodied in a very young Antonio Banderas at the beginning of his film career. Far different from the macho characters he has chosen to portray in subsequent films produced in the United States, Banderas starts out in productions by Almodóvar in roles that call for indecisiveness, stuttering, and even impotence as aspects of the "new"

masculinity. Such crossovers of gender and sexuality have created a prolific gray space for the demons of desire to surface as part and parcel of both the masculine and the feminine.

4. Lev writes of the potential confluences between the permitted and the prohibited: "Amenábar highlights the tension between the craving for the real that motivates the consumer of snuff (and pornography in general) and the impossibility of any film's perfect meshing with this fetishized reality" (34). With these words the critic signals perfectly the real/staged/simulacral aspects of performance associated with the consumption of such real or desired films, as well as the imaginary's notion of what one might have access to if only a "perfect" cinematic example could be found. The mentioned "craving" for reality television or snuff footage is both an indicator of how the marketplace has created a consumer of produced images as the "real" and an indictment of the trappings of modernity that attempt to hide some sort of suppressed, primitive, premodern urges and desires. Bosco is the perfect example of the economically privileged student whose tastes run to underground tapings of the ruthless exercise of power over bound and restrained women. His appearance to the contrary, Bosco harbors the dark side within himself and people are taken in by his amenable countenance. As Lev points out in addition, Bosco's name sends the spectator back to the triptychs of Flemish artist Hieronymous Bosch to find an equal in the representation of hell on earth. In the modern version of evil, however, it is more difficult to see the darkness since it has been clouded by our contemporary ideals of beauty and by an even more subtle disguise—a clean-cut student—than the grotesque creatures of Bosch's fevered imagination. The traditional allegory has turned into the boy next door who lures an innocent into the obscure depths of the family mansion. Once again, the spectator finds horror in the domestic domain.

CHAPTER 7. A FEW LAST WORDS

1. The letters written in response to this article and published in the magazine section on June 16 are, if anything, chilling indications of the easy banalization of horror and how the immediacy of excess too quickly fades to a dismal, gray discourse of loss.

2. One is reminded that in Benjamin's view of both texts and cities, in the labyrinthine twists and turns of modernity "there is continual movement but no progress" (Gilloch 20). Perhaps the "going forward" of history is no longer part of the myth of progress but rather a violent rupture with the traditional sense of advancing toward some set goal.

Works Cited

Allen, Dennis W. "The Marketing of Queer Theory." *College Literature* 25.1 (Winter 1998): 282–88.

Amores perros. Dir. Alejandro González Iñárritu. Altavista Films/Zeta Films, 2000.

Arendt, Hannah. *Eichmann in Jerusalem: A Report on the Banality of Evil*. New York: Penguin, 1994.

Arroyo, José. "Pup Fiction." *Sight and Sound* 11.5 (May 2001): 28–30, 39–40.

Bakhtin, Mikhail. *The Dialogic Imagination*. Ed. Michael Holquist. Trans. Caryl Emerson and Michael Holquist. Austin: U of Texas P, 1981.

Ballard, J. G. *Crash*. 6th ed. New York: Farrar, Straus, and Giroux, 1996.

Baudrillard, Jean. *Simulacra and Simulation*. Trans. Sheila Faria Glaser. Ann Arbor: U of Michigan P, 1994.

Baumgarten, Marjorie. "*Danzón*." *The Austin Chronicle* 29 Jan. 1993 1-2. Online review. <http:// www.auschron.com/film/pages/people/7.html>.

Baxter, John. *Buñuel*. New York: Carroll and Graf, 1998.

Benjamin, Walter. "D: [Boredom, Eternal Return]." *The Arcades Project*. Trans. Howard Eiland and Kevin McLaughlin. Cambridge, MA: Harvard UP, 1999. 101–19.

———. "On Some Motifs in Baudelaire." *Illuminations*. Ed. Hannah Arendt. Trans. Harry Zohn. New York: Schocken, 1968. 155–200.

————. "The Work of Art in the Age of Mechanical Reproduction." *Illuminations*. Ed. Hannah Arendt. New York: Schocken, 1985. 217–51.

Bentham, Jeremy. *The Panopticon Writings*. Ed. Miran Bozovic. London: Verso, 1995.

Berardinelli, James. "*Live Flesh* (Carne trémula): A Film Review." Online review. 1998. <http://movie-reviews.colossus.net/ movies/l/live_flesh.html>.

Berger, John. *King, a Street Story*. New York: Vintage/Random House, 2000.

Bolz, Norbert, and Willem Van Reijen. *Walter Benjamin*. Trans. Laimdota Mazzarins. Atlantic Highlands, NJ: Humanities Press International, 1996.

Bonfil, Carlos. "Las ciudades imaginarias del cine mexicano." *La Jornada Semanal* 10 junio 2001: 1–6A.

————. "*En el país de no pasa nada.*" *La Jornada Semanal*. junio 19 de 2000: Sección Cultural: 3A.

Bratton, Jacky, Jim Cook, and Christine Gledhill, eds. Introduction. *Melodrama: Stage, Picture, Screen*. London: British Film Institute, 1994. 1–8.

Brooks, Peter. "Melodrama, Body, Revolution." *Melodrama: Stage, Picture, Screen*. Ed. Jacky Bratton, et al. London: British Film Institute, 1994. 11–24.

Buck-Morss, Susan. *The Dialectics of Seeing: Walter Benjamin and* The Arcades Project. Cambridge, MA: MIT P, 1989.

Careaga, Gabriel. *Mitos y fantasías de la clase media en México*. Mexico City: Océano, 1974.

Carne trémula. Dir. Pedro Almodóvar. El Deseo, S. A., 1997.

Coad, Emma Dent. "Designer Culture in the 1980s: The Price of Success." *Spanish Cultural Studies: An Introduction. The Struggle for Modernity*. Ed. Helen Graham and Jo Labanyi. Oxford: Oxford UP, 1995. 376–80.

Conley, Tom. "A Land Bred on Movies." Foreword. *Modes of Representation in Spanish Cinema*. Ed. Jenaro Talens and Santos

Zunzunegui. Hispanic Issues No. 16. Minneapolis: U of Minnesota P, 1998. xi–xxvi.

Danzón. Dir. María Novaro. Cinematográfica Macondo, S. A. de C. V., 1991.

de la Vega, Miguel. "Fernando Cámara, productor de *De noche vienes, Esmeralda*, detalla los contratos y propuestas para distribuirla en todo el mundo." *Proceso* 1090 21 sept. 1997: 51.

Donald, James. "The City, the Cinema: Modern Spaces." *Visual Culture*. Ed. Chris Jenks. London and New York: Routledge, 1995. 77–95.

Durand, Régis. "How to See (Photographically)." *Fugitive Images: From Photography to Video*. Ed. Patrice Petro. Bloomington: Indiana UP, 1995. 141–51.

Edmundson, Mark. *Nightmare on Main Street: Angels, Sadomasochism, and the Culture of Gothic*. Cambridge: Harvard UP, 1997.

El día de la bestia. Dir. Alex de la Iglesia. Lola Films, 1995.

Ensayo de un crimen. Dir. Luis Buñuel. IFEX, 1955.

Evans, Peter. "Back to the Future: Cinema and Democracy." *Spanish Cultural Studies: An Introduction*. Ed. Helen Graham and Jo Labanyi. Oxford and New York: Oxford UP, 1995. 326–31.

Fiske, John. *Understanding Popular Culture*. Boston: Unwin Hyman, 1989.

Flores y Escalante, Jesús. *Imágenes del danzón: Iconografía del danzón en México*. Mexico City: Conaculta/Asociación Mexicana de Estudios Fonográficos, 1994.

Foster, Hal. "Postmodernism: A Preface," *The Anti-Aesthetic: Essays on Postmodern Culture*. Ed. Hal Foster. Seattle: Bay Press, 1983. ix–xvi.

Freud, Sigmund. "The 'Uncanny.'" *Writings on Art and Literature*. Foreword Neil Hertz. Stanford, CA: Stanford UP, 1997. 193–233.

Fuentes, Carlos. *A New Time for Mexico*. Trans. Marina Gutman Castañeda and Carlos Fuentes. Berkeley: U of California P, 1996.

————. *La región más transparente*. México: Fondo de Cultura Económica, 1958.

Garber, Marjorie. *Vested Interests: Cross-Dressing and Cultural Anxiety*. New York and London: Routledge, 1992.

García, Gustavo. "Cine: Bailar con la más fea." *Letras Libres* 14 junio 2001: 1–2.

————. "Melodrama: The Passion Machine." *Mexican Cinema*. Ed. Paulo Antonio Paranaguá. Trans. Ana M. López. London: BFI and IMCINE (Mexico), 1995. 117–27.

García Canclini, Néstor. *Hybrid Cultures: Strategies for Entering and Leaving Modernity*. Trans. Christopher L. Chiappari and Silvia L. López. Minneapolis: U of Minnesota P, 1995.

García Tsao, Leonardo. "One Generation, Four Film-makers: Cazal, Hermosillo, Leduc, and Ripstein." *Mexican Cinema*. Ed. Paulo Antonio Paranaguá. London: British Film Institute, 1995. 209–23.

————. "The Very Latest in Mexican Cinema." *Voices of Mexico* 59 April-June 2002: 44–49.

Gelder, Ken, ed. "Introduction: The Field of Horror." *The Horror Reader*. London and New York: Routledge, 2000. 1–13.

Gilloch, Graeme. *Myth and Metropolis: Walter Benjamin and the City*. Cambridge: Polity Press, 1996.

González Requena, Jesús. "*Vida en sombras*: The Recusado's Shadow in Spanish Postwar Cinema." *Modes of Representation in Spanish Cinema*. Ed. Jenaro Talens and Santos Zunzunegui. Hispanic Issues No. 16. Minneapolis: U of Minnesota P, 1998. 81–103.

González Rodríguez, Sergio. Prologue to *Danzón* (filmscript). Mexico City: El Milagro, 1994. 7–35.

Goytisolo, Juan. "In Memoriam F. F. B. (1892–1975)." *Libertad, libertad, libertad*. Barcelona: Anagrama, 1978. 11–19.

Graham, Helen, and Jo Labanyi, eds. *Spanish Cultural Studies: An Introduction. The Struggle for Modernity*. Oxford: Oxford UP, 1995.

Gunning, Tom. "Phantom Images and Modern Manifestations: Spirit Photography, Magic Theater, Trick Films, and Photography's

Uncanny." *Fugitive Images: From Photography to Video*. Ed. Patrice Petro. Bloomington: Indiana UP, 1995. 42–71.

Habermas, Jürgen. "Modernity—An Incomplete Project." *The Anti-Aesthetic: Essays on Postmodern Culture*. Ed. Hal Foster. Seattle: Bay Press, 1983. 3–15.

Hawkins, Joan. *The Cutting Edge: Art-Horror and the Horrific Avant-garde*. Minneapolis: U of Minnesota P, 2000.

Hayward, Susan. *Key Concepts in Cinema Studies*. London and New York: Routledge, 1996.

Hermosillo, Jaime Humberto, director. *La tarea*. Mexico City: CLASA Films, 1990.

Highmore, Ben. *Everyday Life and Cultural Theory: An Introduction*. New York and London: Routledge, 2002.

Hirschberg, Lynn. "A New Mexican." *New York Times Magazine* 18 March 2001: 32–35.

Hury, Hadley. "*Live Flesh*." Online review. *Memphis Flyer*, 6 April 1998. <http://www.weeklywire.com/ww/archives/authors/memphis_hadleyhury.html>.

Jahiel, Edwin. "*Danzón*." Online review. 1993: 1–2. <http:// www.prairie-net.org/ejahiel/danzon.htm>.

Jameson, Fredric. "Class and Allegory in Contemporary Mass Culture: *Dog Day Afternoon* as a Political Film." *The Jameson Reader*. Ed. Michael Hardt and Kathi Weeks. Malden, MA: Blackwell, 2000. 288–307.

———. "Culture and Finance Capital." *The Jameson Reader*. Ed. Michael Hardt and Kathi Weeks. Malden, MA: Blackwell, 2000. 255–74.

———. "On Magic Realism in Film." *Critical Inquiry* 12.1 (1986): 301–25.

Jay, Martin. *Downcast Eyes: The Denigration of Vision in Twentieth-Century French Thought*. Berkeley: U of California P, 1993.

Jenks, Chris. "The Centrality of the Eye in Western Culture: An Introduction." *Visual Culture*. Ed. Chris Jenks. New York and London: Routledge, 1995. 1–25.

Jordan, Barry, and Rikki Morgan-Tamosunas. *Contemporary Spanish Cinema*. Manchester and New York: Manchester UP, 1998.

Juliá, Santos. "History, Politics, Culture: 1975–1996." *The Cambridge Companion to Modern Spanish Culture*. Ed. David T. Gies. Cambridge: Cambridge UP, 1999. 104–20.

Krauss, Rosalind E. "Reinventing the Medium." *Critical Inquiry* 25 (Winter 1999): 289–305.

Labanyi, Jo. "Postmodernism and the Problem of Cultural Identity." *Spanish Cultural Studies: An Introduction*. Ed. Helen Graham and Jo Labanyi. Oxford and New York: Oxford UP, 1995. 396–406.

Lastra, James. "From the Captured Moment to the Cinematic Image: A Transformation in Pictorial Order." *The Image in Dispute: Art and Cinema in the Age of Photography*. Ed. Dudley Andrew. Austin: U of Texas P, 1997. 263–92.

Latour, Bruno. *We Have Never Been Modern*. Trans. Catherine Porter. Cambridge, MA: Harvard UP, 1993.

León, Magaly. "Los vínculos del miedo: Entrevista con Alejandro González Iñárritu." *unomásuno*. *Sábado* (Suplemento Semanal, nueva época). año 2 no. 102, junio 16 2000: 3, 16.

Lev, Leora. "Tesis." *Film Quarterly* 54.1 (Fall 2000): 34–8.

Levin, Martin. "From the Fringe: Shelf-Life." Book review of Mell Kilpatrick, *Car Crashes and Other Sad Stories*. *Globe and Mail* (Toronto) 8 July 2000: D6.

Loaeza, Soledad. "Cambio por la derecha." *La Jornada* en Internet, 6 julio 2000: 1–2.

López, Ana M. "At the Limits of Documentary: Hypertextual Transformation and the New Latin American Cinema." *The Social Documentary in Latin America*. Ed. Julianne Burton. Pittsburgh: U of Pittsburgh P, 1990. 407–14.

———. "Tears and Desire: Women and Melodrama in the 'Old' Mexican Cinema." *Mediating Two Worlds: Cinematic Encounters in the Americas*. Ed. John King, Ana M. López, and Manuel Alvarado. London: British Film Institute, 1993. 147–63.

Lyman, Rick, with Bill Carter. "In Little Time: Pop Culture Is Almost Back to Normal." *New York Times* 4 Oct. 2002: A1, B10.

Lyotard, Jean-François. "The Sublime and the Avant Garde." Trans. Lisa Liebmann. *Artforum* 22 (1984): 36–43.

Maciel, David R. "El imperio de la fortuna: Mexico's Contemporary Cinema, 1985–1992." *The Mexican Cinema Project*. Ed. Chon Noriega and Steven Ricci. Los Angeles: UCLA Film and Television Archive, 1994. 33–44.

Maltin, Leonard. *"Danzón"* Online review. *Leonard Maltin's 1999 Movie and Video Guide*. New York: Penguin Putnam, Inc., 1999. 1–2.

Márquez, Javier. "El cine después del 11-S." *Cambio 16* 1578 4 marzo 2002: 64–66.

Martin, Michael T. "The Unfinished Social Practice of New Latin American Cinema: Introductory Notes." *New Latin American Cinema: Theory, Practices, and Transcontinental Articulations*. Vol. 1. Ed. Michael T. Martin. Detroit: Wayne State UP, 1997. 15–29.

McDermid, Val. "Kings and Queens of Crime: Essays on Major Crime Writers—Ruth Rendell." Online essay. 2000. <http://www.two books.co.uk/crimescene/cwa/mcdermidonrendell.html>.

McLuhan, Marshall. *Understanding Media: The Extensions of Man*. Cambridge: MIT, 1964.

Meisel, Martin. "Scattered Chiaroscuro: Melodrama as a Matter of Seeing." *Melodrama: Stage Picture Screen*. Ed. Jacky Bratton, Jim Cook, and Christine Gledhill. London: BFI, 1994. 65–81.

Millán, Márgara. *Derivas de un cine en femenino*. Mexico City: UNAM/PUEG (Programa Universitario de Estudios de Género), 1999.

Mitchell, Elvis. "Screen Hype: Be Afraid, Be Very Afraid." *New York Times*. 9 July 2000: A4.

Mitchell, W. J. T. *Iconology: Image, Text, Ideology*. Chicago: U of Chicago P, 1986.

Monleon, José. "1848: The Assault on Reason." *The Horror Reader*. Ed. Ken Gelder. London and New York: Routledge, 2000. 20–28.

Monsiváis, Carlos. "Mythologies." *Mexican Cinema*. Ed. Paulo Antonio Paranaguá. Trans. Ana M. López. London: BFI and IMCINE. 1995. 117–27.

Moretti, Franco. *Modern Epic: The World System from Goethe to García Márquez*. Trans. Quintin Hoare. London and New York: Verso, 1996.

Mulvey, Laura. "Notes on Sirk and Melodrama." *Home Is Where the Heart Is: Studies in Melodrama and Women's Film*. Ed. Christine Gledhill. London: British Film Institute, 1987.

———. "Visual Pleasure and Narrative Cinema." *Film Theory and Criticism: Introductory Readings*. Ed. Leo Braudy and Marshall Cohen. New York: Oxford UP, 1999. 833–44.

Novaro, María. *Danzón*. Filmscript. Mexico City: El Milagro, 1994.

Peñaloza, Patricia. "Los participantes de la cinta sonora de *Amores perros*, en el Hard Rock." *La Jornada* en Internet, 7 julio 2000: 1–2.

Pérez Turrent, Tomás. "Crises and Renovations (1965–1991)." *Mexican Cinema*. Ed. Paulo Antonio Paranaguá. Trans. Ana M. López. London: British Film Institute and IMCINE, 1995. 94–115.

Petro, Patrice. "After Shock/Between Boredom and History." *Fugitive Images: From Photography to Video*. Ed. Patrice Petro. Bloomington: Indiana UP, 1995. 265–84.

Rainer, Peter. "Tales of La Ciudad." Film review. *New York* 9 April 2001: 108, 149.

Rendell, Ruth. *Live Flesh*. New York: Ballantine, 1987.

Rich, B. Ruby. "An/Other View of New Latin American Cinema." *New Latin American Cinema: Theory, Practices, and Transcontinental Articulations*. Vol. 1. Ed. Michael T. Martin. Detroit: Wayne State UP, 1997. 273–97.

———. "Mexico at the Multiplex." *The Nation* 14 May 2001: 34–36.

Rico Godoy, Carmen. *Cómo ser una mujer y no morir en el intento*. Barcelona: Planeta, 1999.

Romney, Jonathan. Review. "*Amores perros*—Dogfights on Film." *The Guardian* 17 May 2000: 1–3.

Ross, Christopher J. *Modern History for Modern Languages: Spain, 1812–1996*. New York: Oxford UP, 2000.

Sandro, Paul. *Diversions of Pleasure: Luis Buñuel and the Crises of Desire*. Columbus: Ohio State UP, 1987.

Saragoza, Alex M., and Graciela Berkovich. "Intimate Connections: Cinematic Allegories of Gender, the State, and National Identity." *The Mexican Cinema Project.* Ed. Chon Noriega and Steven Ricci. Los Angeles: UCLA Film and Television Archive, 1994. 25–32.

Schlossman, Beryl. "Looking Back: Luminous Shadows and the Auras of History." *Nottingham French Studies* 36.1 (Spring 1997): 76–87.

Schneider, Steven. "Monsters as (Uncanny) Metaphors: Freud, Lakoff, and the Representation of Monstrosity in Cinematic Horror." *Horror Film Reader.* Ed. Alain Silver and James Ursini. New York: Limelight, 2000. 167–91.

Schreck, Nikolas. *The Satanic Screen: An Illustrated Guide to the Devil in Cinema 1896–1999.* London: Creation Books, 2001.

Scoffield, Heather. "Fox Fever: Are Mexico's Hopes Too High?" *Globe and Mail* (Toronto) 19 August 2000: A9.

Sconce, Jeffrey. "'Trashing' the Academy: Taste, Excess, and an Emerging Politics of Cinematic Style." *Screen* 36.4 (Winter 1995): 371–93.

Siever, Héctor. "*Amores perros* o el bestial lengüetazo del deseo." *unomásuno. Sábado* (Suplemento Semanal, nueva época) año 2 no. 102, 16 junio 2000: 3.

Sinclair, Iain. *Crash: David Cronenberg's Post-mortem on J. G. Ballard's Trajectory of Roman Fate.* London: British Film Institute, 1999.

Spacks, Patricia Meyer. *Boredom: The Literary History of a State of Mind.* Chicago: U of Chicago P, 1995.

Subirats, Eduardo. *La cultura como espectáculo.* Mexico City: Fondo de Cultura Económica, 1988.

Szuchman, Mark D. "Depicting the Past in Argentine Films: Family Drama and Historical Debate in *Miss Mary* and *The Official Story*." *Based on a True Story: Latin American History at the Movies.* Ed. Donald F. Stevens. Wilmington, DE: Scholarly Resources, 1997. 173–200.

Taylor, Charles. "Is the Serious New Pedro Almodóvar All Grown Up or Just Worn Out?" Online review, Almodóvar's *Live Flesh.* 20

feb. 1998. <http://www.salonmagazine.com/ent/movies/1998/
    02/20live flesh.html>.

Tesis. Dir. Alejandro Amenábar. Las Producciones del Escorpión, 1996.

Tierney, Dolores. "Silver Sling-backs and Mexican Melodrama: *Salón
    México* and *Danzón*." Screen 38.4 (Winter 1997): 360–71.

Torrents, Nissa. "Mexican Cinema Comes Alive." *Mediating Two
    Worlds: Cinematic Encounters in the Americas.* Ed. John King,
    Ana M. López, and Manuel Alvarado. London: British Film
    Institute, 1993. 222–29.

Tuñón, Julia. "Emilio Fernández: A Look Behind the Bars." *Mexican
    Cinema.* Ed. Paulo Antonio Paranaguá. Trans. Ana M. López.
    London: British Film Institute and IMCINE, 1995. 179–92.

Vernon, Kathleen, and Barbara Morris. "Pedro Almodóvar, Postmodern
    Auteur." *Post-Franco, Postmodern: The Films of Pedro
    Almodóvar.* Ed. Kathleen M. Vernon and Barbara Morris.
    Contributions to the Study of Popular Culture, No. 43.
    Westport, CT: Greenwood Press, 1995. 1–23.

Williams, Linda. *Hard Core: Power, Pleasure, and the "Frenzy of the
    Visible."* Berkeley and Los Angeles: U of California P, 1989.

Index

Abre los ojos, 170

accumulation and expenditure, 8, 172
  capital, 2, 3, 167
  desires, 6
  in middle classes, 7, 21

action cinema, 20, 21, 43, 129

addiction
  and boredom, 8, 139, 141, 144, 173
  and desire, 130

affect, 8, 20, 85, 136

Almodóvar, Pedro
  democratic Spain, 133–4, 152
  pasotismo, 110
  recovery industry, 6, 109–12, 114,
    118–20, 127, 129, 130
  visual style, 107
  women, portrayal of, 36, 147
  See also *Carne trémula; Mujeres al
    borde de un ataque de nervios;
    Todo sobre mi madre*

Amenábar, Alejandro, 138, 141
  See also *Tesis*

Amores perros
  car crashes, 23, 85, 86–8, 91–3, 96,
    106
  domestic melodrama, 91, 102, 105,
    166 (*see also* melodrama)
  Generation X, 101

influence of Hollywood films, 83–4,
    86–7, 90, 92, 99, 105 (*see also*
    Hollywood films)
  Mexico City, 86, 87, 88–9, 91, 99,
    104, 106
  plot, synopsis of, 91–3, 96, 98,
    103–4
  post-1968 politics, 85, 88, 98, 102,
    104
  renaissance of Mexican film indus-
    try, 83, 84, 176n
  soundtrack of, 85, 89, 90, 105, 180n
  spectator, 93, 99, 102, 107
  trash aesthetics, 85, 101 (*see also*
    cinema of excess)
  violence in, 85, 86, 88–91, 93, 98,
    99, 104, 105, 169
  See also González Iñárritu,
    Alejandro

anxieties, cultural, 77, 141, 165
  and boredom, 3, 4, 8, 44, 88, 89,
    136, 167 (*see also* boredom)
  represented on screen, 22, 24, 33, 49,
    63, 64, 72, 107, 117–9, 171

apocalypse, 140, 145, 155

artifacts (cultural commodities), 2, 14,
    26, 76, 89, 110, 134, 153

aura
  of authenticity, 12, 40, 56, 57, 75,
    77, 80, 111–2
  of exoticism, 58–9, 153, 172
  and gaze, 9
  of the real, 26, 28, 55
  See also Benjamin, Walter; ruins,
    cultural

Bakhtin, Mikhail, 14, 110
  chronotope (time space), 14, 16, 18,
    19–21, 23–4, 56, 64, 78, 110, 112,
    126, 130, 170
  perception of historical events, 11,
    12, 14–8, 63, 73, 81, 133
  time without event (timelessness), 5,
    8, 28, 31, 56, 59, 60, 62, 64, 66, 67,
    72, 74–5, 129, 168
Baudrillard, Jean
  simulacra and simulation, 16, 59,
    102, 110, 149–50, 151, 155, 181n
Bemberg, María Luisa, 30
Benjamin, Walter
  Angel of History, 8, 79, 103, 110,
    171
  Arcades Project, The, 9
  awakening (power of film), 5, 8,
    9–10, 22, 26, 127, 136, 141–2, 156,
    163, 166, 168–9
  dream state, 14–6, 143, 164, 170, 172
  metaphor of sleepwalker, 9–10,
    14–6, 23, 25, 28, 139, 167
  modernity, 4, 5, 26, 140–1, 143–4,
    146, 165–6
  work of art, 40, 112
  See also modernity; ruins, cultural
boredom
  antidotes to, 20, 21, 44, 50, 58, 67,
    75, 85–6, 101, 136
  and cinema, 7–9, 18–20, 21, 23,
    25–6, 32, 78, 90, 111, 144
  as cultural symptom (pathology), 6,
    8, 15, 17, 86, 115–6, 124, 133,
    166-7
  marketing of, 34, 124

middle-class routine, 6–7, 12, 33, 46,
    56, 62, 129, 140–1
  and politics, 11–2, 14–6, 17–8, 23–4,
    113, 115–6
  as positive force, 5, 7–10, 24
  theories of, 3–6
  work and leisure, 3–4, 15, 18, 47,
    164, 168
  See also addiction; anxieties, cul-
    tural; everyday life; melodrama
Brooks, Peter, 43, 49, 112, 129
Buñuel, Luis
  cinematic influence
    on Almodóvar, 6, 109, 110, 114,
      118–9, 124, 130, 134
    on González Iñárritu, 84, 86,
      92–3, 179n
  critique of bourgeoisie, 115–7, 129
  exile, 84, 111, 134
  Un chien andalou, 9, 85, 119, 127
  See also Conley, Tom

Carne trémula, 112, 118-22
  adaptation of Rendell novel, 120,
    121, 123, 181n
  criminality in, 111, 119–20, 123,
    125–31
  masculinity, 118, 122, 128–9, 131
  melodrama, 110, 119–21, 123, 126,
    130–2 (*see also* melodrama)
  misreadings in, 119, 123, 125–6, 131
  montage and recovery industry,
    110–2, 118–9, 124–6, 130, 131
  new Spain, 121, 122, 128, 132, 134
  photographs as evidence in, 129
  spectator, 110, 112, 119, 123, 125,
    126, 129, 132–3
  See also Almodóvar, Pedro
Children of Franco, 15
cinema of excess, 5, 7–10, 20–2, 25, 33,
    87, 88, 107, 128–9, 131–2, 136,
    158, 168–9
  body genres, 90, 159, 171–2
  extreme cinema, 84, 157–9
  paracinema, 21, 85, 101, 136, 142,
    154, 164–6, 170, 171

spectator, 8, 10, 19–20, 22, 24, 29,
136–7, 154, 157, 164, 170
See also *Amores perros; Tesis*
Como agua para chocolate, 31
Conley, Tom, 113, 123, 131, 134, 182n
consumption, cultural, 14, 18, 20,
23–5, 35, 40, 45, 56, 132, 155
citizens as consumers, 2, 8, 17, 47,
51, 53, 65, 98, 110, 121, 159, 168
and desire, 1, 165
and gaze, 127, 131, 163
Crimen del padre Amaro, El, 179n
Cruz, Penélope, 118, 120, 132

Danzón, 31, 36
Mexican state in, 57, 62, 65–6, 70,
77, 80, 81
middle-age crisis, 56–7, 60, 62–7,
72–8
and performance, 57, 63, 67, 166
plot synopsis of, 59–60, 62–4
reworked cabaretera film, 36, 55–7
Salón México, 57, 58–9, 78–80
road movie, 64
soundtrack, 55–8, 63, 67, 72, 78
spectator, 55, 56, 62–3, 66, 74
transvestite characters (Susy, Karla),
67, 70, 73, 76–8
Veracruz in, 56, 62–7, 70, 72–4, 80,
166
See also Novaro, María; Rojo,
María
De la Iglesia, Alex
banality of horror, 135, 138, 141
influence of Hollywood on, 143
See also *Día de la bestia, El*
desire
fantasies, 2, 3, 25, 35, 43, 50, 63, 77,
105, 113–5, 118, 129, 133, 136–7,
139, 153, 164, 170–1
and the gaze, 11, 21, 26, 31, 33, 36,
48, 119, 122, 161, 165
and materiality, 1, 6–7, 151
and melodrama, 39, 42, 46–7, 57,
130 (*see also* melodrama)
and women, 30, 32, 42, 52, 58, 78,
117

desmemoria, la (amnesia), 23
See also recusado, el
Día de la bestia, El
Basque setting of, 144, 148
and evil, 146–8, 149, 166, 182n
influence of Hollywood films on,
143, 145 (*see also* Hollywood
films)
Madrid in, 143–5, 146–8, 149, 150
millennial anxieties, 145–6, 150 (*see
also* millennium)
plot, synopsis of, 144–50
sight and blindness, 144, 151
soundtrack, 144–5
spectator, 142, 149, 150
See also De la Iglesia, Alex
distraction, 75
as blindness, 11, 15
and excess, 9–10, 17, 18 (*see also*
cinema of excess)
gaze, 19, 20, 88, 131

Ensayo de un crimen
bourgeoisie in, 114, 115, 117, 129,
131
in *Carne trémula*, 109–11, 113, 114,
117, 118, 120, 122, 123, 124–5,
126–8, 130, 131, 133, 134
criminality, 113–5, 122, 123
and class, 116, 117
confession, 128, 166
and desire, 114, 119, 122, 126,
127, 129, 130, 131
evidence of, 118, 125, 127, 128,
129
masculine power (male gaze), 114,
115, 118, 122, 125, 127, 128, 129,
131
melodrama, 114, 115, 117, 118, 129
(*see also* melodrama)
Mexican Revolution, 114–6, 117,
121, 128, 131
music box, 116, 117
narrative adaptation of Usigli, 116
photograph album in, 113, 117
plot, synopsis of, 113–5, 125–8

Ensayo de un crimen—continued
  spectator, 113, 114, 116
  violence, 114, 115, 125, 126–7
  See also Buñuel, Luis
enthrallment
  spell, 99, 141, 152, 161
  trauma, 9, 29, 138, 154
  and vision, 2, 10, 22, 29, 41, 59, 83,
    110, 143
  See also Benjamin, Walter
Erice, Víctor, 138–9, 154, 156
Esquivel, Laura, 31
EU (European Union)
  Europhilia, 17
  Puerta de Europa (Gateway to
    Europe), 122, 145, 148
  Spain's entry into, 18, 22, 25, 132,
    133
  See also Spanish culture, modern
everyday life, 32, 35
  breaking through, 5, 23, 85, 88, 93,
    99, 106, 136–8, 143, 169, 170–1
  material aspects of, 1, 168
  pathology of, 15, 39, 116
  routine, 2, 3, 8, 9, 26, 29, 37, 40, 43,
    54, 56, 63, 64, 65, 114, 173
  See also melodrama

family
  contradictions in, 6, 30, 31–3, 36,
    105, 137
  as haven, 18, 19, 20, 25, 37, 65, 120,
    167
  Holy Family (Marx and Engels), 34
fatigue of the eye, 9, 10, 22, 76, 169
Foucault, Michel, 6, 8
Franco Bahamonde, Francisco
  and bourgeoisie, 116
  on the family, 18, 182n
  post-Franquismo, 15–7, 26, 101,
    113, 119–20, 132–3, 138, 139, 145
Fuentes, Carlos, 7, 59, 87
  A New Time for Mexico, 14
  La región más transparente, 104,
    106, 180n

García Canclini, Néstor, 77
globalization, 1, 14, 22, 25, 31, 55, 65,
    76, 77, 78, 110, 134, 165, 166
  and media, 4, 17, 27, 45, 47, 56, 99,
    107, 111, 137, 167, 168, 173, 179n
González Iñárritu, Alejandro, 6, 84,
    86–8, 93, 101, 103, 105, 169
  See also *Amores perros*
González Requena, Jesús, 20, 22, 23,
    117, 128, 183n
  See also recusado, el
Goya y Lucientes, Francisco de, 141,
    149, 152
Goytisolo, Juan, 15, 16, 17, 176n

Hawkins, Joan
  body genres, 85, 90, 101, 164, 170
  horror films, 173
  snuff films, 153
  time, 143
Hayward, Susan
  melodrama, 48, 50, 52, 53, 60, 171
    (*see also* melodrama)
  mise-en-abîme, 38, 48
  montage, 111
Hermosillo, Jaime Humberto
  domestic melodrama, 31, 36, 40, 41,
    49, 52 (*see also* melodrama)
  point of view, 30, 33, 35, 37, 38, 42
  See also *Tarea, La*
Hollywood films
  as competition, 53, 79, 143, 168
  techniques of, 22, 48, 107, 131, 154
    (see also *Día de la bestia, El*)
  violence in, 25, 164, 169
home
  comfort zone, 15, 18–20, 25–6,
    28–9, 167, 169
  domestic space of melodrama,
    29–32, 34, 37, 38, 40, 45, 49, 60,
    140 (*see also* melodrama)
  women relegated to by Franco, 18
horror
  film genre, 85, 101, 106, 107, 138,
    149, 170, 171, 173
  modern images of, 87, 120, 137, 160,
    165, 171

rhetorics of, 135–6, 152, 161
in society, 4, 11, 12, 25, 139, 141,
    142, 147, 153, 155
hybrid film genres, 21, 22, 85, 141
See also action cinema; melodrama

Jameson, Fredric
    blindness, 140
    figurability (figuration), 23, 127,
        128, 165, 170
    modern culture, 1, 2, 44, 102, 165,
        168, 175n
    obsession, 86

Krauss, Rosalind, 110, 113, 117
See also ruins, cultural

legibility, cultural, 24, 110, 113, 178n
López, Ana, 21, 33, 39
Lyotard, François, 10

Madrid, 2, 36, 118, 119–20, 129, 132,
    143, 150–1, 166, 168, 170
melodrama, 7, 30, 48
    and chiaroscuro, 21–3, 38, 119, 130,
        171
    compared to cinema of action, 20,
        21, 170 (*see also* action cinema)
    conventions of, 20–2, 32, 33, 38, 50,
        51–2, 53–4, 129
    Mexican, 29, 74
    spectator, 31, 40–3, 45, 48–53, 170
    time as ellipsis in, 20–1, 60, 65, 75,
        117
    traces of event in, 20, 76, 77, 78, 80,
        96, 104, 110, 111, 114, 119, 123,
        166
    triangular structure of, 40–1, 42, 43,
        49-50, 52, 91, 112–4, 118, 120,
        121, 123, 126, 130, 171
    See also Brooks, Peter; desire;
        Hayward, Susan; Hermosillo,
        Jaime Humberto; home;
        modernity; nostalgia; spectacle
Mexico (city), 2, 37, 56, 57, 59, 64, 70,
    74, 166, 168, 169
    See also *Amores perros; Danzón*

Mexico (country), 55–7, 62, 70, 83, 99,
    104, 106, 107, 115, 169
    culture under (Carlos) Salinas, 30,
        62, 73, 79
    Ejército Zapatista de Liberación
        Nacional (EZLN), 12, 96
    foxismo (Vicente Fox) and elections
        of 2000, 11, 12, 14, 25, 84, 86, 90,
        98, 102, 105, 106
    PRI (Partido Revolucionario
        Institucional), 11, 12, 26, 49, 57,
        77, 85, 87, 98, 101, 104
    utopian visions, 11, 58, 79, 87, 101,
        103, 105
middle classes
    aesthetics, 6–7, 42, 55, 56, 60, 74
    desires, 46, 57, 58, 63, 67, 118, 171
    and domestic life, 19, 34, 39–40, 48,
        53–4, 78, 79, 103, 166 (*see also*
        family; home)
    myths, 4, 12, 45, 72
    See also accumulation and expendi-
        ture; boredom; melodrama
millennium
    cinematic images, 5, 31, 76, 80–1,
        84, 110–1, 118, 132, 142, 149
    and progress, 1, 109, 136–7, 152
    as transition, 2, 11, 14, 17, 29, 78,
        86, 98, 105–6, 139, 166, 173
modernity
    as banquet, 1, 18, 20, 86, 132, 164–6,
        167, 168, 172
    cityscape of, 5, 87, 129, 143, 146,
        152, 166
    contradictions of, 49, 58, 64, 89,
        130, 131, 136, 137, 138
    and masquerade, 153, 155, 160–1,
        169
    and melodrama, 26, 32, 34, 46, 77,
        78, 141 (*see also* melodrama)
    as struggle, 23, 29, 57, 73, 76, 106–7,
        146, 148, 149, 150
    and technology, 3, 4, 62–3, 44
    See also Benjamin, Walter

Monsiváis, Carlos, 20, 32, 34, 58, 78
  See also melodrama
monstrosity
  art of Goya, 141
  cinematic, 105, 117, 137, 138–9, 152,
    159
  social, 78, 135, 151, 159
movida, la, 17, 132, 139, 152
  See also Almodóvar, Pedro; Spanish
  culture, modern
movie theaters, 18, 25–6, 152
  competition from home video, 30,
    33–4, 42–3, 46–7, 50–1, 164, 168
Mujeres al borde de un ataque de
    nervios, 36
Mulvey, Laura, 51–2, 163

NAFTA (North American Free Trade
    Agreement), 14, 22, 79, 87
New Latin American Cinema, 28, 31,
    39, 42
  and spectator, 32–5
  See also Rich, B. Ruby
New World Order, 30, 64, 77, 107
nightmare, 22, 103, 140
  and art of Goya, 141, 152
  and excess, 101, 151
  and history, 150, 173
Nosferatu, 182n
nostalgia, 3, 27, 47, 56, 57, 89, 133
  as commodity, 18, 65
  and melodrama, 50
Novaro, María, 55–6, 58, 59, 75–9
  See also Danzón

panopticon (Bentham), 15, 38
paralysis, cultural, 4, 6, 9
Petro, Patrice, 3–5, 9, 10, 28, 44, 67, 76
photography, 59
  captured images, 2, 23, 30–1, 75, 98,
    102, 146
  compared to cinema, 4, 27–8, 111
popular culture
  cinema, 20, 85
  power of, 5, 45–6, 58
  theories of, 25, 77
  See also Benjamin, Walter

pornography, 33, 37, 143, 157, 159,
    177n
  See also Williams, Linda
privatization, 2, 18, 53, 57, 62

recusado, el, 23, 128
  See also González Requena, Jesús
repression
  and boredom, 6, 7, 11, 44
  politics of, 12, 29, 65, 134
  and representation, 28, 30–1, 37, 41,
    46, 89, 129, 139, 149
revelation, 8, 9, 10
Rich, B. Ruby, 28–9, 31
  on secrets in Latin American
    cinema, 42, 53, 59, 177n
  See also New Latin American
    Cinema
Ripstein, Arturo, 180n
Rojo, María, 76
  and danzón, 56, 58, 59, 77
  as director, 33, 36, 54
ruins, cultural, 8, 14, 18, 23–6, 30, 104,
    172
  debris, 107, 109, 110, 130, 134, 171
  mourning of, 55, 56, 75, 80
  phantoms, 105, 160
  remnants, 112, 139, 164
  residues, 105
  September 11, 2001, 24, 25
  vestiges, 55, 59, 137
  See also Krauss, Rosalind

Salón México, 57–9, 78–80
  See also Danzón
saturation, 8–9, 14, 17, 26, 29, 165,
    168–9
Sconce, Jeffrey, 21, 85
  See also cinema of excess
September 11, 2001, 24, 25, 26, 167
shock value, visual, 8–10, 14, 22, 84,
    136, 166, 171
simulacra, 33, 59, 96, 102, 110, 149–50,
    151
  See also Baudrillard, Jean
Spacks, Patricia Meyer, 3, 4, 6, 85,
    167, 171

Spanish culture, modern, 15, 122, 128,
    131–2, 138
    Barcelona Olympics (1992), 133
    and democracy, 133, 143, 145, 161
    desencanto, 133, 139
    end of difference, 18, 132, 133, 151
    1990s, 11, 17, 122, 133–4, 142–8,
        150–2, 169, 170, 182n
    See also Almodóvar, Pedro;
        Amenábar, Alejandro
spectacle
    and cinema, 30, 44, 75, 106, 116,
        136, 137, 143, 150
    masquerade, 114, 125
    of melodrama, 38, 39, 47 (see also
        melodrama)
    social, 18, 59, 76, 90, 132, 144, 149
sublimation, 58, 78

Tarea, La, 30, 33–4, 35–8
    domestic melodrama, 33, 35–40, 42,
        43, 44–5, 46–9, 50, 52, 53 (see also
        melodrama)
    mise-en-abîme, 32, 38, 42, 44, 48, 51
    pornography, 37, 42, 43, 45, 46 (see
        also pornography)
    sequence shot, 36, 41, 42, 43–4, 48,
        51, 52
    soundtrack, 35–6
    voyeurism, 35, 37–8, 39, 40–3, 47

woman as director in, 35–42, 44, 46,
    47, 48–9, 51, 52, 53
    See also Hermosillo, Jaime
        Humberto
Televisa (Mexican media conglomer-
    ate), 177n
Tesis
    horror, 152, 155, 157, 160, 166
    Madrid, 151–2, 155
    pleasure, 157, 161, 171
    plot, synopsis of, 154–6
    snuff films, 143, 152, 153–4, 155,
        159, 161
    spectator, 142, 153, 155, 156–9, 161
    violence, 152, 154, 156
    See also Amenábar, Alejandro
Todo sobre mi madre, 147
Torrent, Ana, 140, 154, 156
    See also Tesis

uncanny, the, 158–61
    and boredom, 6, 146
    evocation of, 2, 11, 24, 28, 127, 141,
        149, 153–5, 161, 171
    Heimlich/Unheimlich (Freud), 29,
        138–9, 154, 159–60

Williams, Linda, 42, 90, 153, 177n
    See also cinema of excess; pornog-
        raphy